'We're Rooted Here and They Can't Pull Us Up'
Essays in African Canadian Women's History

Despite the increasing scope and authority of women's studies, the role of Black women in Canada's history has remained largely unwritten and unacknowledged. This silence supports the common belief that Black people have only recently arrived in Canada and that racism is a fairly recent development. This book sets the record straight.

The six essays collected here explore three hundred years of Black women in Canada, from the seventeenth century to the immediate post–Second World War period. Sylvia Hamilton documents the experiences of Black women in Nova Scotia, from early slaves and Loyalists to modern immigrants. Adrienne Shadd looks at the gripping realities of the Underground Railroad, focusing on activities on this side of the border. Peggy Bristow examines the lives of Black women in Buxton and Chatham, Ontario, between 1850 and 1865. Afua P. Cooper describes the career of Mary Bibb, a nineteenth-century Black teacher in Ontario. Dionne Brand, through oral accounts, examines labourers between the wars and their recruitment as factory workers during the Second World War. And, finally, Linda Carty explores relations between Black women and the Canadian state.

This long overdue history will prove welcome reading for anyone interested in Black history and race relations. It provides a much-needed text for senior high school and university courses in Canadian history, women's history, and women's studies.

PEGGY BRISTOW is a researcher in the Centre for Women's Studies at the Ontario Institute for Studies in Education in Toronto. DIONNE BRAND is a poet, filmmaker, and writer living in southern Ontario. LINDA CARTY is a sociologist teaching at the University of Michigan, Flint. AFUA P. COOPER is a doctoral student in history at the University of Toronto. SYLVIA HAMILTON is a filmmaker and writer living in Halifax. ADRIENNE SHADD is a researcher and writer living in Toronto.

Contents

vi   Contents

Acknowledgments

Just as the slave women who, in the darkness of night, clandestinely taught slaves to read and write, this book was given birth after hours, after we finished our paid work, after we put our children to bed and tended to our other roles in our families and communities. However, there are many individuals who supported and encouraged this endeavour through their assistance in providing information and leads, and in locating numerous documents and photographs. In particular, we acknowledge the efforts of Ruth Edmonds Hill, audiovisual coordinator of the Schlesinger Library, Radcliffe College, Cambridge, Massachusetts; Elise Harding Davis, curator of the North American Black Museum, Amherstburg, Ontario; Alice Newby, curator of the Raleigh Township Centennial Museum, North Buxton, Ontario; Gwendolyn Robinson, author and researcher, Chatham, Ontario; Everette Moore, Ontario Black History Society, Toronto; the staffs of the National Archives of Canada, Ottawa, and the Archives of Ontario, Toronto (in particular Leon Warmski of the latter); and Gail Benjafield, Special Collections, St Catharines Public Library, St Catharines, Ontario.

We are especially grateful to Pat Murphy for her sharp editorial skills and expertise. We would also like to thank Annette Henry, who started out with us and collaborated in the initial stages of the manuscript. Thanks also are due to our supportive friends Beulah Worrell and Lucy Tantalo, and our families for their unending support of our work in the time spent away from them: to Marishana, Majorie, Alyson and family, Anthony, Terrence, Malcolm, Andrew and Aunt Lyla (Annie), Shani, Bev, mother Marie and sisters Ada and Janet, Akil, Lamarana, and Alpha.

No work is without struggle and we have had our share. We are indebted to Peggy Bristow, who first had the idea for this book and was the glue that held the project together, coordinating it from its inception, and persevering with us through its various stages right to the end.

Finally, we thank the University of Toronto Press, especially History Editor Gerald Hallowell, Laura Macleod, Agnes Ambrus, and John St James for their support.

Contributors

PEGGY BRISTOW has given workshops on the integration of Black women's studies in the secondary-school curriculum. She is on the advisory board of *Resources for Feminist Research / Documentation sur la recherche féministe*. Her most recent writing on African Canadian women's organizations appears in *And Still We Rise: Feminist Political Mobilizing in Contemporary Canada*, edited by Linda Carty. A researcher at the Centre for Women's Studies at the Ontario Institute for Studies in Education, she is currently pursuing doctoral studies in the Department of History and Philosophy at OISE.

DIONNE BRAND is a Toronto writer. She was born in the Caribbean and has lived in Toronto for the past twenty years. She has an MA in Philosophy of Education and is working on a Ph.D. in Women's History.

Brand has published five books of poetry. Her poems and other writing have appeared in several Canadian journals, including *Poetry Canada Review*, where her columns on Caribbean poetry have also appeared. Her poetry is included in various anthologies including the *Penguin Book of Caribbean Verse* and *Poetry by Canadian Women* (Oxford). Her book of poetry *No Language Is Neutral* was nominated for the Governor General's Award in 1991.

Brand is the associate director and writer of the NFB Studio D documentaries *Older, Stronger, Wiser* and *Sisters in the*

Struggle. Her most recent publication is *No Burden to Carry: Narratives of Black Working Women in Ontario, 1920s–1950s* (1991).

LINDA CARTY is a sociologist who teaches at the University of Michigan, Flint Campus. She has taught in women's studies programs at the University of Toronto and Oberlin College in Ohio. A number of her publications address the structural location of women of Colour in advanced capitalist countries and Third World countries, the state and economic development in the Caribbean, and the historical significance of colonialism and imperialism to the international division of labour. Recent publications include *And Still We Rise: Feminist Political Mobilizing in Contemporary Canada* (Women's Press 1993), 'Women's Studies in Canada: A Discourse and Praxis of Exclusion,' in *Resources for Feminist Research* (1992), and 'Black Women in Academia: A Statement from the Periphery,' in *Unsettling Relations* (Women's Press/South End).

AFUA COOPER is a Ph.D. candidate in the Department of History at the University of Toronto, where she is doing research on Ontario Black women's history. As well, she has done extensive research on Black teachers and Black education in nineteenth-century Ontario. Afua lectures on a continuous basis on aspects of Canadian Black history throughout the province of Ontario. In addition, she has published three books of poetry, the last of which, *Memories Have Tongue*, was the first runner-up in the prestigious Casa de las Americas Award (1992). Her poetry has been published in several anthologies in Great Britain, North America, and the Caribbean. She has given numerous readings throughout Canada and beyond.

SYLVIA HAMILTON is a filmmaker and writer who lives in Halifax, Nova Scotia. Her primary area of interest is the social and cultural history of people of African descent in Nova

Scotia, with a focus on the history of African Nova Scotian women. She researched, wrote, and co-directed the award-winning documentary *Black Mother Black Daughter* (1989), an exploration into the lives and experiences of Black women in Nova Scotia. She researched and directed *Speak It! From the Heart of Black Nova Scotia* (1993), a documentary about issues facing African Nova Scotia youth. Both films were produced by the National Film Board of Canada. Her historical and literary writings have been published in anthologies, newspapers, and journals. She is pursuing a master's degree in education at Dalhousie University and continuing her work in film and video production.

ADRIENNE SHADD was born in North Buxton, Ontario, a descendant of nineteenth-century abolitionist and newspaper-woman Mary Ann Shadd Cary. She obtained a BA from the University of Toronto and an MA in sociology from McGill University in Montreal.

Shadd is a freelance researcher and writer whose work includes articles on the regional dynamics of racial inequality and the history of Black women in Canada. She is formerly research editor and contributor to *Tiger Lily*, a journal by women of Colour. In addition, she was recently the guest editor of a special issue of the *International Review of African American Art*, entitled 'Celebrating the African Canadian Identity' (Fall 1992). She is currently working on several book projects, including a history of Black women in Canada.

TO BE SOLD,

A BLACK WOMAN, named PEGGY, aged about forty years ; and a Black boy her son, named JUPITER, aged about fifteen years, both of them the property of the Subscriber.

The Woman is a tolerable Cook and washer woman and perfectly understands making Soap and Candles.

The Boy is tall and strong of his age, and has been employed in Country business, but brought up principally as a House Servant—They are each of them Servants for life. The Price for the Wowan is one hundred and fifty Dollars—for the Boy two hundred Dollars, payable in three years with Interest from the day of Sale and to be properly secured by Bond &c.—But one fourth less will be taken in ready Money.

PETER RUSSELL.

York, Feb. 10th 1806.

Enslaved woman and son advertised for auction sale by owner Peter Russell, member of Executive Council in Ontario

Harriet Tubman (1820?–1913) is the best-known 'conductor' to have worked on the Underground Railroad.

Maria Weems escaping in male attire. From William Still's
Underground Rail Road Records

Mary Ann Shadd Cary

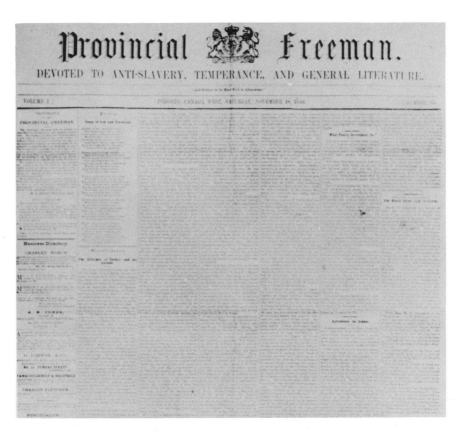

Newspaper started by Mary Ann Shadd Cary

Masthead, *Voice of the Fugitive*, 16 July 1851, published by
Henry Bibb, often with the assistance of his wife, Mary Bibb

Martha Barton ca. 1887   Una Gibson ca. 1904, Shelburne

People in front of church, ca. 1904

Graduates ca. 1921. Ethel Gibson (front row, left) was a midwife delivering children through many rural communities in
the Kingston County area of Nova Scotia. Her mother had
also been a midwife. For twenty-four years (1908–32) Ethel
lived in Boston, Massachusetts, where she went to nursing
school, graduating as a nursing assistant. The photo is of her
graduating class. Back row, left–right: Mary (Blocker) Washington, Ethel Jenkins, Lucinda McWilliamson. Front row,
left–right: Ethel Gibson, Daisy Bacota

Teacher Cleata Morris and students of S.S. #10 Chatham, 1948

Members of the Hour-A-Day Study Club in Windsor, Ontario, with Mary McLeod Bethune in 1954

'WE'RE ROOTED HERE
AND THEY CAN'T PULL US UP'

Introduction

We are six Black women who share a collective concern that the history of Black people in Canada and of Black women in particular is missing from the pages of mainstream Canadian history. Black people in Canada have a past that has been hidden or eradicated, just as racism has been deliberately denied as an organizing element in how Canada is constituted.

We are of diverse social and political backgrounds and experiences two of us are fifth- and sixth-generation Canadian, and four of us came to Canada as immigrants from the Caribbean. Through our discussions we recognized that we share a common experience around racism within Canadian society. Specifically, the educational system has maintained and perpetuated the common perception that Black people were either non-existent in the development of Canada, or only arrived in Canada through recent migration from the Caribbean and Africa.

This misconception continues to the present and means that Black children entering the schools have no sense of Blacks being here for generations and, hence, that there is a 400-year presence and contribution of African Canadians in this country. These children naturally feel invisible and marginalized. Of equal importance to us is that such a distorted sense of history minimizes the claims of African people to a role in the making of Canada. Further, this distortion suggests that racism is a new phenomenon to this country.

The idea for the book came from Peggy Bristow, who works at a Women's Resource Centre in Toronto where students have been increasingly requesting writings on Black women's history in Canada. She has had to tell them that there was nothing beyond the one or two articles or pamphlets that the centre had on hand.[1] As a group, we came together and decided that, just as women could not wait for male historians to rewrite mainstream history to include women, we could not expect white women to include us in women's history.

We decided, therefore, to write about African Canadian women for two primary reasons. First, as women, our experiences have always differed significantly from those of men. While we are subjected to racism as are Black men, gender compounds this situation. How we have managed historically to survive both racial and gender subordination deserves special attention.

Second, we wanted to write a feminist history. So much of history, regardless of the epoch, has been claimed and told by men, who have had no interest in situating women in that history. The inclusion of women is a very recent phenomenon, a product of contemporary feminism. White feminist scholars have taken pains to locate women in the restructuring of Canadian history. However, as with white male history, race is neglected. In white Canadian feminist historiography, Black women pioneers such as Mary Ann Shadd Cary or Addie Aylestock are accorded no recognition as the *first* woman publisher and editor of a newspaper in Canada in the 1850s or the *second* Canadian woman to be ordained as a minister in 1951.

A number of Black women have taken up the writing of Black history. In fact, there is a tradition of writing in the Black women's community that has been overlooked. A Black feminist historiography would begin with the writings of newspaper editor and publisher Mary Ann Shadd who, as early as 1852, wrote *A Plea for Emigration to Canada West*, a treatise informing Blacks in the United States about the benefits of emigrating to Canada West. She also wrote articles on women's rights, and informed her readers through the *Provincial Freeman* newspaper of suffragist meetings in Canada West and the United States. Numerous Black women have continued this tradition of writing into the twentieth century. They include Pearleen Oliver, *A Brief History of the Coloured Baptists of Nova Scotia, 1782–1953* (1953) and *One of His Heralds: A Sketch from the Life of Agnes Gertrude Waring* (n.d.), Charlotte Bronte Perry, *The Long Road: A History of the Coloured Canadian in Windsor, Ontario, 1867–1967* (1967) and *One Man's Journey: The Biography of Alderman Dr. Roy Prince Edward Perry* (1982), Enid D'Oyley and Rella Braithwaite, *Women of Our Times* (1973), Rella Braithwaite, *The Black Woman in Canada* (1977), Rella Braithwaite and Tessa Benn-Ireland, *Some Black Women* (1993), Carrie Best, *That Lonesome Road: The Autobiography of Carrie M. Best* (1977), Velma Carter and Wanda Leffler Akili, *The Window of Our Memories* (1981), Velma Carter, *The Black Canadians: Their History and Contributions* (1989), Dorothy Shadd Shreve, *Pathfinders of Liberty and Truth* (1940) and *The Afri-Canadian Church: A Stabilizer* (1983), Arlie Robbins, *Legacy to Buxton* (1983), and Gwendolyn and John Robinson, *Seek the Truth* (1990). *Legacy to Buxton*, which examines the lives of the Buxton settlers and their descendants, is a rich accounting of the 140-year history and culture of that community. Oliver, who led the fight for the hiring of the first Black nurses in Nova Scotia in the forties, deals with the history of the African United Baptist Church in that province. Of interest is her report on the first Black women's conference ever to be held in Canada in 1917. Braithwaite and D'Oyley's chapbook *Women of Our Times* is significant as the first attempt to address specifically the history of Black women. And Carter and Leffler Akili's *The Window of Our Memories*, which captures and preserves the oral histories of a people, is a tribute to Alberta's Black pioneers.

Though not necessarily feminist approaches to Black history or Black women's history, all these books were pathbreaking efforts to redress the exclusion of Black people in general and Black women in particular from the pages of Canadian history.

In the last twenty years, several general historical accounts of Black people in Canada have appeared. Most notable among them are Robin Winks's *The Blacks in Canada: A History* (1971), James W. St G. Walker's *The Black Loyalists: The Search for a Promised Land in Nova Scotia and Sierra Leone 1783–1870* (1976) and *A History of Blacks in Canada* (1980), and Daniel G. Hill's *The Freedom-Seekers: Blacks in Early Canada* (1981). Each of these texts was written for different audiences and takes a different approach to the history. Winks's *The Blacks in Canada* is the most comprehensive survey of Black history in Canada and can be a valuable resource for researchers given its extensive reference to primary sources. However, the author takes tremendous liberties in his interpretations of Black aspirations and expectations. His constant editorializing on Black intention and organization, and his presumptions and conclusions about what is good for Black people mar the value of the work.

By contrast, Walker's texts offer a much less judgmental approach to Black community organization and initiatives. Another strength of Walker's *The Black Loyalists* is that it focuses on one group of early Black settlers in Nova Scotia, thereby allowing for a more detailed examination of one particular group in a specific location.

Hill's *The Freedom-Seekers* offers a popular history of Black achievement from the earliest times up to 1865. He provides interesting accounts of the daily lives of Black families of the period through interviews with descendants of the early settlers. His unique collection of photographs and other documents enriches the text, and his personal connection to the material distinguishes his approach from those of Winks and Walker.

Missing from all the works of these authors, however, is any exploration of gender as a fundamental category of analysis. Though Hill, to a greater degree, identifies individual women, the context he places them in is primarily a familial one. They are rarely seen as historical actors in their own right. In effect, the work that these women performed and the energies they expended in the survival of those early communities are minimized.

A number of other works exist that are written in a more popular style. Among these are Headley Tulloch's *Black Canadians: A Long Line of Fighters* (1975) (which he wrote for his son because, he explained, there was nothing in the school curriculum on Black history), Leo Bertley's *Canada and Its People of African Descent* (1977), and Colin Thompson's *Blacks in Deep Snow* (1979).

The growth of women's history in Canada over the last twenty years has not reflected the lives of Black women. Even though the white middle-class bias in women's history has partially been redressed in recent years by studies of working-class and immigrant women, Canadian women's history remains primarily that of white women. From early works such as Janice Acton et al., *Women at Work: Ontario, 1850–1930* (1974) or *The Neglected Majority: Essays in Canadian Women's History* (1977), edited by Alison Prentice and Susan Mann Trofimenkoff, to more recent publications like Veronica Strong-Boag and Anita Clair Fellman's *Rethinking Canada: The Promise of Women's History* (1986), the Cleo Collective's *Quebec Women: A History* (1987), and Strong-Boag's *The New Day Recalled: Lives of Girls and Women in English Canada, 1919–1939* (1988), barely a mention is made of the existence of Black women on the historical landscape. In other texts such as *Canadian Women: A History* (1988), by Alison Prentice et al., the authors make mention of Black and other women of Colour now and again, but an analysis of race is not central to the historical narrative. Indeed, it would appear that Black and other racial-minority women are included only as an afterthought. One of the most glaring examples is the way the latter book trivializes the trail-blazing nature of Mary Ann Shadd's contribution by introducing her name after a series of journalists who followed her. (Cora Hinds is given the credit as the first woman journalist in Canada when she went to work for the Winnipeg *Free Press* in 1881!) And *No Easy Road: Women in Canada 1920s to 1960s* (1990), edited by Beth Light and Ruth Roach Pierson, makes a genuine attempt to include more women of Colour in its collection of documentary papers. However, all these works fail to use race as a theme or unit of analysis. Hence, individual accounts or stories of prejudice and discrimination come across as isolated incidents, giving the impression that race and racism do not fundamentally shape the lives of both white and Black women.

There is a fundamental difference in the writing and study of Black history in this country and the United States. In the case of the latter, Black history has long been acknowledged as a legitimate field of historical inquiry, while in Canada even the Black historical presence has yet to be acknowledged. Indeed, it is still possible for someone like Gerald Caplan, a former history professor at the Ontario Institute for Studies in Education, to deny that slavery existed in this country.[2] When Women's History Month, which is celebrated in October, began its first newsletter, a suggested list of readings in women's history did not include a single title from a Black or a First Nations author.[3] This kind of denial is pervasive throughout Canadian society and continues to present impediments to the development of an African Canadian historiography.

In our discussion of how this book was to take shape, we recognized all the omissions in Canadian history and what sustains them. We agreed that these omissions are part and parcel of the endemic racism that fuels the Canadian intellectual tradition. The vision of Canada as an entire culture of Anglo and/or Franco existence is narrow and inaccurate. This Eurocentric perspective, a cornerstone of white supremacy, fails to accommodate any other peoples in its structuring. It renders irrelevant the historical fact that First Nations peoples were here before the arrival of Europeans. In the practice of a Eurocentric intellectual thought, any mention of First Nations peoples has existed in the context of white explanation and white interpretation. The manifestations of this practice continue today in the form of First Nations peoples' lives and history being told by whites, although this practice is now under challenge by First Nations writers and scholars.

Throughout all levels of the educational system we have been told, in our attempts to recover the history of African Canadians, that the 'evidence' does not exist; and when this 'evidence' is produced it is seen as marginal to the dominant historical narrative.

This book, therefore, seeks to offer an interpretation of aspects of Canadian history from a decidedly new point of view. The chapters combine original research and traditional sources. In drawing upon the latter, the book does so from a unique, unprecedented vantage-point, thereby offering a fresh analysis and a challenge to prevailing notions of Canadian history.

The title for the book came from Adrienne Shadd's research on Harriet Tubman, who had made a speech denouncing the nineteenth-century colonization movement back to Africa. She had likened Blacks to a field of onions and garlic that cannot be easily uprooted. Whites had brought Black people here to do their drudgery, and now were trying to root them out and ship them back to Africa. 'But,' she said, 'they can't do it; we're rooted here, and they can't pull us up.' Her speech was very well received.[4]

The papers in this collection cover the history of Black women in Canada from their arrival in the seventeenth century to the immediate postwar period, some three hundred years. Nova Scotia's colonial past is the oldest in Canada. It is a history that includes the legacy of slavery and the establishment of centuries-old communities of people of African descent. Sylvia Hamilton's chapter surveys the presence of Black women in Nova Scotia in an attempt to situate them within this historical context. It documents not only the practice of slavery, but the equally strenuous efforts by Black women to resist this oppression. Using specific examples, and naming names, the chapter offers a view into the lives of early settler women such as Lydia Jackson and Mary Postell, and shows how gender as well as race circumscribed their experiences in Nova Scotia.

A great deal has been written about the Underground Railroad and the role of Harriet Tubman, the woman whose name has since become synonymous with that institution. However, little attention to date has been paid to the plight of the average woman who escaped on the Underground Railroad, as well as to those who, once arrived on Canadian soil, aided the escape of others. Through primarily published slave narratives, Adrienne Shadd provides a dramatic account of heroism and support along 'the Road.' She explores why women represented only approximately 20 per cent of successful fugitives and details some of the more spectacular case studies of women who escaped to Canada. The tremendous dangers involved and the various methods that were used in these women's quest for freedom are illustrated. In addition, the chapter pays tribute to the role of women in the eventual abolition of American slavery itself.

Focusing on two areas in southwestern Ontario, the Elgin Settlement and the town of Chatham, Peggy Bristow reconstructs the lived experiences of women in these communities during the period 1850–65. Through the use primarily of census data, official government reports, and newspaper accounts, she recovers the multiplicity of women's voices through a re-interpretation and re-examination of these documents.

Afua Cooper addresses Black education by examining the teaching life of Mary Bibb, one of the few nineteenth-century Black women who gained access to education at a normal school. On coming to Canada in 1850, Mary Bibb opened a school for Black children, of vital necessity in a community that prevented them from attending the local common school owing to the prejudice of whites. Mary Bibb tried to get a government grant to continue her school, but without sufficient support the school floundered. She later started another independent school that enjoyed longevity. The essay delineates her struggles with a patriarchal educational system in her fight to provide education for Black children.

The difficulties Black women encountered in the eighteenth and nineteenth centuries continued into the twentieth. Dionne Brand looks at Black women between the wars, their role in domestic work up to the Second World War, and their entry into industrial labour as part of the recruitment of women for the war effort. Using Black women's oral accounts against historical accounts of the period, which in the main ignore Black women as agents in this period, the essay reveals the particular role that Black women played during the interwar years.

The collection ends with Linda Carty's paper, which provides a sociological overview of the relationship between Black women and the Canadian state. She attempts to determine the government's role in structuring this relationship, focusing on the historical development of waged work for Black women and Canada's postwar immigration policies regarding Black women.

The following collection of essays does not presume to provide all the answers. Rather, the essays only scratch the surface and begin the debate about the nature of a truly Black feminist women's history in Canada. In addition, the absence of studies on the West and Quebec constitute important gaps that need to be addressed in future texts. In that sense, the book is very much a preliminary work and some essays are, in fact, part of larger, ongoing works in progress. However, we are merely carrying on in the tradition begun by Black woman writer/activist Mary Ann Shadd Cary well over a century ago and continued in the twentieth century by many others. It is to these women that we dedicate this book.

NOTES

1 After this volume went into production, Dionne Brand, a contributor to the present book, launched *No Burden to Carry: Narratives of Black Working Women in Ontario, 1920s–1950s* (Toronto: Women's Educational Press 1991), a collection of oral histories of sixteen older Black women in Ontario. It is the first work to deal with Black women's his-

tory from a scholarly feminist perspective, and thus is an important addition to the literature.

2 Gerald Caplan, 'Our racial record tolerable – compared to U.S.,' *Toronto Star*, 10 May 1992

3 *Women's History Month Newsletter*, October 1992, published by Status of Women Canada

4 From an article entitled 'New England Coloured Citizens' Convention,' *The Liberator*, 26 August 1859, as cited in Earl Conrad, *Harriet Tubman* (Washington: Associated Publishers 1943), 110

1

Naming Names, Naming Ourselves:
A Survey of Early Black Women
in Nova Scotia

SYLVIA HAMILTON

This paper looks at the lives of some early Black women who came to Nova Scotia: enslaved, Loyalist, Maroon, and Refugee. The period surveyed begins in the mid-1600s and concludes with the early years of the twentieth century. While researchers and historians have written generally about Nova Scotia's 'indigenous' Black community, they have paid little attention to the specific condition of Black women in this community. Since Black women, for the most part, have been left out of this history, it has perhaps been assumed that their status and experience were the same as that of males within the community, circumscribed only by race. While race has been a major determinant of the Black woman's status, gender has also sharply delineated her condition in Nova Scotian society.

From her first arrival in Nova Scotia, the Black woman has struggled for survival. She has had to battle slavery, servitude, sexual and racial discrimination, and ridicule. Her tenacious spirit has been her strongest and most constant ally; she survives with strong dignity and an admirable lack of self-pity and bitterness. She survives, but not without struggle. This work is a first reading of a multi-layered story of struggle and survival. It offers a historical context that underscores the continuum of Black women's struggle for equality and dignity.

African people, wherever they may be in the diaspora, have a long tradition of oral history; stories are passed down through song, folk-tales, sermons, poetry, and personal histories. For example, within African Baptist churches in Nova Scotia, the names of those who have died are read into church records, preserved so they will not be forgotten. By naming we recognize, unify, and empower ourselves. It is key to the survival of a people.

Beginnings

Very little of what one reads or sees about Nova Scotia reveals that people of African descent have lived there since the 1600s. Nova Scotia is called 'Canada's Ocean Playground,' but provincial-government and corporate advertising, audiovisual tourist displays, and public-relations brochures reflect only people of European ancestry: the Scots, the Celts, the French, and the Irish among others. There is very little mention of Nova Scotia's first people, the Micmac.

People of African descent live in forty-three communities throughout Nova Scotia, which is populated by over seventy-two different ethnic groups.[1] To understand the lives of Black women in Nova Scotia, one must begin by learning something about their people and their environment. The African presence in Nova Scotia began in 1605 when the French established a colony at Port-Royal (now Annapolis Royal). A Black man, Mathieu de Costa, accompanied French fur trader Pierre Du Gua, Sieur de Monts, and explorer Samuel de Champlain to the new colony. De Costa was one of Sieur de Monts's most useful men, as he knew the language of the Micmac and therefore served as interpreter for the French.[2]

And to His Assigns for Ever: A Slave Is a Slave Is a Slave

On Saturday next, at twelve o'clock, will be sold on the Beach, two hogshead of rum, three of sugar, and two well-grown negro girls, aged fourteen and twelve, to the highest bidder.[3]

Black slaves were imported into Nova Scotia from various places including the colonies, as early as 1686. That slave-sellers clearly saw the property value of young women is shown in the advertisement quoted above, which appeared in 1769. Once the establishment of Halifax was complete in 1751, at least ten slaves were no longer needed. An advertisement offering them for sale appeared in the Boston *Evening Post*. The slaves being sold were skilled tradesmen, including carpenters and sailmakers.[4] During this same period, a Black woman named Hagar was a cook in the household of Malachy Salter, a prominent Halifax magistrate and legislator. There was also a boy named Jack. At one point, when his wife was visiting Boston, Salter wrote asking her to buy another slave: 'Jack is Jack but rather worse. I am obliged to exercise the cat or stick almost every day. I believe Halifax don't afford another such idle, deceitful villain. Pray purchase a negro boy if possible.[5] Since Black women were often enslaved with their children, it is possible that 'idle' Jack may have been Hagar's son.

A census return for Nova Scotia in 1767 lists the total population of the province at 13,374. Recorded in the census are 104 people of African descent, spread throughout 12 of the 30 townships surveyed. Of this number 49 were female and 55 were male; the majority were found in Halifax and area. Given the period, and the clear evidence of slavery in Nova Scotia, it may be assumed that the people listed were slaves.[6]

Slaves had value and were property, along with clothing, furniture, horses, wine, and other household possessions. Unlike other property, with the exception of animals, slave women offered owners distinct advantages over furniture and even male slaves: they could increase the master's wealth by 'breeding' other 'slaves.' John Wentworth, a former governor of New Hampshire who became governor of Nova Scotia in 1792, commented on this capacity in a letter accompanying nineteen slaves he sent to his cousin in Dutch Guiana: 'The women are stout and able and promise well to increase their numbers.'[7] (Wentworth's involvement with Black women also figures later in this paper in connection with the Maroon women.) The treatment of slaves as property is demonstrated by their frequent sale at public auction with other possessions and their inclusion in wills and estate records. The age and gender of the slaves did not appear to have any bearing on how they were acquired or disposed of. 'To be sold at public auction on Monday, the 3rd of November, at the house of Mr John Rider, two slaves, viz. a boy and a girl, about eleven years old; likewise a puncheon of choice cherry brandy, with sundry other articles.'[8] Historian T.W. Smith points out that slavery in Nova Scotia was extended 'under the tacit permission of law and sanction of society.'[9]

During Nova Scotia's period of slavery, Black female slaves were called upon to do more than domestic chores for their masters. Sylvia was a servant of Colonel John Creighton of Lunenburg. On 1 July 1782 the town was invaded by soldiers from the strife-ridden American colonies. Sylvia shuttled cartridges hidden in her apron from Creighton's house to the fort where he and his soldiers were engaged in battle. When the house came under fire, Sylvia threw herself on top of the colonel's son to protect him. During the battle she also concealed her master's valuables in a bag that she lowered into a well for safe keeping.

Typically, it was not Sylvia who was publicly recognized or rewarded for her efforts, but her master and a militia private. A year later the provincial house of assembly dealt with the event and voted 'that there be paid to John Creighton, Esquire Colonel of Militia, for the County of Lunenburg for himself, a non-commissioned officer, and one private who were made prisoners at Lunenburg and carried to New England, and who were afterwards set free, the sum of £106.19s out of the arrears of the land tax due from the counties of Lunenburg and Queen's County, when the same shall be paid into the treasury.'[10] That slave women were treated harshly by their masters is documented in the public record. Why would Sylvia risk her life to protect his progeny and property? Was it her sense of loyalty, or an essential sense of decency, of humanness and caring for children? Whatever her motivation, it stands in stark contrast to the behaviour of some of her white female contemporaries, one of whom, as we will see later, refused to cancel the indenture of a young Black girl servant to enable her to reunite with her family.

Who owned slaves is an area for inquiry. Of particular interest are ministers who were slave-masters. Public records clearly document that some of Nova Scotia's most prominent and influential families (including a governor) were slave-owners. These men of the cloth adjusted their Christian beliefs and principles and found biblical approval for their actions when they purchased slaves. Ministers not only owned slaves, they baptized and christened their own and the slaves of others. The slaves of John Wentworth were christened by Reverend Dr Breynton in February 1784 at Halifax's St Paul's Church, before they were sent away to Dutch Guiana. It was common practice for masters to baptize their slaves so they might have 'salvation'; such conversion rarely resulted in emancipation. Lunenburg's Presbyterian minister John Seccombe kept a journal in which he noted that 'Dinah, my negro woman-servant made a profession and confession publickly and was baptized, July 17, 1774.'[11] For Dinah, the Christian concept of salvation and freedom for the baptized would have been a painful irony. Dinah had a son, Solomon, who was brought to the province as a slave, and who died in 1855 at the age of ninety; no record has been found of the date of Dinah's death.

The slave-owning ministers did not go unchallenged, especially within their own ranks. One case demonstrating this challenge, and the tenacity of slave-owners, involved Truro's well-established Presbyterian minister, Reverend Daniel Cock. In 1788, Reverend Cock owned two slaves, a mother and her daughter. The mother had been given to him, but he sold her because of her 'unruly conduct.' The daughter was purchased by Reverend Cock. Reverend James McGregor, also a Presbyterian minister at nearby Pictou, was outraged that his colleague would hold fellow human beings in bondage. In protest, Reverend McGregor refused to take communion with parishioners who would tolerate such behaviour. After having written a personal letter to Reverend Cock urging him to release the young Black woman, he took further public action. He published a tract entitled 'A Letter to a Clergyman, Urging Him to Set Free a Black Girl He Held in Slavery,' which was widely distributed throughout the Truro area. A number of local ministers, insulted by this action, quickly rose to Reverend Cock's defence. Since the records confirm that some of these ministers were themselves slave-owners, it is probable they correctly read between the lines of Reverend McGregor's tract: 'Reverend Sir, let me ask you, Does not your practice in keeping a slave contradict your daily prayers? It surely does. Do you not pray for the downfall of Babylon? Yes. Then you pray in effect for the total abolition of slavery ... I would entreat you, Reverend Sir to consider what a baleful influence your example will have upon others. Doubtless it has already drawn others into the sin, and it may draw others into it for generations after you are rotten in your grave. Many will shield themselves against strong arguments with this: Surely when the Reverend Mr. ——, a good minister does it, there cannot be any harm in it.'[12] In spite of Reverend McGregor's public attempt to embarrass and to use moral suasion, Reverend Cock did not free the young girl, who became known as 'Deal McGregor' because of Reverend McGregor's effort to free her. She continued as Reverend Cock's slave until he died in 1805.

In writing about this case, one modern historian has commented that the information about the incident was drawn from 'biased sources,' since the account was described by one of McGregor's descendants. The Reverend Cock could not speak in his own defence because his papers were apparently lost in a fire. (However, this historian did not ask why there is no record of the women speaking in their own defence.) After all, it must be asked, what defence (Christian or otherwise) can there be for enslaving women and their children?[13]

The mother and daughter enslaved by Reverend Cock were not the only mother/daughter pairs held together in slavery. In his will, Thomas Robinson left property to his daughter

Arcadia Cannon: 'I give and bequeath to my daughter Arcadia Cannon Two hundred Pounds in cash, Nova Scotia currency, to be paid to her by my executors, together with my Negro woman Priscilla and her child Sally.'[14]

These cases confirm that slavery was well entrenched before the arrival of the United Empire Loyalists in 1783. Their arrival, bringing with them slaves they called 'servants for life,' greatly increased the number and visibility of slaves in the province. The Loyalist migration would also mean that, for the first time, there would be large numbers of free Black people in Nova Scotia, a situation not found elsewhere in North America in the late 1700s.

The Loyalist Sojourn

In 1783, at the end of the American War of Independence, British officials had to evacuate their Loyalists, including thousands of former slaves, from the American colonies. In 1775, at the beginning of the war, Virginia's governor, Lord Dunsmore, had issued a call to 'indentured servants' and 'negroes' to enlist in the British army. Four years later, then British Commander-in-Chief Sir Henry Clinton set forth the Philipsburg Proclamation: 'to every negro who shall desert the rebel Standard, full security to follow within these lines, any occupation which he think proper.'[15] Primarily, these offers were tactics aimed at weakening the colonists' position rather than expressions of concern for the slaves and their condition. On the contrary, white colonists loyal to Britain were allowed to keep their slaves. During the war, slaves fought in active combat and served as spies, pilots, guides, nurses, and personal servants. Estimates are that 100,000 slaves – men and women – fled to the British side during the war.

New York, the last British base, became the site of the final Loyalist evacuation. In the postwar years, former slaves lived in fear that their former masters would come to claim them. Boston King and his wife Violet, once slaves, were among the group waiting in New York in anticipation of the voyage to Nova Scotia and freedom. Boston King's memoirs reveal the alarm and the danger: 'This dreadful rumour filled us all with inexpressible anguish and terror especially when we saw our old masters coming from Virginia, North Carolina, and other parts, and seizing upon their slaves in the streets of New York, or even dragging them out of their beds.[16] Boston and Violet King eventually made the voyage to Nova Scotia, settling in Birchtown, near Shelburne, on Nova Scotia's south coast.

Judith Jackson, who considered herself a free Black Loyalist, also waited. She had been owned by John Mclean, who lived in Norfolk, Virginia, before he fled to safety behind British lines. Though he had sold her to Johnathan Eilbeck, she believed that she was a free person. Upon escaping to the British Army she immediately began to work for Lord Dunsmore, doing laundry and other chores. At the end of the war, Judith Jackson was in New York, waiting to leave for Nova Scotia. In hand she carried her 'freedom certificate' issued by British Brigadier General Samuel Birch. Eilbeck arrived in New York, clearly intending to take her back to Virginia. He took Jackson's clothes, her money, and her child, whom he sent on to Virginia while he filed an appeal to a board of commissioners claiming he owned Jackson. The board, set up to hear claims from owners and slaves, ruled that Judith Jackson was the rightful property of Eilbeck.[17]

The American colonists did not want to be deprived of their slave property, especially since their economic well-being depended on the institution of slavery. Article Seven of the Provisional Peace Agreement signed in 1782, stated that there would be no 'destruction or carrying away of Negroes or other property of the American Inhabitants.' Consequently, the colonists wanted these terms respected. Complicating this situation for the British was their commitment to those Black people, former slaves, who had escaped to fight for the British.

A high-level meeting between General George Washington and British Commander Guy Carleton was held in 1783 to discuss the issue of slave property.[18] Washington's position was that all slaves who had been owned by Americans should not be taken away. Carleton, however, insisted that he would evacuate any slave who had responded to the Dunsmore and Clinton proclamations. Carleton kept a detailed register of 774 former slaves, so that compensation could be paid should claims filed by the Americans be found legitimate. This document, known as Carleton's 'Book of Negroes,' records the name, age, and a brief physical description of each Black person leaving New York.[19]

Verifying the exact number of free Black Loyalists who came to Nova Scotia and the number of slaves who came with their masters is difficult because of the variation in numbers given in the records of the period. Carleton's 'Book of Negroes' lists 3000 free Black Loyalists who left between April and November 1783. Many who left earlier or later are not recorded. It is further estimated that at least 1200 slaves came during this same period with white Loyalists.[20] After a two-week-journey from New York to Nova Scotia, the Black settlers – free and slave – arrived in Nova Scotia. Settlements were established in Digby, Halifax, Preston, Annapolis, Shelburne, Birchtown, and Saint John (in 1783 New Brunswick was part of Nova Scotia).

The Black Loyalists believed they were coming to a land where they could exercise their liberty and establish themselves. This soon proved not to be the case: '1785, May 12, It is ordered that 50 Handbills be immediately printed forbidding Negro Dances and Negro Frolicks in this Town of Shelburne.'[21] Not only did the Black Loyalists expect to move freely, they expected to receive the government grants of land and provisions promised all Loyalists regardless of colour. Rarely were their expectations met. Government-hired surveyors were slow in completing their work; the Black petitioners were clearly not a priority. Most, if they received any land at all, were given a few hectares of rocky tracts unsuitable for farming. It was much the same with the distribution of provisions and implements of husbandry.

The settlers sought waged work in the fishing, lumbering,

and boat-building industries. In many cases, just to survive they were forced to indenture themselves, sometimes for a year or more. Often, employers did not provide the food and clothing they had promised in return for the indenture, nor could they be relied upon to respect the agreements, as shown in the case of Lydia Jackson, discussed later in this paper. Out of necessity, many of the Black Loyalists were obliged, as one of them put it, 'to cultivate the lands of a white man for half the produce, which occupies the whole of our time.[22]

Census records for the period reveal the marketable skills to be found among Black Loyalists. A census taken in Birchtown, the largest of the Black communities, in 1784 listed thirty-eight occupations, including weavers, doctors, bricklayers, tailors, butchers, and blacksmiths. The women were weavers, seamstresses, cooks, and hat-makers.[23] However, despite their skills, these early Black settlers were forced to take whatever wage white employers decided to pay. Consequently, Black Loyalists were hired in preference to white disbanded soldiers, who demanded higher wages.

This situation, along with frustration and disputes over land grants and generalized poverty, precipitated Nova Scotia's – and perhaps Canada's – first race riot, in Shelburne in the summer of 1784. Benjamin Marston, the government surveyor for Shelburne recorded the event in his diary: 'July 26: Great Riot today. The disbanded soldiers have risen against the Free negroes to drive them out of Town because they labour cheaper than they–the soldiers.'[24] By the second day of the riot, white soldiers had destroyed twenty houses owned by Black Loyalists. The event was so serious that Governor John Parr sailed to Shelburne to review the crisis.

Freedom for Black people, for Black women, was elusive, regardless of the promises made by the British at the close of the American War of Independence. The case of Mary Postell illustrates the precarious situation of Blacks and the fight they were prepared to wage to leave the American colonies. In 1787 Mary Postell was sold by Jesse Gray of Argyle, Shelburne County, to William Monaghan. Gray, the owner of several

Black women slaves, sold her for one hundred bushels of potatoes. He was tried in the Shelburne county court on a charge of misdemeanour. The charge was not related to having sold a slave; rather, it was that Gray had sold a slave he did not own. However, when Gray provided the court with proof that he had owned Postell (in the southern colonies) he was acquitted. Postell then became the property of Monaghan.

Though she was 'property,' Mary Postell held on to and fought for her freedom. Four years later, she took Jesse Gray to court, charging him with stealing her children. She complained to the court in April 1791; Gray was ordered to appear to answer to the charges and Monaghan was also called to appear to give evidence. The case was heard in July 1791. Postell took the stand, providing the court with a sworn testimony detailing her life well before she arrived in Nova Scotia with her two children, Flora and Nell, as one of Jesse Gray's servants. After Gray had sold her in 1787, he took Nell and Flora. Gray, who gave unsworn testimony, stated he had sold Postell to Monaghan, and that he had sold the child Flora but still had the child Nell in his possession. After several witnesses testified, including Black Loyalists Scipio and Diana Wearing, the case was finally resolved in November 1791. Gray was found not guilty of a misdemeanour.

We can only imagine what conversations may have taken place between Mary Postell and other Black women also owned by Gray. The year before Mary was sold by Gray, he had sold a woman named Molly, who also took him to court to fight for her liberty. She too lost her fight. Other Black Loyalist women took court action on behalf of themselves and their children. Susannah Connor was fortunate; she won her case against John Harris, who held indenture papers for her son and was planning to leave Nova Scotia taking the young boy with him. When the court ruled the indenture had to be cancelled, Connor won custody of her son.[25] Black women were bold and decisive despite their 'official' status as powerless slaves. They filed formal charges against their masters, forcing them into an arena that white men normally dominated and controlled. Some women lost the battle, but that they fought says much about their tenacity and will to survive.

If freedom was elusive for those ostensibly free, the situation for Black slaves was grim. Many slaves could hold no hope of being set free, even upon the death of their owners. Annapolis merchant Joseph Tottan left his wife Suzannah the use of 'slaves, horses, cattle, stock, etc.' and 'to each of three daughters, a negro girl slave ... to her executors, administrators and assigns for ever.'[26] Even in death, Black people, Black females were not considered equal human beings.

The line was clearly and firmly established, setting down a pattern for the future: Black women, regardless of age, were property and at the service of not only the white male slave-owners, but also their wives, sons, and daughters. Some slave women seized their freedom. Determined owners placed newspaper notices offering rewards for their return. Detailed descriptions, such as the following by John Rock, were given to aid capture: 'Ran away from her master, John Rock on Monday the 18th of August last, a Negro Girl named Thursday, about four and a half feet high, broad-set with a lump over her right eye. Had on when she went away a red cloth petticoat, a red biaze bed-gown and a red ribbon about her head. Whoever may harbour said Negro girl, or encourage her to stay away from her said master, may depend upon being prosecuted as the law directs; and who ever may be so kind as to take her up and home to her said master shall be paid all costs and charges with two dollars reward for their trouble.'[27] 'Thursday' was found, re-enslaved, and ultimately listed in John Rock's personal inventory after his death; final estate reports noted that she had been sold for twenty pounds.[28]

While Black women slaves were being sold, left in wills, traded, and otherwise used, Black Loyalist women, evidently free, worked to earn a living for themselves and their families. At the same time, they worked to set-up communities. In 1787 Catherine Abernathy, a Black Loyalist teacher, instructed children in Preston, near Halifax. She taught a class of twenty children in a log schoolhouse built by the people of the community. Abernathy also held regular church services in her home on Sundays.[29] As an educator, Abernathy established a tradition of Black women teachers that would be continued to the present day. Her contemporaries Violet King and Phillis George, the wives of ministers, carved another path: Black women working actively beside their partners as they ministered in the church and community, while providing a stable base for their families. In their own right, the women were religious and spiritual leaders.

Violet King had been a slave in Wilmington, North Carolina, before she escaped, seeking freedom with the Loyalist forces. Along with her husband, Boston, who was twelve years younger, she sailed to Nova Scotia with other Black Loyalists in 1783. Settling in Birchtown, near Shelburne, Violet was converted to the Methodist faith by preacher Moses Wilkinson. According to Boston King, after her conversion, Violet began to preach to others and was 'not a little opposed by some of our Black brethren.'[30]

What must it have been like for Phillis George in Shelburne in the late 1780s? Her husband travelled extensively, setting up Baptist churches in Nova Scotia and New Brunswick. David George preached to and baptized Blacks and whites alike, not a popular undertaking at the time. The Georges had three children; money and food were scarce. On one occasion, a gang of fifty white former soldiers, armed with a ship's tackle, surrounded their house, overturning it and what contents it had. Some weeks later, on a Sunday, a white mob arrived at the George's church. They whipped and beat David, driving the Baptist minister into the swamps of Shelburne. Under the cover of darkness, George made his way back to town, collected Phillis and the children, and fled to neighbouring Birchtown.[31]

While David George and Boston King left personal testimonies as part of their legacies, the lives of Violet King, Phillis George, and other Black Loyalist and slave women await reconstruction. That much richness remains to be uncovered can be seen in the life of Rose Fortune. A descendant of Black Loyalists, Rose Fortune lived in Annapolis Royal in the mid-1800s. She distinguished herself by establishing a baggage service for travellers arriving by boat at Annapolis from Saint John and Boston. A modest wheelbarrow and her strong arms were her biggest assets. Rose's activities were not only commercial. Concerning herself with the well-being of the young and old alike, she declared herself policewoman of the town, a first in North America, and, as such, took upon herself the responsibility of making sure that young children were safely off the streets at night.[32]

Black Loyalists had been promised enough land to start new lives in Nova Scotia. However, then the land grants were allocated, Black Loyalists, if granted any land at all, received much less than their white counterparts.[33] Dissatisfaction with this blatant inequality, coupled with an unyielding desire to build a better future for their families, led many to leave for Sierra Leone, West Africa, where Black Loyalists were determined to create a new life. John Clarkson, a British naval officer sent to Nova Scotia to organize the move to Sierra Leone, detailed what he saw in his diary: 'It is not in my power to describe the scandalous and shameful conduct shewn to the free blacks by many of the White people in both provinces (New Brunswick and Nova Scotia) although Government allowed to many of them from 60 to 100 acres of land, the greatest part have never been in possession of more than one or two acres and they have so completely worked the land up that it will not yield half crops ... By the account given in by many of the free Blacks who gave their names in this morning there cannot be a doubt that their complaints were founded on facts. For they have certainly been much oppressed and are not in a deplorable state.'[34]

After living through nine harsh years, Black settlers, Loyalist and slave, were so desperate that they risked everything they had to leave. Some were forced to steal their children from their masters. Others, such as the Ceasar Smith family, feared they would have to leave their children behind. The

Smith family had lost all their possessions and their home in a fire. Destitute, they agreed to indenture their young daughter Phoebe to William Hughes, an English shipwright. The family decided to join the group going to Sierra Leone, but Phoebe had three years' indenture left to serve. William Hughes would not release the child. John Clarkson believed that, if the child was left behind with no family, she would be sold as a slave.

Clarkson decided to speak directly to Ann Hughes, William's wife and the mother of their ten children. He appealed to her to think of what Phoebe's mother must be feeling: 'I saw Mrs. Hughes, and solicited her in the most affecting way to induce her to give up the child – I called upon her as a mother, and described the distressed state of Smith's whole family at the thought of leaving the girl behind, and brought to her recollection the circumstances which occasioned the child to be indented for five years, which happened in consequence of Smith's family having lost all they had in the world, by their house being burnt down, that the poor Mother was constantly in tears about her child and I therefore hoped she would feel the case, as if it were her own and do as she would be done by: but could not make the least impression.'35 Ann Hughes refused to release Phoebe; the Smith family sailed to Sierra Leone without her. In other cases, the husband might be enslaved, but would plead for his wife and family to go so they might have a chance for a better life.

The severity of the physical abuse meted out to Black women and the utter disregard for them as human beings is graphically revealed by the story of Lydia Jackson. A young Black woman, Jackson had been abandoned by her husband and invited by Henry Hedley to live in his house as a companion for his wife Mary. Jackson was in their home for a few days before he demanded she pay board or indenture herself to him for seven years. Although she had no money, Jackson would not agree to an indenture. Hedley persisted and she finally agreed to an indenture of one year.

Lydia Jackson could not read or write. Taking advantage of

the situation, Hedley drew up an indenture for thirty-nine years and told her to sign it with her mark. A day after she signed, Hedley advised her that she would finish her one-year term at the home of a doctor in Lunenburg. Upon her arrival at the home of Dr Bulman, he told her she had been indentured to him for thirty-nine years for the sum of twenty pounds, which had already been paid to Hedley. Bulman and his wife Jane considered Lydia Jackson their property to do with as they wished. Clarkson recorded her story in his journal: 'Dr. Bulman turned out to be a very bad master, frequently beating her with the tongs, sticks, pieces of rope &c. about the head & face, his wife likewise was by no means backward to lend him her assistance on these occasions. For some words she had spoken with the least intention of giving offence took occasion to knock her down, and though she was then in the last month of pregnancy, in the most inhuman manner stamped upon her whilst she lay upon the ground.'[36] Lydia Jackson gathered her courage and filed a complaint against Bulman. A lawyer represented her in court, but Bulman's power and influence in the community held the day. Bulman also declared he would sell her as a slave in the West Indies.

In the interim, Bulman sent her out of town to his farm, where his servants had full authority to beat and punish her. After three years, still undefeated, she slipped into the woods and eventually made her way to Halifax, where she found a way to have a 'Memorial' prepared, outlining her case for presentation to the governor, whom John Clarkson notes 'paid little or no attention to it.' She went further, to the chief justice, who promised to look into her case. Hearing about the emigration plan, Jackson went to Clarkson for help. He pursued her case with Dr Bulman, and consulted a lawyer about a settlement for her wages. Her situation was not hopeful, given Bulman's position, and Clarkson advised her to leave Bulman to 'his own reflections.' Clarkson does not say whether Lydia finally became part of the exodus; he does comment that he had encountered many others like her.

On New Year's Day 1792, prayers were offered at Halifax's St Paul's Church for a safe voyage of the fifteen transport ships leaving for Sierra Leone. Phillis and David George and their family, along with twelve hundred other Black Loyalists, ended their sojourn in Nova Scotia. On one of the ships, the *Eleanor*, was a passenger who had a special request for John Clarkson. A 104-year-old Black woman asked to be taken on to the deck to see Clarkson; she asked him to take her 'that she might lay her bones in her native country.'[37]

Black Loyalist women who left Nova Scotia continued to break ground upon settling in Sierra Leone. Mary Perth had taught herself to read the Bible when a slave in Virginia. She would often wait until dark and, taking her child with her, would go to preach to slaves in nearby plantations. When she made her escape from her master in 1776, she took three young women with her.[38] Mary Perth came to Nova Scotia in 1783 with her husband Ceasar, and left with other Black Loyalists in 1792. In Sierra Leone, Perth owned her own home and set up a boarding house. She was a Methodist and active in her church. At the age of sixty-six she remarried and carried on her business ventures. Mary Perth, Martha Hazeley, and Sophia Small were the first three retailers to open shops in Freetown, Sierra Leone.[39]

The exodus of Black Loyalists depleted the Black population. Approximately two thousand Black Loyalists and an undetermined number of slaves were left scattered throughout Nova Scotia to fend for themselves against a white populace that was so clearly hostile.

Maroon Women

As the Black Loyalists were settling in Sierra Leone, events in Jamaica forced a second wave of Black immigrants to sail for Nova Scotia. A proud people, the Maroons were descendants of runaway slaves who for over one hundred and fifty years had waged war against British colonists in Jamaica. Finally, in 1738, the British signed peace treaties with the Maroons, treaties that were later broken and led to further fighting in 1795. An agreement was struck with the Trelawny Town Maroons, considered the largest of the Maroon communities. Though one of the agreed-upon terms was that the Maroons would not be sent away, this condition was not respected by colonial authorities.[40] In 1796, 543 Maroon women, men, and children were exiled to Nova Scotia. Upon their arrival the men were put to work on reconstruction of the third fortification at Citadel Hill in Halifax.

Of the Maroon women very little is recorded. We do know they were used for the 'entertainment' of some of the province's leaders: Governor John Wentworth is known to have taken a Maroon woman as his mistress, while Alexander Ochterloney, a commissioner placed in charge of the Maroons, 'took five or six of the most attractive Maroon girls to his bed, keeping what the surveyor of Maroons, Theophilus Chamberlain called a "seraglio" for his friends.'[41] Governor Wentworth bought land in the Preston area, where he maintained both a farm and a summer home and employed Maroon labour. Sarah Colley, who in 1804 bore a child, George Wentworth Colley, from her relationship with Wentworth, has many descendants in present-day East Preston.[42] Harriet Diggs Colley, related by marriage to James Alexander Colley, died in 1991 at the age of ninety-eight. She left 148 grandchildren, 316 great-grandchildren, 86 great-grandchildren, 45 great-great-grandchildren, and six great-great-great-greatgrandchildren.[43]

The government of Jamaica allocated funds to the government of Nova Scotia for maintaining the Maroons. Local white settlers saw in this new group of Black settlers the potential of a labour pool that might replace the workers lost when the Black Loyalists left the province. While the presence of the Maroons was beneficial to the government and to local merchants, the Maroons were not happy with the increasing efforts, such as those advanced by local churches, to regulate their lives. They informed the agent who had brought them to Nova Scotia of their desire to be re-settled in another British colony. In 1880, the Maroon interlude ended when the majority sailed from Nova Scotia to Sierra Leone, where Black Loyalists had been sent only four years before them. Historian Mavis C. Campbell points out the varied roles played by Maroon women ranging from agriculturists to warriors. Nanny, the most celebrated woman warrior, remains a national hero.

Campbell's recent original work on Maroon societies examines the origins and development of Maroon communities in Jamaica. Such communities were visible examples of the resistance of slaves to the system established to suppress and exploit them. A comprehensive picture of Maroon women will emerge only through extensive research into their lives in Jamaica, Nova Scotia, and Sierra Leone.[44]

In the early 1800s, the court were compelled to become involved in public debate on the legality of slavery. While slaves were being sold, left in wills, and traded as common property, slaves themselves challenged the legality of slavery in the courts. Former owners also tried to prove ownership or receive compensation for runaways. One noted case in 1802 elicited opinions from several lawyers, one of whom wrote: 'And why a Negro, so made an article of traffic, should not be as much the property of a company trader, as ostrich feathers, Indigo, or Gold dust, is an enigma which I am unable to unravel.'[45] Drawing upon practice both in Britain and in the colonies, and the 23d Act of George II, the lawyers continued their arguments in support of slavery, reiterating that 'Negroes, even in this province have always been allowed to pass by will as personal estate ... They have uniformly been sold, in the common course of traffic as other chattel interests are or were sold, and warranted by bill of sale to be the property of the seller.'[46] Whether or not slavery was upheld or sanctioned by the courts, owners continued to buy and sell slaves even as slaves continued their quest for liberty by escaping from their masters.

In 1808, fearing the continued economic impact of the loss of this property, owners appealed to the Nova Scotia legislature. They sought passage of an act 'securing them their property or indemnifying them for its loss.' During this legislative session, Thomas Ritchie, the representative for Annapolis, brought forward an act 'to regulate negro servants within the province.' He received support for his efforts when the bill passed second reading in January 1808. The bill, however, never became law.[47]

Some slaves left Nova Scotia not of their own volition. Slaveowners sold their slaves out of province to Upper Canada, the American colonies, and the West Indies. Historian T.W. Smith recounts the story of a slave woman: 'An aged woman at Annapolis used to recall to her latest days a scene witnessed by her in childhood, when a slave woman was put on board a schooner from a wharf at the lower end of the town to be taken away, her screaming child clinging to her till torn from her by sheer force.'[48] The last recorded slave sale appeared in a Halifax paper in 1820: five years after the Black Refugees arrived, thirteen years before an act of the British parliament abolished slavery in 1833.[49]

The Women among Them

The last major migration of African people to Nova Scotia occurred from 1813–16, after the War of 1812. It is the memory of this group that is strongest in Nova Scotia, for their descendants live on in Black communities such as Hammonds Plains, Preston, Beechville, Conway, Cobequid Road, and Three Mile Plains.

While the Treaty of 1783 officially ended the American War of Independence, it did not prevent continuing animosity between Britain and the newly independent states. For its part, Britain routinely searched American vessels, and both sides were guilty of not respecting the conditions of the treaty. This situation culminated in the War of 1812. A proclamation issued by British Vice-Admiral Alexander Cochrane offering transportation for anyone in the colonies wanting to leave was widely circulated among the slave population in the former colonies; it paralleled the earlier edict issued by Henry Clinton during the War of Independence. Two thousand former slaves, mostly from the states in the Chesapeake Bay area, and known as the Black Refugees, were transported by ship to Nova Scotia.[50]

When the Refugees arrived, they were initially housed in a former prison at Melville Island in Halifax Harbour. The first years of settlement fully tested their will and capacity to survive. The first three winters were the worst ever recorded in Nova Scotia. Epidemics of smallpox threatened the lives of many Refugees. There was little, if any, work. And few provisions were provided by the governing authorities. In spite of the conditions, the Refugees were resourceful. Looking to their environment for sustenance, they picked blueberries, raspberries, and strawberries. Lakes offered trout and eel, while forests abounded in wildflowers, wildlife, and trees. From the later the Refugees made brooms, baskets, barrels, firewood, and wreathes. Some of the earliest sketches and photographs of the Halifax city market show Black women selling baskets overflowing with mayflowers. Basket-weaving for them was not an activity used to fill idle time: it was work that brought in money vital to the survival of the family.[51]

The Refugees set down long roots, intertwined from community to community. The Refugee women were the planters. When, in 1836, the provincial government tried to send the people of Preston to Trinidad, it was the women who objected: 'They all appear fearful of embarking on the water – many of them are old and have large families, and if a few of the men should be willing to go, the Women would not. It is objected among them that they have never heard any report of those who were sent away a few years ago to the same place, and think that if they were doing well some report of it would have reached them. They seem to have some attachment to the soil they have cultivated, poor and barren as it is.'[52]

Census records for the late 1800s list Black women in many occupations, including dressmaker, shopkeeper, basket-maker, private teacher, weaver, farmer, and washerwoman. Although they were settled in communities with some of the worst agricultural land in the province, many women farmed. In the 1881 census, Matilda Carter, 86, of Preston was noted as a female farmer. The same census listed Elizabeth Taylor, 60, a widow also in Preston who headed a household of eight. Mary Giggie, 48, a farmer in Hammond's Plains, headed a household having three children.[53]

The involvement and presence of Black women vibrates throughout the social, educational, cultural, and religious life of the Black community. Between 1824 and 1891, a network of African Baptist Churches were organized in Black communities throughout Nova Scotia. In 1854, these churches were re-grouped into the African Baptist Association. Women were active in most of the churches, where they taught in Sabbath schools, and in nearby day schools. While women were listed in the membership of church registers, the first woman delegate did not attend an association annual meeting until 1891. Historian Pearleen Oliver writes that it would be another thirty-seven years before African Baptist women would establish their own organization.[54]

On 3 September 1917, the women of the African Baptist churches gathered in East Preston. Women of African descent have long carried water – the source of life – from a well to their homes (in many places they still do). When the women in East Preston came together, they gathered around a well near the church, since the church did not have a space they could use. This gathering became known as 'The Women at the Well.' The ladies' auxiliary they set up was charged with the responsibility for the 'stimulation of the spiritual, moral, social and educational, charitable, and financial work of all the local churches of the African Baptist Association.' They elected Maude Sparks as their president. The five vice-presidents were Jane Hamilton, Martha Middleton, Rufus Marsman, Margaret Upshaw, and Julia Williams. Bessie Wyse became official organizer responsible for organizing auxiliaries in all African Baptist Churches belonging to the association. By 1919, the position of official organizer became a permanent one responsible for 'women's work' in the churches.[55] Some of these same women later organized an auxiliary to provide support for the Nova Scotia Home for Coloured Children. While the mandate of the African Baptist Women's Auxiliary tied their work to local churches, the church meant Black communities: for Black communities, the African Baptist churches were the focus of social, educational, political, economic, and spiritual work.

In 1920, many of the same women organized the first 'Congress of Coloured Women.' Some fifty delegates gathered at Halifax's Cornwallis Street Baptist, the 'Mother Church' of the African Baptist Association. Proceedings included a prayer service, a roll-call of officers and delegates, and a presentation of papers. Topics included the history of coloured people in Nova Scotia, education, social and mission work, and the needs of young women working in domestic service. A photograph of delegates commemorates the event, which was reported in the local and regional newspapers of the time as the first event of its kind ever held in Nova Scotia, and Canada.[56] These examples highlight the continuing work of African Nova Scotian women within their communities in the early part of the 1900s and underscore the necessity of further research to present a thorough study of their history and experiences.

Conclusion

Many and varied are the roles Black women have played and continue to play within their own and the broader community. It has often been said that Black women are the backbone of the Black community: organizers, fund-raisers, nurturers, care-givers, mourners, and orators. Eva Cromwell, a contemporary leader within the African Baptist Women's movement, has commented that she believes in an adage older people used: Bloom where you're planted. Women of African descent in Nova Scotia, against all odds, have indeed bloomed where we have been planted.

NOTES

An earlier version of this paper, titled 'Our Mothers Grand and Great: Black Women of Nova Scotia,' was published in *Canadian Women Studies / Les cahiers de la femme* 4, no. 2 (Winter 1982).

1 While the term 'Black' is most commonly used to identify people of African origin, 'Afro–Nova Scotian' and 'African Canadian' have come into contemporary usage to identify people of African origin whose ancestry is Nova Scotian. These terms claim a valued heritage that predates slavery and colonialism and that affirm the right to self-definition. The term 'African' was common throughout Nova Scotia and in the late 1700s and the 1800s, within both the Black and the wider communities. The main Baptist church organization, which was established in 1854 and continues to function, is the African United Baptist Association. There were also African Methodist and African Orthodox churches; the latter still exists in Sydney, Nova Scotia. A separate school for Black children in Halifax in the mid-1800s was known as the 'African School.' 'People of Colour' was also used by Black people to describe themselves, and that term appears in public petitions on record for the period. In this paper both 'Black' and 'African Nova Scotian' are used.

2 *Pierre Du Gua, Sieur de Monts*, ed. William Inglis Morse (London: B. Quaritch 1939), 51.

3 T. Watson Smith, 'The Slave in Canada,' *Collections* of the Nova Scotia Historical Society, 10 (Halifax, 1989), 10. Smith cites Rev. G.W. Hill, 'Memoir of Sir Brenton Haliburton, Late Chief Justice of the Province of Nova Scotia' (Halifax: James Bowes & Sons 1864), 56. Smith's work is a valuable documentary study of the existence of slavery in Canada. In his preface, Smith acknowledges the difficulty in preparing the work because historians have 'almost wholly ignored the existence of slavery in Canada.' For a review of slavery in French Canada, see Marcel Trudel, *L'esclavage au Canada*

Français: Histoire et conditions de l'esclavage (Quebec: Presses de l'université Laval 1960).

4 Smith, 'Slave in Canada,' 9.

5 Ibid., 7.

6 Census return for Nova Scotia, 1767, Public Archives of Nova Scotia.

7 *Collections of the Nova Scotia Historical Society* 20 (1921), 53: John Wentworth, 24 Feb. 1784.

8 Smith, 'Slave in Canada,' 10.

9 Ibid., 20.

10 Mather Byles DesBrisay, *History of Lunenburg County* (Bridgewater: Bridgewater Bulletin), 68.

11 Ibid., 261.

12 Smith, 'Slave in Canada,' 54; James McGregor, 'A Letter to a Clergyman, Urging Him to Set Free a Black Girl He Held in Slavery' (Halifax, 1788), 175–7.

13 Robin W. Winks, *The Blacks in Canada* (Montreal, New Haven: McGill-Queen's University Press with Yale University Press 1971), 104.

14 Smith, 'Slave in Canada,' 55.

15 James W. St G. Walker, *The Black Loyalists: The Search for a Promised Land in Nova Scotia and Sierra Leone 1783–1870* (London and New York, 1976), 84. This work provides a comprehensive examination of the history of Black Loyalists and has been an invaluable source in the preparation of this chapter.

16 Boston King, 'Memoirs of the Life of Boston King, a Black Preacher,' *Methodist Magazine*, 1798, p. 157.

17 Ellen G. Wilson, *The Loyal Blacks* (New York, 1976), 68.

18 Walker, *Black Loyalists*, 10–11.

19 'Book of Negroes,' Public Archives of Nova Scotia, RG 1, vol. 423.

20 Smith, 'Slave in Canada,' 32.

21 *A Bibliography of Canadian Imprints, 1751–1800*, ed. Marie Tremaine (Toronto: University of Toronto Press 1952), 217.

22 King, 'Memoirs'; Marion Gilroy, *Loyalists and Land Settle-*

ment in Nova Scotia, Public Archives of Nova Scotia, no. 4 (Halifax, 1937). This publication provides a detailed listing of land grants given to all Loyalists after their arrival in Nova Scotia in 1783.

23 Muster Book of Free Blacks at Birchtown, 1784, Public Archives of Nova Scotia, MG 100, vol. 220, no. 4.

24 Walker, *Black Loyalists*, 48, citing W.O. Raymond, 'The Founding of Shelburne and Early Miramichie, Marston's Diary,' *Collections of the New Brunswick Historical Society* 3 (1907), 265.

25 General Sessions of the Peace, Shelburne, 1786, 1787, 1791, Public Archives of Nova Scotia, MG 4, vol. 141.

26 Smith, 'Slave in Canada,' 53–4. In 1968 when a small Black girl died, the St Croix cemetery near Windsor, Nova Scotia, refused to allow her to be buried within its gates. See *Chronicle Herald*, 12 Oct. 1968, p. 1.

27 Ibid., 12–13.

28 Ibid.

29 Walker, *Black Loyalists*, 84.

30 King, 'Memoirs,' 158.

31 David George's narrative appears in 'An Account of the Life of Mr. David George (as told to Brother John Rippon),' *Baptist Annual Register* 1 (1790–3), 473–84.

32 The memory of Rose Fortune is kept alive by her descendants, the Lewis family of Annapolis Royal. Daurene Lewis is an accomplished weaver whose work is well known in Nova Scotia and internationally. She holds the distinction of having been the first Black woman elected to a town council in Nova Scotia, and is recorded as being the first Black woman mayor in Canada. She was mayor of Annapolis Royal between 1985 and 1988.

33 Gilroy in *Loyalists and Land Settlement*, identifies the name, date, situation (that is, location), number of acres, and the origin or rank of each Loyalist. Black Loyalists are identified in the Origin or Rank column as 'Negro.'

34 *Clarkson's Mission to America 1791–1792*, ed. Charles B. Ferguson (Public Archives of Nova Scotia, Halifax, 1971), 46–7.

35 Ibid., 103–4.
36 Ibid., 89.
37 Ibid., 167.
38 Wilson, *Loyal Blacks*, 35.
39 Christopher H. Fyfe, *A History of Sierra Leone* (London, 1962), 101–2.
40 *Nova Scotia and the Fighting Maroons: A Documentary History*, ed. Mavis C. Campbell, Studies in Third World Societies, no. 41 (Williamsburg, Virginia, 1990), x, xvi. See also Campbell's *The Maroons of Jamaica 1655-1796: A History of Resistance, Collaboration and Betrayal* (Granby, Mass.: Bergin & Garvey 1988).
41 Colonial Records Office, 217/69, Chamberlain to Wentworth, 20 June 1798.
42 Nova Scotia Museum *Reports*, 1934–5, 45–6; Bridglal Pachai, *Beneath the Clouds of the Promised Land: The Survival of Nova Scotia's Blacks*, vol. 2: 1800–1989 (Halifax: 1991), 35.
43 Halifax *Mail Star*, Obituary, 17 June 1991.
44 Campbell, *Maroons of Jamaica*, 1–13.
45 Public Archives of Nova Scotia, 'Opinions of Several Gentlemen of the Law on the Subject of Negro Servitude in the Province of Nova Scotia,' Halifax, 1802, p. 7.
46 Ibid., 10–12.
47 Smith, 'Slave in Canada,' 117.
48 Ibid., 121.
49 Ibid., 113.
50 John Grant, *The Immigration and Settlement of the Black Refugees of the War of 1812 in Nova Scotia and New Brunswick* (Hantsport, NS: Lancelot Press 1990), 41.
51 Nearly two hundred years later, this tradition continues because there are women who learned the craft from their mothers, who in turn learned it from their mothers. One of those women is the late Edith Clayton. Born in Cherrybrook, she began weaving maplewood baskets when she was eight years old: it is a tradition reaching back six generations of her family. Until her death in 1990, Edith Clayton made and sold baskets, taught classes in basket-weaving, and

gave demonstrations throughout Nova Scotia and across Canada, preserving and passing on a significant and uniquely African–Nova Scotian aspect of the province's heritage. Her daughter Clara (Clayton) Gough not only continues her mother's basketry, but is innovating new designs and techniques. For an examination of the Clayton technique, see Joleen Gordon, *Edith Clayton's Market Basket: A Heritage of Splintwood Basketry in Nova Scotia* (Halifax, 1977); see also Sylvia Hamilton, 'A Glimpse of Edith Clayton,' *Fireweed*, issue 18, 1984.

52 *Journal of the House of Assembly*, 1837–8, Appendix 9, 10, June 1836.

53 Census records for 1881, Public Archives of Nova Scotia, RG 12, reels 13648, 13649.

54 Pearleen Oliver, *A Brief History of the Colored Baptists of Nova Scotia, 1782–1953* (Halifax, 1953), 39. See also Frank Stanley Boyd, ed., for P.E. McKerrow's 1895 work, titled *A Brief History of the Coloured Baptists of Nova Scotia and Their First Organization as Churches A.D. 1832* (Dartmouth: Afro Nova Scotian Enterprises 1975). McKerrow's book was originally published in 1895 by the Nova Scotia Printing Company. He recounts the origins and development of African Baptists in Nova Scotia.

55 'Minutes of the African United Baptist Association of Nova Scotia' (Halifax, 1917), 29–30.

56 *Sunday Leader*, 13 June 1920, p. 17.

2

'The Lord seemed to say "Go"': Women and the Underground Railroad Movement

ADRIENNE SHADD

I did not realize it then; but now I see that she was a brave woman.
John Little (1856) of his wife, who endured three months escaping with him from Tennessee to Canada West, ca. 1840[1]

I inquired of the Lord concerning the matter. I prayed most all night, and the Lord seemed to say 'Go.'
Mrs Armstrong of Colchester, Upper Canada, who rescued five of her children from bondage in Kentucky, 1844[2]

Between 1815 and 1865, and particularly after the passage of the Fugitive Slave Act of 1850,[3] it is estimated that tens of thousands of African-Americans sought refuge on Canadian soil. Some of these settlers were free Blacks migrating from northern free states and upper slave states. Others were fugitive slaves, for whom the road to freedom was made via the legendary Underground Railroad.[4]

Thus far, few studies have focused on the plight of women on the Underground Railroad and the tremendous difficulties they found in escaping and successfully eluding capture. In his classic work *The Underground Rail Road*,[5] William Still paid homage to the women of the Road when he wrote: 'In justice ... to the heroic female who was willing to endure the most extreme suffering and hardship for freedom, double honors were due.'[6] This paper, therefore, examines the experiences of women who escaped to Canada West before the American Civil War, drawing primarily on published accounts of Underground Railroad (UGRR) workers and exslaves. It argues that the much smaller percentages of successful women fugitives must be understood by examining the impact of gender on the fugitive-slave phenomenon and the many additional constraints hampering the escape of these women. The paper also surveys the fugitive community in Canada West and the role that women played in assisting the escape and resettlement of others, once they themselves had obtained their freedom.

The story of the Underground Railroad – a series of secret routes or 'trains' through northern states to 'terminals' in Canada – has been told many times. Some fugitives, once they reached the non-slaveholding northern states, received aid through organized systems that spirited them to freedom. This aid sometimes involved 'conductors' who personally transported 'passengers' from point A to point B, and/or 'stationmasters' who received and hid arrivals at transfer points. At times, in the operation of transporting passengers, elaborate disguises were devised to fool slave-catchers, or secret compartments in wagons or carriages were created. During the 1850s, transportation by boat or train became a more common method of conveying fugitives. However, many freedomseekers received little or no systematic aid – there might be assistance in the form of pointing out directions, or a meal. Sympathizers might even take in runaways for a few days. However, the trip was primarily the result of the slaves' own locomotion north and into Canada. Some scholars argue that the vast majority of fugitives attained their freedom without any organized help whatsoever,[7] thereby compounding further the hazards and dangers of escape.

In this context, how difficult would it be for women, particularly women with children, to make the trip north? American studies reveal that the majority of fugitive slaves – as many as 80 per cent – were men between the ages of 16 and 35.[8] In his book, Still recorded the stories of 892 fugitives, of whom 311 were reportedly on their way to Canada. Although we cannot be sure exactly how many of these actually arrived on British soil,[9] it is interesting to compare the percentage that were women. Of 311 escapees, only 63, or 20 per cent, were women, a figure consistent with overall rates of women fugitives. Likewise, Benjamin Drew's *A North-side View of Slavery* records the stories of 114 freedom-seekers, of whom only 18 (16 per cent) were women. While the latter figure cannot be considered representative in a statistical sense, and is perhaps influenced by the male bias of the author,[10] the numbers do give an indication of the far lower percentages of women who were able to obtain their freedom in this way.

Deborah Gray White's analysis of the female fugitive phenomenon in *Ar'n't I a Woman?* offers a number of persuasive reasons why women made up proportionately fewer fugitives as compared with men. The age profile of the average fugitive – between 16 and 35 years – covered precisely a woman's peak childbearing years. Women were more likely to be pregnant, nursing an infant, or having at least one small child to care for at this stage of their lives.[11]

Moreover, a slave woman, by necessity, had to be more concerned for the welfare of her child. Often, in a slave family, the decision about who would escape was based on who could run without encumbrance. No matter how painful it was for the slave woman and children to see their husband and father leave, at least the separation occurred with the knowledge that the offspring would be cared for by their mother. If the latter were sold, there was at least the *possibility* that a woman and her young children might be sold together. There was less chance that a father would be sold together with his children because, for example, fathers could not nurse small infants and children under one year of age, who were not bottle-fed in those days. A fugitive mother simply did not have the same assurances that her babies would be properly cared for if she became a fugitive.[12] Moreover, a strict nineteenth-century code of ethics dictated that, even for slaves, a mother's place was to remain with her children, at any cost.[13] Clearly, for one reason or another, not all slave women abided by this social dictate.

Mary Jones escaped with four-year-old Susan Bell, whose mother had fled to Canada three years earlier under circumstances that obliged her to leave her child, then only one year old. Apparently the latter, an invalid who had never walked, had been left in the care of friends who were to look after her until she could be safely delivered to her mother. The mother's terrible anxiety was reportedly evident in numerous letters penned concerning little Susan, and how and when her escape might be effected. The Vigilance Committee of Philadelphia, led by William and Letitia Still, among others, ran a well-organized Underground depot that aided hundreds of fugitives by providing food, shelter, clothing, and free passage to destinations in the North. (William and Letitia, Black abolitionists from Philadelphia, personally received many of these refugees in their home.) The committee was gratified to be able to help this woman and child, and to reunite the child with her mother.[14] However, as Gray White observes, 'the physical relief which freedom brought was limited compensation for the anguish (these mothers) suffered,' a fact known only too well by slave-owners, who would keep a tight hold on slave children in order to prevent their mothers from taking flight.[15]

Yet slave women did brave the odds and attempt escape with one or more children when they could. Indeed, of 151 fugitive women advertised for in 1850 New Orleans newspapers, not one was listed as having run away without her children.[16]

In one phenomenal case recorded by Still, Ann Maria Jackson, aged forty, fled from Maryland on foot with *seven* of her offspring. The children ranged in age from three or four up to sixteen years. Still's comment about this woman's escape is noteworthy: 'The fire of freedom obviously burned with no ordinary fervor in the breast of this slave mother, or she never would have ventured with the burden of seven children, to escape the hell of slavery.'[17]

Apparently, two of her children had already been sold and Ann Maria's husband, a freeman with whom she had been allowed to live, went insane because of it and had died in the poorhouse the previous fall (1857).

It almost broke my heart ... when [my master] came and took my children away as soon as they were big enough to hand me a drink of water. My husband was always very kind to me, and I had often wanted him to run away with me and the children, but I could not get him in the notion; he did not feel that he could, and so he stayed, and died broken-hearted, crazy. I was owned by Joseph Brown ... This Fall he said he was going to take four of my oldest children and two other servants to Vicksburg. I just happened to hear of the news in time. My master was wanting to keep me in the dark about taking them, for fear that something might happen. My master is very sly ...[18]

Fortunately, this brave woman and her family were recovered by UGRR workers just outside of Wilmington, Delaware. Although there were spies stationed along the route, a carriage was sent to pick them up and the party was spirited on without incident to Philadelphia and the Vigilance Committee. A letter from Hiram Wilson, a missionary and UGRR agent in St Catharines, later confirmed their safe arrival in Niagara Falls.

Niagara City, Nov. 30th, 1858

Dear Bro. Still: I am happy to inform you that Mrs. Jackson and her interesting family of seven children arrived safe and in good health and spirits at my house in St. Catharines, on Saturday evening last. With sincere pleasure I provided for them comfortable quarters till this morning, when they left for Toronto. I got them conveyed there at half fare, and gave them letters of introduction to Thomas Henning, Esq., and Mrs. Dr. Willis, trusting that they will be better cared for in Toronto than they could be at St. Catharines. We have so many coming to us we think it best for

some of them to pass on to other places. My wife gave them all a good supply of clothing before they left us. James Henry, an older son is, I think, not far from St. Catharines, but has not as yet reunited with the family. Faithfully and truly yours,
HIRAM WILSON.[19]

The success of this particular family belied the incredible dangers involved in fleeing with young children. For instance, two days before arriving in Cincinnati, Charlotte and Josiah Henson and their family of four exhausted their supply of provisions. Henson, who carried his youngest toddlers, aged two and three, in a knapsack on his back, was unable to prevent their cries of hunger during the night. His fear of detection was overwhelming.[20] In one of numerous escape attempts, Malinda and Henry Bibb and their young daughter fled one night from their Louisiana slaveholder. They spent eight or ten days in the Red River swamps trying to make some headway before finally being overtaken by slave-catchers. Bibb, who later established the *Voice of the Fugitive* newspaper (1851–3) in Sandwich, Canada West, was forced to make his next bid for freedom without Malinda or his child.[21]

Occasionally, tragedy accompanied unsuccessful escape attempts, revealing the incredible lengths to which women fugitives were driven in attempting to rescue their children from bondage. Margaret Garner had escaped from Kentucky with her husband, in-laws, and four children, but the party was captured in Ohio. Rather than see her offspring returned to slavery, this woman determined to save them in the only way she knew how. She grabbed a butcher knife and slit the throat of one little girl with the intention of killing the other three and then turning the knife on herself. However, she was overpowered and prevented from completing her desperate action. Canadian Underground Railroad conductor Alexander Milton Ross has provided a telling quotation from Margaret Garner, who is described in later trial testimony as a 'womanly, amiable, affectionate mother.' 'The child is my own, given me of God to do the best a mother could in its behalf. I have done the best I could; I knew it was better for them to go home to God than back to slavery.' This unfortunate individual was led back into bondage by the national guard with her remaining two children and the dead body of the third.[22]

Fugitive women with children caused Underground workers to suffer far greater worry and anxiety than was the case with single men. William Still was always nervous when transporting women and children because they stood a greater chance of being caught. 'Females,' he observed, 'undertook three times the risk of failure that males were liable to, not to mention the additional trials and struggles they had to contend with.'[23] Lawyer James Bigelow, a UGRR associate in Washington, DC, who sometimes conducted his activities under the assumed name 'William Penn,' also expressed apprehension. Referring to two women, each of whom had two children, he wrote: 'None of these can walk so far or so fast as scores of *men* that are constantly leaving. I cannot shake off my anxiety for these poor creatures.'[24]

In another case, Harriet Shephard led an escape from Chestertown, Maryland, on 1 November 1855 with her five children, an aunt and uncle, and three young men. The children were too young to walk very far and Mrs Shephard was penniless and unable to hire a 'conductor,' even if she had known someone willing to risk the penalty if caught helping them. She decided to make off with two horse-drawn carriages (four head of horses), and the group managed to find their way to Wilmington, Delaware. Here, UGRR workers split them into two parties, the couple and three young men being sent to Norristown, Pennsylvania, and the mother and five children secreted in Kimberton. However, the conductor at Kimberton was fearful of betrayal by a 'coloured woman' who knew of their escape and route through Wilmington. After considerable manoeuvring, the parties were sent to Philadelphia, where 'they were completely divided and disguised,' then sent on to Canada in a private compartment on one of the regular trains.[25]

Many female Underground Railroad travellers either did

not have children, or had children who had been sold away from them. Only 17, or 27 per cent, of Still's above-mentioned 63 cases of women escaping to Canada came with children. Others had no choice but to leave their children behind. Louisa Bell, who escaped to Toronto in July 1855, was the mother of Robert, six years old, and a little girl, Mary. She was forced by circumstances to make the heart-wrenching decision to leave her little ones 'in the hands of God.'[26]

Other factors that restricted flight for women had to do with the sexual division of labour on the slave farm or plantation: men, having been trained in more skills, had a greater chance of being hired out as artisans or craftsmen. They were also more likely to be chosen to assist in the transport of crops to market, and of supplies and other materials back to the plantation. Therefore, their knowledge of the outside world made escape far easier for them than for women. The nature of female bondage restricted movement away from the immediate environment. This lack of mobility was further reinforced in the 'abroad marriage' (a marriage between two slaves in different locations) whereby the husband normally did the travelling to visit his wife, rather than vice versa. Under these circumstances, potential fugitive women were forced to consider their lack of familiarity with the surrounding countryside, and the fact that they would be more conspicuous as women travelling alone or in groups.[27]

Some managed to overcome the latter obstacle by disguising themselves as men. Fifteen-year-old Ann Maria Weems eluded capture dressed in male attire, disguised as a young male coachmen to her 'master' (actually a UGRR conductor). Apparently, she played her role so well that members of the Philadelphia Vigilance Committee were astounded by her male appearance and boyish manner. Miss Weems was eventually sent on to Canada West to be educated at the 'Buxton Settlement,' a farming colony established for fugitive Blacks near Chatham.[28]

This particular mode of deception – dressing up in men's clothing – was evidently quite successful as it was employed by countless other women. Two such cases of women fugitives reaching the Windsor area were reported in the above-mentioned *Voice of the Fugitive* newspaper between November 1851 and August 1852.[29]

However, many women made their quest for freedom in the company of their husbands, fiancés, brothers, or unrelated male companions. Sometimes, as we have seen, they escaped in larger groups of men and women. Forty-three of the sixty-three above-mentioned Canada-bound females escaped in such company (68 per cent). Only fifteen came alone, although often under circumstances in which the fiancé would first secure a means of escape for his companion, then follow himself. In other instances, the woman would follow her mate, who was waiting anxiously at the other end of the line until such time as she could make her pre-planned getaway.

For example, Frances Hilliard, described as a beautiful young woman of twenty-nine years, assisted her husband to escape from his owner. One year later she followed him to Canada with the aid of a Black hand who hid her on a steamer sailing from Richmond to Philadelphia. In escaping, she left her mother, Sarah Corbin, and sister Maria, behind. The Vigilance Committee in Philadelphia sent her on to Toronto, but she was not able to find her husband there. As she could read and write very well, she wrote back the following:

Toronto, Canada, U.C., October 15th, 1855

MY DEAR MR. STILL: Sir – I take the opportunity of writing you a few lines to inform you of my health. I am very well at present, and hope that when these few lines reach you they may find you enjoying the same blessing. Give my love to Mrs. Still and all the children, and also to Mr. Swan, and tell him that he must give you the money that he has, and you will please send it to me, and I have received a letter from my husband saying that I must come on to him as soon as I get the money from him. I cannot go to him until I get the money that Mr. Swan has in hand. Please tell Mr. Caustle that the clothes he spoke of my mother did not know anything about them. I left them with Hinson Brown and he promised to give them to Mr. Smith. Tell him to ask Mr. Smith to get them from Mr. Brown for me, and when I get settled I will send him word and he can send them to me. The letters that were sent to me I received them all. I wish you would send me word if Mr. Smith is on the boat yet – if he is write me word in your next letter. Please send me the money as soon as you possibly can for I am very anxious to see my husband. I send to you for I think you will do what you can for me. No more at present, but remain

Yours truly, FRANCES HILLIARD

Send me word if Mr. Caustle had given Mr. Smith the money that he promised to give him.[30]

Occasionally, women escaped together. In one case, Charlotte Giles and Harriet Elgin cleverly donned suits of mourning, complete with heavy black veils, and prevailed upon a friend to get them on the train bound from Baltimore to Philadelphia. Unbeknownst to them, the master of one of the women was fast on their heels. He boarded the train while it was still in the Baltimore depot, searching for his 'property.' Approaching the two mourners, who were by this time playing up their grief-stricken roles to the hilt, he peered under their veils, and asked each her name. 'Mary' and 'Lizzie' were their mournful replies. The excited gentleman rushed on to the next car and, after searching the entire train, disembarked, to the utter relief of the young ladies. They reached Philadelphia and were welcomed by the Vigilance Committee.

The dangers to those left behind, if secrecy was not maintained once fugitives reached their destinations, are revealed in this same case. One of the women – Charlotte Giles – moved on to Niagara Falls, Canada West, after one week in Syracuse, New York. She apparently wrote back to Baltimore for her clothes to be sent to her, but the letter, containing the details of their escape, must have been intercepted. As a result, a

Black man named James Adams who had helped them onto the train was arrested. The former 'owner' sued the rail company, but after it was proved that he had spoken to the two women 'in mourning' and failed to recognize them, the jury found the railway company not guilty and Adams was released.[31]

The act of fleeing in disguise assumed even more drastic form in the case of the young woman who escaped in a box in the winter of 1857. The inconspicuous parcel was shipped from Baltimore to Philadelphia overnight by her lover, arriving at its destination the following morning (around 10 a.m.). But the woman inside, described as a seamstress and ladies' servant for a wealthy Baltimore family, was close to death when rescued. She was pregnant at the time, and it took three days for her to fully revive. She was later sent on to Canada.[32]

If this case sounds unusual, it is only one of numerous known similar incidents. On 31 January 1857 another local Black newspaper, the *Provincial Freeman*, reported that a female refugee had arrived in Chatham two nights before from Kentucky, 'carefully boxed up' and sent by train under the charge of a sympathetic railway conductor. 'She is now walking about our streets as happy as a lark and as free as air,' wrote the *Freeman*.[33]

But danger defined the existence of the fugitive bondwoman. Even when in the company of men, women had to draw upon incredible courage in their bid for freedom. A party of six 'took out' from Loudon County, Virginia, on Christmas Eve 1855 by 'borrowing' their master's horses and carriage. After two days of travel, in which they suffered from the biting cold and hunger, they were met by a party of six white men and a boy, who demanded to know who they were and where they were going. Their pretensions of freemen and women were not accepted by the latter, who demanded that the six surrender themselves forthwith.

At this juncture, the fugitives verily believing that the time had arrived for the practical use of their pistols and dirks, pulled them out of their concealment – the young women as well as the young men – and declared they would not be 'taken!' One of the white men raised his gun, pointing the muzzle directly towards one of the young women, with the threat that he would 'shoot', etc. 'Shoot! shoot!! shoot!!!' she exclaimed, with a double barrelled pistol in one hand and a long dirk knife in the other, utterly unterrified and fully ready for a death struggle. The male *leader* of the fugitives by this time had 'pulled back the hammers' of his 'pistols', and was about to fire! Their adversaries seeing the weapons, and the unflinching determination on the part of the *runaways* to stand their ground, 'spill blood, kill, or die', rather than be 'taken', very prudently 'sidled over to the other side of the road', leaving at least four of the victors to travel on their way.[34]

Two of the party were captured, but the remaining four – Mary Elizabeth and her husband Barnaby Grigby, alias John Boyer, Emily Foster, alias Ann Wood, and Frank Wanzer, alias Robert Scott – were later received by the Philadelphia Vigilance Committee and sent on to Canada West. Frank, the leader, and his intended, Emily, decided to 'tie the knot' at the Underground Railroad station in Syracuse. UGRR Superintendent Reverend J.W. Loguen, himself a former escaped slave, performed the happy ceremony. A letter written to William Still, dated 28 January 1856, by Agnes Willis of the Ladies Society to Aid Coloured Refugees in Toronto attested that the party was well and had found temporary employment. 'They are all in pretty good spirits, and I have no doubt they will succeed in whatever business they take up. In the meantime the men are chopping wood, and the ladies are getting plenty sewing.'[35]

Once safely landed on free British soil, many Black women were not content simply with getting on with the business of establishing themselves as freewomen. They were bound and determined to rescue their families and friends from the jaws of the 'peculiar institution.' As we saw in the case of little

Susan Bell, her mother did not rest until she was reunited with her in Canada, an event that took three years to accomplish. Likewise, Jefferson and Louisa Pipkins escaped in a party of six men and women from Baltimore in April 1853. Over three years later, they were still trying to find a way out for their four offspring. A letter received by Still from Jefferson Pipkins asked for assistance on behalf of himself and his wife Louisa:

September 28, 1856

TO WM. STILL.   SIR: I take the liberty of writing to you a few lines concerning my children, for I am very anxious to get them and I wish you to please try what you can do for me. Their names are Charles and Patrick and are living with Mrs. Joseph G. Wray in Murphysborough, Hartford County, North Carolina; Emma lives with a Lawyer Baker in Gatesville, North Carolina and Susan lives in Portsmouth, Virginia and is stopping with Dr. Collins sister a Mrs. Nash you can find her out by enquiring for Dr. Collins at the ferry boat at Portsmouth, and Rose a coloured woman at the Crawford House can tell where she is. And I trust you will try what you think will be the best way. And you will do me a great favour. Yours respectfully,

Jefferson Pipkins

P.S. I am living at Yorkville near Toronto Canada West. My wife sends her best respects to Mrs. Still.[36]

In rare instances Black women are known to have actually 'conducted' other family members out of bondage. Levi Coffin, the well-known Quaker Underground 'stationmaster,' met one of these women on a visit to Upper Canada in 1844. Mrs Armstrong had escaped to Canada with her husband and youngest child, only a few months old, two years before. However, seven other children had been left behind. Against her husband's better judgment, this woman decided to rescue them, or die trying. She dressed up in men's clothing and travelled through Ohio into Kentucky, finally reaching her old master's farm in the early part of the night. Hiding near a spring, Armstrong waited, knowing that some of her children were accustomed to get water at that particular spot. 'I had not been there long before my eldest daughter came. I called her name in a low voice, and when she started up and looked round, I told her not to be afraid, that I was her mother. I soon convinced her, and her alarm passed away.' Mrs Armstrong gave instructions to her daughter, who was able to bring all but two – who slept in the master's room – away the following night. 'I started with the five, and hastened back to the [Ohio] river as fast as we could go in the dark. We found the skiff waiting for us, and soon crossed. On the other side, a wagon was ready to take us in, and the man with it drove us a few miles to a depot of the Underground Railroad.' Mrs Armstrong and her offspring arrived safely at Fort Malden (later renamed Amherstburg). By the time of her meeting with Coffin, she had already made arrangements with friends in Ohio to get her two other children out and have them sent to her.[37]

Most rescue attempts by females were probably never recorded, but a single leaf of a diary kept by Daniel Osborn, a stationmaster in Alum Creek, Ohio, was found, and provides a record of forty-seven fugitives passing through that town from 14 April to 10 September 1844. Under the date of 21 August the following is entered: 'A coloured woman who had been to Canada and went back and got four of her children and one grandchild / and a man and wife from Kentucky.'[38] Could this 'coloured woman' have been Mrs Armstrong?

Ironically, although few women are recorded as having been Underground Railroad conductors, the name of one – Harriet Tubman – is virtually synonymous with the institution. She was born about 1820 on a large plantation in Bucktown, Maryland. Although she married a free Black by the name of John Tubman around 1844, they lived together only about five years before Harriet escaped to the North in 1849 and began her active Underground Railroad work.[39]

Between 1851 and 1857, Harriet Tubman's home base of

operation was St Catharines, Ontario. The woman who made an estimated nineteen trips into slave territory and rescued over three hundred from bondage brought a party of eleven, including her brother and his wife, to St Catharines in 1851. At one point she is listed as renting a boarding house on North Street behind the B.M.E. Church. Here refugees stayed with her until they could get established.[40]

Tubman earned money to finance her activities by cooking and cleaning for people in the town. The passengers on her trips were often the relatives of men from Canada who would ask her to conduct their families out of slavery. She personally rescued many of her own family members during this time, including her parents in June 1857, after her father was arrested for helping someone else escape on the Underground Railroad.

In all, eleven trips were made south during those years, and she would average about two trips per year. Her method of operation, and the many strategies she employed, have been covered extensively in numerous books, articles, and dramatizations of her life. However, her significance to the anti-slavery movement, indicated by the thousands of dollars offered for her capture, cannot be overstated.[41]

The life of Harriet Tubman has come to symbolize in many ways the struggle of African people for freedom and justice. However, although Harriet's incredible life and deeds took a course that few women (or men) would emulate, her courage and tenacity in the face of all odds were certainly not unique in the history of African-Canadian women.

Because of the obvious dangers, most did not elect to conduct others out of slavery personally. However, some became involved in receiving escaping slaves and assisting them after they arrived in the province. Notable in this regard was abolitionist and newspaper editor Mary Ann Shadd Cary, who arranged through letters to Elizabeth J. Williams, her free Black aunt in Wilmington, Delaware, to have fugitives forwarded northward to Chatham. One letter from Elizabeth Williams went as follows:

Wilmington, [Delaware]
Jan[uary] 18, 1858

Mary A.S. Cary
My Dear Mary Ann [——] Some time a go I wrote to you concerning Mrs. [V]easy and r[equ]ested an answer but none has ever
come. [I]f you remember I told you that she was a fugitive that
her owners live in Baltimore and that there is a Coulred man living in fall river that knows her owners and She lives in continuel
dread of him. She wants to come to Canada in the Spring. She is
a good seamster and [what i] want to know is weather you [think]
She can make a living by her neadle there and weather you
would be willing to let her come to your house for a Short time
and weather you would be willing to ade her in litting [sic] work
when She first Comes out there. You will find her a real [n]ice
woman and I know you will like her and all she wants is to have
some one to go too when she firs arives [as is] a stranger their
She does not want [to] come to live on you for She [words illegi-
ble] industress working woman and a very pleasant [agreeable
lady?] [rest of letter – 7 lines – virtually illegible]

E.J. Williams[42]

Shadd Cary would then assist such fugitives by taking them
in or finding other accommodations, employment, and otherwise easing their transition to freedom. Such activity carried
out by Cary and others – a vital component of Underground
Railroad work – contributed to the influx of tens of thousands
of freedom-seekers in the decades prior to the American Civil
War.[43]

Indeed, many a family participated in some small way in
the assistance of recently arrived refugees. When 15-year-old
Ann Maria Weems escaped from Maryland dressed as a young
man, she was sent on to the Buxton Settlement and readily
taken in by one of the families there. Clarissa Bristow was
another young fugitive aided by a Buxton family in this way.[44]

In essence, assistance in one form or another was a community affair. When a woman with five children arrived in

Windsor on 14 April 1854, Shadd Cary's paper, the above-mentioned *Provincial Freeman*, reported what took place next. 'The colored people called a meeting at once and collected over $6 to meet their immediate wants, besides assisting them in other ways. Such promptness in relieving the wants of fugitives frequently takes place in that thriving little town, we know of one old father there, (father Freeman) who has given away hundreds of meals since the passage of the Fugitive Bill.'[45]

Black Canadian newspapers were an important source of communication for newly arrived fugitives who were unable to make direct contact with loved ones for lengthy periods. A distressed notice first appeared in the 30 June 1855 edition of the *Provincial Freeman* (published by Shadd Cary and her family first in Windsor, then Toronto, and finally Chatham, Canada West, between 1853 and 1859). It read:

Mrs. Martha Ann Moseby, wife of William Moseby, from Richmond, Virginia, is now in this city [i.e., Toronto], and is anxious to ascertain where her husband is. He was known to some by the name of Wm. Dandridge. If friends in Detroit or Amherstburg, or at any other place in which this paper is taken, should know of such a person, they will confer a great favour upon his distressed wife, by communicating the intelligence to him, or by sending word to her. A letter addressed to Orpheus Ruffin, of this city, will meet with prompt attention.[46]

Among the many important services these newspapers provided, they enabled fugitives themselves to place notices in the advertisement sections, which could run almost indefinitely if need be. The following ad ran in the *Freeman* from 10 November through 8 December 1855:

INFORMATION WANTED

Ellen NETTLETON wants to find her husband, GEORGE NETTLETON. She got parted from him at one of the Stations west of Hamilton, and don't know the place he has gone to. He had two young children with him. She is in Chatham, a stranger and without money.

Exchanges will serve the cause of humanity by making the above known.

Commercial Hotel, Chatham.[47]

As in the United States, vigilance committees were organized in Canada West whose primary duty was to prevent fugitives from being captured and transported across the border into slavery. An 1858 circular listed Mary Ann Shadd Cary as secretary of the Chatham committee, which included three other women in a group of thirteen. Lucie Stanton Day, a teacher and the first Black woman college graduate (Oberlin College, 1850) was on the committee. She had accompanied her journalist-abolitionist husband to Chatham during the 1850s. Mary Ellen Pleasant, who had run a successful boarding house in San Francisco, also accompanied her husband to Chatham in 1858. Mary Ellen's antislavery activities preceded her move to Canada, as tradition credits her with rescuing newly arrived slaves held illegally by their masters in California. Amelia Freeman Shadd, also a teacher, noted artist, and former student at Oberlin, established a school for Black children in Chatham. She married Isaac D. Shadd, brother of Mary Ann, and played an important part in the cultural life of Chatham's Black community. Shadd Cary and Stanton Day were also listed as collecting agents for the organization.[48]

The Chatham committee was reportedly one of the most aggressive of the Canadian vigilance committees and saved several Blacks from being returned to slavery in the 1850s. The best known incident occurred in September 1858, when a young boy of ten was spotted in the London train station in the company of a white man, W.R. Merwin, apparently about to return him to slavery in the South. The committee was telegraphed in advance of the train's arrival in Chatham and quickly assembled a crowd of over one hundred men and women – Black and white – who forcibly removed the young man, Sylvanus Demarest, from the train. Railroad officials brought charges against seven of the principals, but later dropped them when it was discovered that the kidnapper was not the owner of the boy, but a slave agent intending to sell him into slavery. Merwin returned to New York, glad to escape with his life. Demarest, actually a free-born from New Jersey, remained with the Shadd family until his mother could be located.[49]

Vigilance committees could be less formal in their make-up, but this in no way implied that they were less well-organized or less successful in their efforts. One of the most spectacular cases on record occurred in Niagara in 1837. By several accounts, the action of the women made the difference to the final outcome. A fugitive slave, Solomon Mosely, or Moseby, had stolen his master's horse to effect his escape and was considered a felon by agreement of the Canadian and American governments. When he was arrested at Niagara, the Upper Canadian authorities consented to hand Mosely over to the Americans, even though the result would be his return to slavery.

Understandably, the Black community was outraged by this decision. They correctly reasoned that the extradition was initiated to re-enslave Mosely more so than to punish him for theft. Several hundred – led by teacher Herbert Holmes – came together to prevent the fugitive's extradition at any cost. For three weeks, members of the group held vigil outside the jail, with guards posted twenty-four hours to alert them in case the sheriff tried to remove Mosely during the night.

On the day set for extradition, the crowd swelled to over four hundred. According to one account, the women stood on the bridge near the jailhouse, singing hymns and forming a solid non-violent mass. It was hoped that in the time spent and confusion created in dispersing them, the prisoner would be able to escape. Two hundred Black men lined up on each side of the road and across in front of the emerging police phalanx.

Meanwhile, the prisoner emerged from the jailhouse in

handcuffs, under heavy police guard. He was helped into a wagon surrounded on all sides by armed officers. The gates were opened. Holmes quickly rushed the horses, bringing them to a standstill. A man named Green drove a fence rail into the spokes of the hind wheels, effectively locking the wagon. Mosely then leaped from the wagon and jumped a rail fence, escaping into the distance.

The deputy sheriff, on horseback with a drawn sword, had got into an altercation with a large fat woman who would not make way for him. When he realized what had transpired, he yelled 'Fire!' and 'Charge!' Holmes and Green were killed instantly.[50]

Anna Jameson, a British writer travelling through Upper Canada at the time, was another eyewitness to the incredible scene. Her description of the women's actions elaborates on other reports of the extraordinary role they played in the uprising. 'They had been most active in the fray, throwing themselves fearlessly between the black men and the whites, who, of course, shrank from injuring them. One woman had seized the sheriff, and held him pinioned in her arms; another, on one of the artillery-men presenting his piece,[51] and swearing that he would shoot her if she did not get out of his way, gave him only one glance of unutterable contempt, and with one hand knocking up his piece, and collaring him with the other, held him in such a manner as to prevent his firing.'[52] By more than one account, at least one woman swirled a large stone in a stocking at her adversaries, and others filled their aprons with stones and threw them.

Shortly after the incident, Jameson interviewed one woman whose eloquent leadership had contributed to the success of her people. Her name was Sally Carter.[53] The brief portrait of this woman, herself a former fugitive from Virginia, is inspirational.

She came out to speak to us. She was a fine creature, apparently about five-and-twenty, with a friendly animated countenance; but the feelings of exasperation and indignation had evidently not yet subsided. She told us ... that, so far from being ill-treated, she had been regarded with especial kindness by the family on whose estate she was born. When she was about sixteen her master died, and it was said that all the slaves on the estate would be sold, and therefore she ran away. 'Were you not attached to your mistress?' I asked. 'Yes,' said she. 'I liked my mistress, but I did not wish to be sold.'

Jameson asked if she were happy in Canada.

She hesitated a moment, and then replied, on my repeating the question, 'Yes – that is, I *was* happy here – but now – I don't know – I thought we were safe *here* – I though nothing could touch us *here* – on your British ground, but it seems I was mistaken, and if so I won't stay here – I won't – I won't! I'll go and find some country where they cannot reach us! I'll go to the end of the world, I will!' And as she spoke, her black eyes flashing, she extended her arms, and folded them across her bosom, with an attitude and expression of resolute dignity, which a painter might have studied; and truly the fairest white face I ever looked on never beamed with more of soul and high resolve than hers at that moment.[54]

Despite Jameson's patronizing comment, such was the stuff of which Black women in Upper Canada were made.

Although not without the loss of two lives, and the brief imprisonment of thirty or forty individuals, the fugitive Mosely was never recaptured. He went to Montreal and afterward to England, finally returning to Niagara, where he was joined by his wife. She had more recently escaped from slavery.[55]

Whether travellers on the Underground Railroad, or those who aided and abetted its operation, Black women were integrally involved with this important 'institution.' For the Underground Railroad touched all levels of Black society where it existed, slave and free, educated and uneducated, abolitionist and non-abolitionist, male and female. Indeed, the popular myth of a clandestine system of liberal white abolitionists and sympathizers helping poor, destitute Black fugitives is a distortion of the reality. As we have seen, large numbers of Black people – Black women – aided on the Underground Railroad with money, time, energy, and commitment.

Moreover, if, as it has been claimed, the Underground Railroad was one of the greatest forces that led to the Civil War and the eventual abolition of slavery, then every woman that escaped dealt an economic setback to her owner and hence to the system of slavery itself. Unlike the case for male slaves, female slavery had as much to do with women's reproductive capacities as their labour. This was because the plantation labour force could be augmented through childbirth with little additional outlays of capital, thereby increasing production and hence the slave-master's wealth. Particularly after Congress outlawed the overseas slave trade in 1807, this reproductive function became an important source of additional profit.[56] Therefore, the economic loss associated with flight had to be weighed not only against the loss of a woman's labour, but also against that of her unborn children, a factor that slaveholders understood only too well. Similarly, every woman who aided a slave to escape, or prevented his or her recapture dealt an economic blow to the slaveholding system.

But what of these women of the Underground Railroad? As we have seen, they risked their lives in escaping to freedom or in helping others to escape. That more women were not able to take flight has its explanation in the nature of female slavery itself, and the tremendous constraints on women, particularly during their childbearing years. Often, we tend to lionize Harriet Tubman, one of the few women invariably associated with the secret movement north. Harriet Tubman is viewed as an exception, a woman of uncommon valour whose actions went beyond the bounds of the ordinary or the usual. However, it is hoped this paper has placed Harriet's incredible life in context, as one of untold thousands of hitherto unknown women who endured similar risks and hardships and exhibited similar courage and tenacity in the fight for freedom and justice for themselves and their people. These women's actions in bringing about the eventual emancipation of Blacks in America is only now being realized. To the women of the Underground Railroad, we pay tribute!

NOTES

This paper is part of a work in progress that has been made possible by the Canada Council Explorations Program, the Ontario Arts Council Writers' Reserve program, and the Toronto Arts Council Research/Development Awards to Writers. I thank them for their generous support. In addition to the collective, I would like to thank Professors Frederick Case and James Walker for their valuable comments and suggestions on an earlier draft of this paper.

1 Benjamin Drew, *The Refugee: A North-side View of Slavery* (Reading, Mass.: Addison-Wesley 1969), 153.
2 Levi Coffin, *Reminiscences of Levi Coffin* (London: Sampson Low, Marston, Searle & Rivington 1876), 263.
3 This bill, an appeasement to southern pre-slavery interests, allowed a citizen to arrest and detain any person of African descent suspected of being a runaway slave. In practice, free Blacks as well as runaways were often kidnapped by bounty-hunters and taken off to slavery. Alleged runaways did not have the benefit of jury trials.
4 While contemporary estimates ranged from 15,000 to 75,000, Robin Winks – author of the most comprehensive text on African-Canadian history to date, *The Blacks in Canada: A History* (New Haven and London: Yale University Press 1971) – concluded that, after examining every source and its validity (pp. 234–40), 'by 1860, the black population of Canada West alone may have reached forty thousand, three-quarters of whom had been or were fugitive slaves or their children, and therefore beneficiaries of the Underground Railroad,' (240). However, ground-breaking new research by Michael Wayne that looks at the census-enumerated African population of 1861 suggests that a more

conservative figure of about 22,500 to 23,000 is appropriate. Moreover, Wayne also estimates that no more than 20 per cent of all Blacks living in the province were fugitives from slavery, and not more than 33 per cent could be construed as fugitives and their descendants. (Over 40 per cent of the census-enumerated Black population were Canadian-born in the 1861 census!) Michael Wayne, 'The Myth of the Fugitive Slave: The Black Population of Canada West on the Eve of the American Civil War' (unpublished paper, University of Toronto 1993). I thank Professor Wayne for sharing this paper with me.

5 William Still, *Underground Rail Road Records*, rev. ed. (Philadelphia: William Still 1883). Many of the cases of fugitive women referred to below are taken from Still's book, which, unlike other fugitive-slave collections that often do not provide the details of escape of the women (e.g., Benjamin Drew, *A North-side View of Slavery*, or Charles Blockson, *The Underground Railroad* [New York: Prentice Hall 1987]), furnishes a wealth of information on the operations of the Philadelphia Vigilance Committee and those it aided. Although representing one of the most organized systems of the Underground Railroad, Still was one of the few conductors to keep a fairly thorough record of its operation, including the names of those he saw, their places of origin, their owners, information on their lives as slaves, and details of their escape. In so doing, he risked the security of the UGRR and his own freedom. For our purposes, however, this documentary was invaluable in illustrating the many methods by which women escaped, and how they reached the North and Canada.

6 Ibid., 80.

7 James W. St G. Walker, *A History of Blacks in Canada* (Hull, Que.: Minister of Supply and Services 1980), 48–50; Larry Gara, *The Liberty Line: The Legend of the Underground Railroad* (Lexington, Ky.: University of Kentucky Press 1967), esp. chap. 3.

8 Herbert G. Gutman, *The Black Family in Slavery and Free-*

dom, 1750–1925 (New York: Vintage Books 1976), 265; Deborah Gray White, Ar'n't I a Woman? Female Slaves in the Plantation South (New York: W.W. Norton 1985), 70.

9 Winks (p. 239) states that there is evidence (usually in the form of letters) of only 117 actually reaching the Canadas. However, Still (p. 610) claims to have omitted a large number of cases from the book, especially during the early period of operation, because their stories were not properly recorded. Moreover, given that the Vigilance Committee was clearly advising most, if not all, fugitives to go on to Canada because of the dangers of re-enslavement after the passage of the 1850 Fugitive Slave Act, many whose destinations were not provided may have in fact reached Canada. In addition as Winks himself admits, some fugitives changed their names, thereby making it difficult to trace them in the Canadian census or other public records. And, too, it was not safe to record fugitives' destinations in case the records were confiscated by pro-slavery forces. Therefore, we will never know exactly what percentage of Still's cases came to Canada. The point is that the numbers of women escaping to Canada were far fewer, consistent with the figures of other fugitive-slave studies.

10 Drew, as a male writer, may well have been inclined to speak to more men than women. This, therefore, would also have been a factor in the disproportionate number of men interviewed for the book.

11 Gray White, 70.

12 Ibid., 70–1.

13 Jacqueline Jones in Labor of Love, Labor of Sorrow: Black Women, Work and the Family, from Slavery to the Present (New York: Vintage Books 1986) argues that familial responsibilities, moreover, were relished by slave women, and afforded them the opportunity to control their own lives outside of the watchful eye of the slave-master. See, for example, pp. 35–6.

14 Still, 463–4.

15 Gray White, 71.

16 Judith Kelleher Schafer, 'New Orleans Slavery in 1850 as Seen in Advertisements,' *Journal of Southern History*, February 1981: 46, 43; cited in Gray White, 71.

17 Still, 513.

18 Ibid., 513–14.

19 Ibid.

20 Josiah Henson, *An Autobiography of the Reverend Josiah Henson* (Reading, Mass.: Addison-Wesley 1969), 59–63; Gray White, 71-2.

21 Gilbert Osofsky, *Putting' On Ole Massa: The Slave Narratives of Henry Bibb, William Wells Brown and Solomon Northrup* (New York: Harper & Row 1969); Gray White, 72.

22 Alexander Milton Ross, *Recollections and Experiences of An Abolitionist; from 1855 to 1865* (Toronto: Rowsell and Hutchison 1875), 125–6; Levi Coffin, *Reminiscences*, 557–67; Wilbur H. Siebert, *The Underground Railroad from Slavery to Freedom* (New York: MacMillan 1898), 302–3.

23 Still, 80; Gray White, 72.

24 Still, 188; Gray White, 72.

25 Still (39–40, 302–3) was probably referring to a hidden area in the freight car, where runaways were often hidden by sympathetic railway employees.

26 Ibid., 264.

27 Gray White, 75–6.

28 Still, 177–87.

29 *Voice of the Fugitive* 1, no. 24, 19 November 1851, and 2, no. 17, 12 August 1852. See also the fugitive-slave narrative of William and Ellen Craft, *Running a Thousand Miles for Freedom* (New York: Arno Press and the *New York Times* 1969). Their tale is perhaps the most famous case of this kind; Ellen dressed up as a young master (since she was very light-skinned) and escaped with her husband, who played the part of her body servant. They successfully made their way to England.

30 Still, 288–9.

31 Ibid., 215, 222–3.

32 Ibid., 608–10.
33 *Provincial Freeman* 3, no. 23, 31 January 1857.
34 Still, 125.
35 Ibid., 124–8.
36 Ibid., 136–7. In most cases where this kind of help was re-
    quested to free family members and friends, the Vigilance
    Committee had a strict policy. It could only assist those
    who had made their way to Pennsylvania, a free state. It
    would not further endanger committee members by entering
    slave territory to rescue others. In all likelihood, therefore,
    the Pipkins were not able to help their children with the aid
    of the Philadelphia Vigilance Committee. Still hints at this
    in his précis to the letter from Mr and Mrs Pipkins (p. 137).
37 Coffin, 262–4.
38 Siebert, *Underground Railroad*, 345–6.
39 Earl Conrad, *Harriet Tubman* (Washington: Associated Pub-
    lishers 1943); Sarah Bradford, *Harriet Tubman: The Moses
    of Her People* (Secaucus, NJ: Citadel Press 1961).
40 Gail Benjafield, 'St. Catharines: The Open Door,' *The
    Downtowner* 6, no. 3 (May–June 1990), 2; 1858 Assessment
    Roll for the Town of St Catharines, Special Collections,
    Brock University.
41 See Conrad, *Harriet Tubman*; Bradford, *Harriet Tubman*.
42 C. Peter Ripley et al., eds, *The Black Abolitionist Papers:
    Volume II Canada, 1830–1865* (Chapel Hill, NC: University
    of North Carolina Press 1986), 386.
43 Ibid.
44 Joyce Middleton, 'The Women of the Elgin Settlement and
    Buxton,' in *65th Annual North Buxton Homecoming and
    Labour Day Celebration*, North Buxton, 2, 3 and 4 Septem-
    ber 1989, 25.
45 *Provincial Freeman* 1, no. 6, 29 April 1854.
46 Ibid., vol. 2, no. 17, 30 June 1855.
47 Ibid., vol. 2, no. 28, 10 November 1855 – vol. 2, no. 32, 8
    December 1855.
48 Ripley et al., eds, *Black Abolitionst Papers*, 392–8.
49 Ibid., 392; Jim Bearden and Linda Jean Butler, *The Life and*

Times of Mary Shadd Cary (Toronto: NC Press 1977), 198–200; Elijah M. Leonard, *The Honourable Elijah Leonard: A Memoir* (London, Ont., n.d.), 47–8; Daniel G. Hill, *The Freedom-Seekers: Blacks in Early Canada* (Agincourt, Ont.: Book Society of Canada 1981), 41–2.

50 Janet Carnochan, 'A Slave Rescue in Niagara Sixty Years Ago,' *Niagara Historical Society Papers*, no. 2 (1897), 14–16.

51 The term 'piece' refers to a firearm or artillery weapon.

52 Anna Jameson, *Winter Studies and Summer Rambles in Canada* (Toronto: McClelland & Stewart 1923), 98–9.

53 Janet Carnochan, 'A Slave Rescue in Niagara Sixty Years Ago,' *Niagara Historical Society*, paper no. 2 (1897), 18.

54 Jameson, *Winter Studies*, 99–100.

55 Jameson, 96–100; Carnochan, 'A Slave Rescue,' 8–18; Winks, *The Blacks in Canada*, 169–70; Alison Prentice et al., *Canadian Women: A History* (Toronto: Harcourt Brace Jovanovich Canada 1988), 102–3; William Renwick Riddell, 'The Slave in Canada,' *Journal of Negro History* 5 (1920), 347–50.

56 Gray White, 68–70; Jones, *Labor of Love*, 12.

3

'Whatever you raise in the ground
you can sell it in Chatham':
Black Women in Buxton and Chatham,
1850–65

PEGGY BRISTOW

On 30 June 1855, Mary Ann Shadd Cary wrote in the *Provincial Freeman*, 'To colored Women we have a word – we have broken the 'Editorial Ice' whether willingly or not for your class in America, so go to editing as many of you who are willing and able as soon as you may, if you think you are ready.'[1] As the first woman in Canada to establish, publish, and edit a newspaper,[2] Shadd Cary was one of the many Black women in Chatham in the mid-nineteenth century who chose living in British North America over the denial of legal, economic, social, and political rights to Black people in the United States.[3] She publicly challenged her Black sisters to carry on the struggle against racism, sexism, and classism, in the tradition of Maria Stewart, who decades earlier had lectured on racism and sexism in the United States;[4] Rebecca Jackson, who refused to be contained by the dictates of society and travelled around the United States as a spiritual woman, preaching;[5] Sojourner Truth, who, at a women's convention in Akron, Ohio, in 1851 declared, 'Look at me! I have ploughed and planted and gathered into barns and no man could head me. And ain't I a woman? ... I have borne thirteen children and seen most all sold off to slavery and ain't I a Woman?';[6] and Harriet Tubman, who made at least nineteen trips to the southern United States to lead her people out of slavery on the Underground Railroad.[7]

Of these five women, only two, Mary Ann Shadd and Harriet Tubman, lived in nineteenth-century Canada.[8] These two women, however, were a part of the larger community of Black women in the Americas, all of whom shared inferior status based on race. But they also shared a tradition of resistance and survival. This holds true for all women of African descent in the Americas: Canada, the Caribbean, and Latin America. It is crucial to an understanding of Black women's history in Canada to locate our experiences within this broad framework, while recognizing the particular time and place. Like the rebel woman Nanny, of Jamaica, and her sister Cudgoe,[9] Maria Stewart, Rebecca Jackson, and Sojourner Truth in the United States, Mary Ann Shadd Cary and Harriet Tubman in Canada, and the countless other Black women whose words were not recorded, we are all part of that tradition.

In reconstructing the lives of Black women in Canada, this article focuses on two areas in southwestern Ontario from 1851 to 1865. Kent County was selected primarily because the area had a relatively large Black population during the period. Kent County was one of the administrative districts set up in Ontario during the mid-1840s,[10] and it included eleven townships and the village of Chatham, which later became the county's town. This study looks at the lives of those women living in the county town of Chatham. It also examines the lives of those women living on the Elgin Settlement in Buxton, which is situated approximately twelve miles from Chatham, in Raleigh Township, also part of Kent County.

My research into Black women's lives in Kent County includes the analysis of census data, government reports, city directories, church records, minute books of organizations, correspondence of government officials, personal letters, diaries, newspaper accounts, and secondary sources. Personal letters were a rare discovery. In addition to several letters written by Mary Ann Shadd Cary, the *Black Abolitionist Papers* includes a letter written by Mary Jane Robinson. An open letter in the *Provincial Freeman*, addressed to relatives and friends in the United States, is another important discovery. The diary of a white woman, Elizabeth Russell, also sheds some light on moments in the lives of enslaved Black women. There were no official birth and death registers until the latter part of the nineteenth century, but some church records note the births and deaths of Black people. While the census provides insights into the economic, social, and political situations of women, the way the data is classified gives short shrift to women.[11] Newspapers, however, provide important shadings in the landscape of the research.

A history of Black women's lives in Canada must start with our arrival here as slaves. Black women, like Black men and like First Nations peoples, were enslaved here, beginning with the seventeenth century,[12] first by the French and later by the British. We were brought to labour.[13] The words of General James Murray, British Administrator in Canada in 1763, underscore that role. In a letter to the governor of New York he wrote, 'I must most earnestly entreat your assistance, without servants nothing can be done, had I the inclination to employ soldiers, which is not the case, they would disappoint me, and Canadians will work for nobody but themselves. Black slaves are certainly the only people to be depended upon.'[14] Murray is clearly referring to Black men. He did not, however, lose sight of the slave woman's value, for he added: 'so that they might have a communication with the Ladys and be happy – for each a clean young wife, who can wash and do the female offices about a farm.[15]

The Quebec Act set up by the British Parliament in 1763 reaffirmed that 'all His Majesty's Subjects within the provinces, Upper and Lower Canada, would continue to hold and enjoy their property and possessions.'[16] But as Winks points out, the most important legal protection given to slavery by Britain was contained in the Imperial Act of 1790 to encourage immigration into British North America. Britain permitted free importation into North America, the Bahamas, and Bermuda of all 'Negroes, household furniture, utensils of husbandry or cloathing [sic].' No one could sell such goods for a year after entering the colonies; and furniture, utensils and clothing were not to exceed in value fifty pounds for every white and two pounds for every Negro slave. Free Negroes were not encouraged. All white settlers over fourteen years old were to take an oath of allegiance; children and Negroes, slave or free, were not expected to do so since they were unable to swear.[17] All sixty slaves on Matthew Elliot's farm near Amherstburg knew what the ring driven into the black locust tree at the front of the house meant. Anyone of them could be tied to the ring and flogged. Some fled across the border to Ohio.[18] A debate thirty years later in the Ontario legislature led to a bill prohibiting the 'further importation of slaves into the province,' but it did not free one enslaved person.[19] The bill, introduced by Governor Simcoe, drew heated debate from the members of the legislature, many of whom were slave-owners. Simcoe was no doubt influenced by the British Antislavery and Abolitionist movement. Writing about this bill, William Renwick Riddell, notes: 'Contrary to the common idea, it was bitterly opposed especially by the farming class, who urged that the operations of farming could not go on unless they had the help of their slaves. It was found that it would probably be impossible to carry a Bill abolishing Slavery immediately, and a compromise was arranged which met to some extent the objections of the farmers. The compromise Bill was carried in the House of Assembly and on being sent up to the Legislative Council, it was readily carried in that House; and received the Royal Asent [sic] at the close of the Session of 1793. The anger and hard feelings roused by this interference with the property of the people did not abate, and White [the Attorney General] was, in consequences of his advocacy of this measure, never able to gain a seat in any subsequent Parliament.'[20] Governor Simcoe adds: 'The greatest Resistance was to the Slave Bill. Many plausible Arguments of the dearness of Labour and the Difficulty of obtaining Servants to cultivate Lands were brot forward ... The matter was finally settled by undertaking to secure the property already obtained upon Condition that an immediate Stop should be put to the Importation and that Slavery should be gradually abolished.'[21] Enslaved Black people continued to be disposed of as and when the owners saw fit. For example, Amy Pompadour was given by her white mistress, Elizabeth Russell, to a 'Mrs. Captain Denison of York.'[22]

In some cases, slave-owners advertised in the newspapers. Four years after the bill to limit the importing of slaves into Ontario, the following advertisement appeared in the *Gazette*: 'wanted, to purchase a negro girl from seven to twelve years of age, of good disposition. For fuller particulars apply to the subscribers, W. and J. Crooks, West Niagara.'[23] In the *Niagara Herald* another advertisement read: 'for sale, a negro man and woman, the property of Mrs. Widow Clement. They have been bred to the business of the farm. Apply to Mrs. Clement.'[24]

At the turn of the nineteenth century, Peter Russell, the receiver general of Ontario, placed an advertisement in the *Gazette* and the *Oracle*: 'For sale, Peggy, aged 40, 150 dollars ... Jupiter, age 15, 200 dollars, payable in three years, secured by bond, but one-fourth less would be taken for ready money. The woman is a tolerable washer-woman, and perfectly understands making soap and candles.'[25]

Sylvia Hamilton, in this book, points to acts of resistance by enslaved Black women and men in Nova Scotia. Moreover, during French rule, Marie-Joseph Angelique set fire to her mistress's house in Montreal in the spring of 1734.[26] Angelique took such action when she realized that she was to be sold. For this act of resistance Angelique 'was arrested, convicted of arson and sentenced to hang. A rope was tied around her neck, signs bearing the word "Incendiary" were fastened on her back and chest, and she was driven through the streets in a scavenger's cart. Worse was to come: she was tortured until she confessed her crime before a priest; and hanged in public.'[27]

Resistance takes many forms.[28] A glimpse into the lives of Milly and Peggy, two enslaved Black women, is provided through the eyes of Elizabeth Russell. In her diary, Russell concludes that Milly was 'addicted to pilfering and lying.'

Peggy, by contrast, is supposed to have had a demonic character, as she was deemed 'a corrupter of children'[29] Peggy, however, would make the decision to escape from the Russell household. In 1803 Peter Russell ran the following notice in the *Gazette*: 'York, September 2nd, 1803 – the subscriber's black servant Peggy, not having his permission to absent herself from his service, the public are hereby cautioned from harbouring or employing her without the owner's leave. Whoever will do so after this notice may expect to be treated as the law directs.'[30] Once Peggy was captured, Russell could then advertise her for sale.[31] By 1833, when the proclamation of the abolition of slavery was made by an Imperial Act of the British Government,[32] Black people had settled in many areas of southwestern Ontario. The Elgin Settlement in Buxton, Raleigh Township, and the county town of Chatham, both in Kent County, are the two areas to which I now turn my attention.

Raleigh Township's Elgin Settlement, Buxton

Black families, through their hard work and dedication, built the Elgin Settlement in Buxton. Most came from the United States. Indeed, most Black people who settled in Canada came from the United States, and by 1850, when the U.S. Congress passed the Fugitive Slave Law making it legal to capture Black people and return them to slavery, many Black people saw Canada as the promised land.[33] How many Black people settled in Canada during this period is not known. Figures derived from census data differ from other sources. How many were fugitives from U.S. slavery and how many were 'free' is also not clear.

The *Provincial Freeman* of 25 March 1854 reported: 'The entire number of Fugitives in Canada may be estimated at from 30,000–35,000 of whom from 3,000–5,000 have annually escaped since the passing of the Fugitive Slave Law.'[34] According to records, the Elgin Settlement had some two hundred Black families ten years after its founding.[35] The introduction to the Black Abolitionist Papers notes: 'They all found that Canada offered freedom and perhaps the welcoming embrace of friends or family who had preceded them. Blacks and philanthropic whites organized relief efforts.'[36] Mary Jane Robinson's letter to her friend Sarah in New York sums up the feelings of most Black settlers: 'Come to a land of liberty and freedom, where the coloured man is not despised nor a deaf ear turned to them. This is the place to live in peace and to enjoy the comforts of life.' And no doubt referring to the situation in the United States, she adds: 'I hear that OLD FILLMORE is a screwing you all up tighter still, but don't stay there, come to Queen Victoria's land, where they are not making laws to oppress and to starve you.'[37]

The establishment of the Elgin Settlement occurred at a time when the rising bourgeoisie in Ontario worried about 'salvaging the children of the lowest classes from ignorance and crime.'[38] The Presbytery of Toronto, therefore, agreed to create and support a mission church and school. Ex-Presbyterian minister, and former Louisiana slaveholder, William King had initially written to the Presbyterian Synod in Toronto, and later Lord Elgin, the governor at the time, informing both parties that the children of refugee Blacks were 'growing up in ignorance and vice,' and that a school and church would 'meet their spiritual wants and ... improve their social and moral condition.'[39] Black women (and men) had long known that education was crucial in their struggles to fight racist and sexist oppression.[40]

William King, who was born in Ireland in 1812 and raised a Presbyterian, emigrated with his family to the United States, where he eventually taught school. Married to Mary Mourning Phares, the daughter of a southern slaveholder, King purchased his first slave, Talbert, in February 1842 for $1,000 U.S. from his brother-in-law. In his autobiography, written many years later, King stated that 'one could not get faithful and trustworthy servants unless you bought them.'[41] In November 1843, King purchased land and two slaves, Fanny and Molly, and their children Sarah and Peter. He paid $2,300

U.S. for this property. Mary's dowry included Amelia and her mother, who had raised Mary from the time she was seven years old. On the death of slaveholder Phares, Mary and William King inherited six additional slaves: Ben, Emaline, Robin, Ise, Stephen, and Harriet. Soon after, Mary died and the Kings' only surviving daughter, Johanna, also died.[42]

By the late 1840s, King had emigrated to Ontario and started to plan for his experiment.[43] Earlier in 1843 he had returned to Edinburgh to study theology. In November 1846 he came to Canada as a missionary with the Free Church of Canada, which was supervised by the Toronto Presbytery. The Free Church of Canada was established by the Free Church of Scotland. In 1843 a large disruption had occurred when two congregations left the Church of Scotland to form the Free Church of Scotland. The Free Church of Scotland had strong ties with the Glasgow Emancipation Society, which had been opposed to churches having fraternal ties with slaveholding Christians. The fellowshipping question eventually divided the Free Church. Antislavery and abolitionist activities in Glasgow and Paisley thus gave impetus to the activities in Canada West as far as the Presbytery was concerned. Members of the Toronto Presbytery had been tied to the British antislavery struggle, which had come to believe that slavery was now a sin and that it was morally wrong for Christians to engage in it.[44]

In his autobiography King suggests that Black people were conditioned to believing that slavery was natural. His slaves, he said, 'had come to consider that slavery was their natural condition. They did not know what freedom meant ... They thought that to be free was to be like their master, to go idle, and have a good time.'[45] King's ideas did not differ from those of the ruling élite in the Americas. Angela Davis and others have pointed out quite the contrary. Davis notes the various forms that resistance took. 'It involved, for example, the clandestine acquisition of reading and writing skills and the imparting of this knowledge to others. In Natchez, Louisiana, a slave woman ran a "midnight school" teaching her people between the hours of eleven and two until she had "graduated" hundreds.'[46]

As early as March 1849, when rumours were abounding of the plan to establish a settlement in Raleigh Township, irate white members of the Western District Council sent a petition to the Ontario legislative assembly protesting the settlement of any Black people in the area.[47] Black people had long been living in several townships in Kent County, including Raleigh Township, and in other counties in southwestern Ontario.[48] The debate protesting the plans raised the question of whether settlement colonies should exist for any particular group of people. The protesters referred to 'frontier settlements by colonies of the Roman Catholic population of Ireland,' and argued 'that colonies of any peculiar classes are an evil, and that the general welfare will best be promoted by fostering the growth of a national Canadian character of settlements in which people of every nation, and every creed, will be found living side by side on terms of amity and friendship.'[49]

It was clear, however, that race was the issue. The Toronto *Globe* carried, in its 25 August 1849 issue, a letter addressed to the editor which reported that about four hundred people had assembled in front of the Royal Exchange in the town of Chatham to protest plans for the settlement.[50] Four days later, the *Examiner*, another Toronto newspaper, also reported on the protest meeting: 'A large public meeting was held in the town of Chatham, Western District on the 18th instant, for the purpose of adopting means to prevent the furtherance of the objects of "The Elgin Association" a benevolent Society designed to create an Asylum for the Coloured Race in the township of Raleigh. The Sheriff of the District was in the Chair, and the following series of resolutions were passed.'[51] The resolutions, blocked out in their entirety in the *Examiner*, I later discovered reprinted in a 1964 issue of the *London Free Press*: 'It was resolved: That in the opinion of this meeting, it would be unconstitutional, impolitic and unjust government, to sell large portions of the public domain in SETTLED PARTS of this province, to foreigners, the more so, when such persons belong to a different branch of the human family, and are BLACK.'[52] Organized protests were not confined to Kent County; white settlers in two other counties joined in as well. Protesters appealed to the Canadian Parliament, the Synod of the Presbyterian church, and the wider community. They published a lengthy printed address to 'all inhabitants of Canada' and widely circulated it in August 1849. An excerpt follows:

Fellow Subjects – Canadians by birth or adoption, we address you and we call your attention to a subject of vital importance, connected as it is, with the future destinies of our country ... The Imperial Parliament of Great Britain has forever banished slavery from the empire. In common with all good men we rejoice at the consummation of this immoral act ... Every member of the human family is entitled to certain rights and privileges and nowhere on earth are they better secured, enjoyed or more highly valued than in Canada. Nature, however, has divided the same great family into distinct species for good and wise purposes, and ... it is our duty to follow her dictates and to obey her laws. Believing this to be a sound and correct principle, as well as a moral and a Christian duty, it is with alarm we witness the fast increasing emigration and settlement among us of the African race ... It is also with a feeling of deep resentment that we look upon the selection of the township of Raleigh, in this district, as the first portion of our beloved country which is to be cursed with a systematic organization for setting the laws of nature at defiance ... would the people of any of the old settled townships of the eastern portion of this province look upon a measure which has for its avowed project, the effect of introducing several hundreds of Africans into the very heart of their neighbourhood, their families interspersing themselves among them, upon every vacant lot of land, their children mingling in their schools, and all claiming to be admitted not only to political but to social privileges ... Look at your prisons and your penitentiary, and behold the fearful preponderance of their black over white inmates in proportion to the population of each ... Let the slaves of the United States be free, but let it be in their own country.[53]

Earlier in 1840, a group of magistrates in the Western District petitioned the legislature to check the 'rapid importation of this unfortunate race, such as have of late inundated this devoted section of the province, to the great detriment of the claims of the poor immigrant from the mother country.'[54] The plans for the Elgin Settlement went ahead, however, and the governor-general of Canada, Lord Elgin, gave royal assent. Nine thousand acres of clergy reserves were allocated for the settlement, to be sold in 50-acre lots. Decades later, the *Detroit Tribune*, in a series of articles on the settlement, suggested that Lord Elgin saved the day for Canada 'He granted that asylum to the outcast which it has long been Great Britain's glory to afford – thus at once succoring the friendless and saving this country from the terrible disgrace that was about to befall it.'[55] Elgin may have had second thoughts. A year after giving his name to the settlement, he thought that the U.S. Fugitive Slave Law could have unwelcome ramifications for Canada, which might be 'flooded with blackies who are rushing across the frontier to escape from the bloodhounds whom the Fugitive Slave Bill has let loose on their track.'[56]

As Black settlers struggled with racism on a daily basis, they questioned the 'freedom' and 'equality' they understood to be theirs in British North America. Furthermore, they sought confirmation from government officials about their right to buy land anywhere in Canada. Some Black settlers in Canada were particularly concerned about the proposed settlement, and questioned whether it meant that Black people would be segregated.[57] Certainly, Black children were already being excluded from attending the common schools with white children.[58]

The all-male committee set up to manage the financial and social affairs of the Elgin Association included six Black men who supported the all-Black settlement for strategic reasons. Adolphus H. Judah, Wilson Ruffin Abbott, and David Hollins had all settled in Toronto. Judah was in the carpentry business and Hollins was a courier. Abbott later moved to the settlement, where his sons attended school. He had worked as a tobacconist before moving into real estate. Henry Garrett and A. Bickford Jones had both settled in London, Ontario. Garrett, a former slave from Virginia, operated a bakery; Jones, a former slave from Kentucky, ran a grocery store. James Charles Brown was born in Maryland and had settled in Chatham. William King was managing director of the association, and a prominent white Chatham lawyer and member of the Reform party, Archibald McKellar, was chairman of the advisory committee.[59] A second administrative group was also set up. This group was in charge of the mission and supervised the community's chapel, schools, and Christian work. In order to give Black settlers time to pay for their property, it was stipulated in their contracts that the land could not be sold to any white people during the first ten years. In order to support these services, King set up a mission fund, and a collection for it was taken every year in all Canadian Presbyterian churches.[60]

Many questions arise. What part did women play in the structure of these organizations? How were decisions made? We are told that King insisted that the settlers were not to receive any help in building their settlement.[61] Yet we know that King solicited help from philanthropic organizations. While settlers were discouraged from accepting gifts, King travelled to England soliciting funds. On one occasion two Black men, Martin Delany and William Day, accompanied him. And, as just mentioned, collections from Presbyterian churches were made available. The issue of begging was a recurring theme throughout this period and one that many in the community abhorred.[62] Yet one must not lose sight of the patronizing missionary zeal with which decisions were made and the tight control that was exercised by King.

The land selected for the settlement was considered fertile – timbered crown land in Kent County. As reported in the *Voice of the Fugitive*, '9000 acres of this block were secured from government by paying the first instalment ... It was divided into lots of 50 acres each and sold to actual colored settlers of approved moral character at $2.50 per annum.'[63] The settlers were expected to clear at least six acres of their land during the first year of occupancy. Given that many historians 'place the amount of land which could be cleared in a year or two to three acres, while others estimate that the amount was between five and ten acres,'[64] settlers faced a tremendous task. In addition, they were expected to build a house a minimum size of 18 feet long and 12 feet high. The house had to sit 33 feet from the road and, as soon as possible, the settlers had to build a fence in front of it. Failure to meet these requirements could bring eviction from the land.[65] Settler James Rapier notes in a letter to his brother, dated 27 January 1857: 'Rev. King told me that you would have to put you up a house to entitle you to the land. The house you have started is of the right dimension providing it was covered and a fence before it. This all has to be done by the first of June next or it is liable to be sold for he sold one about a week ago under the Same circumstances.'[66] The business transaction was made between the association and the male members of the settlement. King and his second wife, Jemima, also lived in the settlement in a large house and retained three of his ex-slaves as their servants. He, however, purchased his land from a white farmer. We hear absolutely nothing about Jemima King during this period.

Women in the Elgin Settlement

In October 1851, the *Voice of the Fugitive* reprinted the second annual report of the Elgin Settlement, stating that forty-five families had settled there.[67] Catherine Riley was the first woman to live in the settlement. In her early thirties, Riley, with her husband Isaac and their three young sons, John, Jerome, and James, had escaped from slavery in Missouri.[68] Their daughter Mary was born on the settlement. Another woman, Eliza Ann Elizabeth Parker, who arrived in Toronto in November 1851 and was reunited with her husband, William, also settled in Elgin. 'The Parkers were joined by their children later.'[69] Catherine Riley and Eliza Parker, other early families, and fifteen slaves freed by William King formed the nucleus of the settlement. Seven of the freed slaves were women:

Fanny, Amelia, Emaline, Mollie, Sarah, and Harriet.[70] When Harriet learned of King's plan to settle the group in Canada, she 'begged him to buy her son Solomon so that they would not be separated.'[71]

Because the manuscript census for Raleigh Township is missing for 1851, I have had to depend on the 1861 census. Settlers were checked to see if they were morally suitable residents. Single women were not encouraged, which leads us to believe that most women on the settlement were married. A handful of single women, perhaps relatives of the married women, also came. Adrienne Shadd, in this collection, describes how young girls like Clarissa Bristow and Ann Maria Weems made their way to Elgin. These young girls were taken in by families.[72] By 1861, twenty-three-year-old Clarissa was married to a farmer, Abraham Johnson, and had three children, including a daughter, Harriet. The couple had twelve children, but only four are known to have survived. Widowed in her early forties, Clarissa provided for her family and kept the property intact.[73]

Arlie Robbins points out that many households consisted of a middle to elderly age group with families and sometimes included four generations. The 1861 census lists Elizabeth and Henry Johnson living with their six daughters. But also in the Johnson household is Hannah Johnson, a forty-five-year-old widow, and a twenty-eight-year-old single farmer, Arron, Louisa and Ezekiel Cooper lived on the settlement with their two sons and daughter Elizabeth. Nancy Euphenia was the second wife of George Hatter, who had escaped slavery in West Virginia. He first moved to the settlement with his first wife Mary Baker, who died.

Margaret Brown and her husband Robert VanVranken came to Elgin and were actively involved in community affairs. White abolitionist John Brown met with Robert when he visited Chatham in 1858 to plan a convention. Margaret's brothers boarded with them on the settlement and worked as labourers. Mary Morgan, who worked as a washer-woman in Haiti after leaving Nova Scotia on one of the colonization schemes offered during the mid-nineteenth century, eventually moved to Elgin. She brought her ten-year-old niece, Margaret Rebecca Neal, and a nephew, Arthur, with her. Since land was sold to men, Mary may have boarded with another family. Her niece, Margaret, eventually married Isaac Charles Johnson, who owned property. Isaac was killed in an accident at the sawmill on the settlement and Margaret inherited his property. Years later she remarried Ezekiel Collins and he moved onto her property.

The Settlement also had settlers who were born in the West Indies. The 1861 census lists Emily Prince, a seventy-seven-year-old woman. Certainly, one family came from Buxton, British Guiana (now Guyana) and settled at Elgin. Some settlers were also born in Canada. Sixty-one-year-old Sarah Jackson who was a widow by 1861 lived on the Settlement with her two single adult daughters.

Some women who came to the settlement had been free and living in the Northern United States. The Fugitive Slave Law threatened these women and their families. Originally from Alabama, Maria Thomas moved to the settlement with her husband, Henry, and their children from Buffalo in 1852.[74] Mary Jane Robinson worked as a laundress in New York City, then moved to Elgin with her husband and children in 1853.[75] Ellen and Wilson Abbott moved with their family from Toronto to Elgin in 1854. Wilson purchased land in Raleigh Township, just outside the settlement. Whatever the marital status and family size of the settlers in 1851, by 1861 most adult women over thirty years old were married and most had been born in the United States (see tables 1, 2, and 3). Interestingly, there were just about as many single women as married women in the 21–29-year age group (tables 2 and 3).

Like women everywhere, women in the settlement had a double and at times triple work load. The large number of children between the ages of one month and sixteen years indicates the demands of child-rearing. While children aged ten years and older would have been expected to help care for their younger siblings, the mother or guardian would have

TABLE 1
Place of Birth of Blacks in Buxton, 1861

Place of birth	Number	% of all females	% of total pop-ulation	Number	% of all males	% of total pop-ulation
Canada	122	35	16	126	31	17
United States	221	63	29	270	67	36
Other	5	1	1	3	1	0
Unknown	1	0	0	4	1	1
Total	349	99	46	403	100	54

SOURCE: Walton, 'Blacks in Buxton and Chatham,' 315; Census of Canada, Raleigh Township, 1861

been ultimately responsible for all her children. No one knows how many women on the settlement read the *Voice of the Fugitive*, which was circulated there. In addition, many could not read or write. However, the *Voice of the Fugitive* was clear about the moral responsibilities of women to their children: 'The most powerful and beneficial of the influences ordinarily at work in the formation of human character is that of woman ... Man in life is what he is, to a great extent, by the power of woman. His infancy being committed to her charge, and his childhood spent in her society.'[76]

All children were expected to work, an activity that would help mould their characters. As reported in the *Voice of the Fugitive*: 'There is no greater defect in educating children than neglecting to accustom [sic] them to work. The parent does not consider whether the child's work is necessary to the child. Nothing is more certain than their future independence and comfort for much depend on being accustomed to work ... it strengthens both body and mind ... it enables them better to bear the confinement of the school-room ... no man or woman is fully educated unless accustomed to manual labour.'[77] The *Voice* also had advice for husbands, entitled 'Gentlemen at home: There are few families, we imagine, anywhere, in which

TABLE 2
Marital status compared with age for all Blacks in Buxton, 1861

Age	Number	% of married females	% of all females
1 mo.–16 yrs.	–	–	–
17–20	4	3	1
21–29	19	16	6
30–39	28	23	8
40–49	38	31	11
50–59	20	17	6
60–69	9	7	3
70–79	2	2	1
80–100	1	1	0
Total	121	100	36

Age	Number	% of married males	% of all males
1 mo.–16 yrs.	–	–	–
17–20	1	1	0
21–29	8	6	2
30–39	22	17	6
40–49	40	31	10
50–59	30	24	8
60–69	20	16	5
70–79	5	4	1
80–100	1	1	0
Total	127	100	32

SOURCE: Walton, 308; Census of Canada, Raleigh Township, 1861

love is not abused as furnishing a license for impoliteness: A husband, father, or brother, will speak harsh words to those whom he loves the best, and to those who love him the best.'[78]

By the time Rebecca Carter, who was married to John Carter, settled at Elgin, she had ten children. Arlie Robbins suggests that the Carter family lived outside the settlement.[79] Her ten-year-old daughter Ann no doubt helped with domestic chores. But Ann would also have shared with her older brothers, the

TABLE 3
Single status compared with age for all Blacks in Buxton, 1861

Age	Number	% of single females	% of all females
1 mo.–16 yrs.	162	79	47
17–20	25	12	7
21–29	18	9	5
30–39	1	0	0
40–49	–	–	–
50–59	–	–	–
60–69	–	–	–
70–79	–	–	–
80–100	–	–	–
Total	206	100	59

Age	Number	% of single males	% of all males
1 mo.–16 yrs.	194	75	49
17–20	24	9	6
21–29	27	10	7
30–39	8	3	2
40–49	4	2	1
50–59	1	0	0
60–69	1	0	0
70–79	–	–	–
80–100	–	–	–
Total	259	99	65

SOURCE: Walton, 307; Census of Canada, Raleigh Township, 1861

oldest of whom was thirteen years old, work outside the house. On arrival at the settlement Rebecca was carrying her eleventh child. She later gave birth to four more children.[80]

Infant mortality reduced the number of live births. Addia Bailey had eight children, but lost a newborn male child in 1860. Jane Calaham spent many sleepless nights caring for her two-year-old child, who died in 1860 after a lingering illness. Mary Jackson lost her three-year-old child in 1860, owing to a cold.[81] Margaret Rebecca Johnson lost two sons under five years and a baby.

Like other settler women, Black women's child-rearing did not keep them from outside work. Land had to be cleared, work that was tedious and strenuous, involving chopping trees and hauling wood. One writer on the work of the pioneer in Canada notes: 'The land is first cleared of brushwood and small timber and then a ring of bark is cut from the lower part of every tree, if this is done in the autumn, the trees will be dead and destitute of foliage in the spring, at which time the land is sown without culture except a little harrowing ... After trees are felled some are split into rails for fences, the remainder cut into logs 12' long and hauled together.'[82] As Hill points out, 'In the middle of the winter of 1849–50 they had to build homes, cut down and burn trees, clear brush and open roads. Because the land was level, they had to dig a drainage before they could sow a crop.'[83] How much clearing could be done depended on the number of hands available. No doubt, many of the women on the settlement would have, like their sisters decades later (after Emancipation) in the United States, 'cut down trees to clear lands for cultivation ... dug ditches, spread manure fertilizer, and piled coarse fodder with their bare hands.'[84]

During the nineteenth century, farming played an important part in the lives of most settlers in Ontario. The economy of the first half of the century was based primarily on agriculture, with wheat being the main crop. Settlers generally first engaged in subsistence agriculture, which may have included selling at local markets, moving later to sales in an export-oriented economy. While most men farmed, women's role in the family economy, as Majorie Cohen and others have pointed out, was crucial to its success.[85] Black women were crucial not only to the success of the family economy, but also to the liberation of their people. Elevating the race from the subordinate position forced on it was a primary concern for all Black people, and so group solidarity and cooperation were constantly stressed. At mid-century, when the Elgin set-

tlement was established, settlers engaged in subsistence agriculture but built a sawmill and grist mill and attempted to
move gradually into regional markets.[86]

Most likely, after a portion of the 50-acre lot had been
cleared and a log house built, gardening started. Gardening
may have begun as the house was being built. There is no
doubt that women contributed to the building of the houses.[87]
Juban Enos, with her sixteen-year-old daughter Mary, four-
teen-year-old Lee, twelve-year-old Sarah, eight-year-old Lu-
cretia, and seven-year-old Rachel, most likely ploughed and
harrowed the land before planting wheat or potatoes. They
may have used spades or hoes, even their bare hands. Taking
care of a garden was a back-breaking task. While children
might have helped in the garden, women must have spent
many hours bent over, weeding and hoeing root crops such
as turnips and potatoes.

The women hoped to provide stable homes so their children
and communities would thrive. Like their sisters in the United
States and the Caribbean, women in Elgin were 'engaged in
a family and survival movement toward self-sufficiency and
self-expression.'[88] Although denied property rights, like all
other women in Canada,[89] that Black women had some access
to land meant they could make some decisions about their
daily lives, thus raising the possibility, however fragile, that
their children would inherit a better way of life. This expec-
tation, shared by the settlers, was voiced by Catherine Riley,
who declared, 'if I do not live to see it, perhaps my children
will, that this will one day be a great place.'[90] Catherine had
earlier expressed some disappointment on her arrival. She
found that white people here did not speak to Black people.

Mary Jane Robinson wrote proudly about the size of her
turnips, in a letter to her girl friend in New York. They were
'as big as the crown of your husband's hat, and cabbage as
large as a water pail. O, don't laugh, for its a fact – for the
ground is so rich it raised everything up in no time.'[91] All
family members helped with the harvest. It is likely that the
atmosphere at the Elgin Settlement would have been similar

to that recorded by another Black family elsewhere in Ontario during the period: 'When they had a threshing all the community would come in and help ... when threshing was finished ... they joined in an afternoon and evening of eating, dancing and revelry. They'd really whoop it up and then sit down to a good home-cooked meal, prepared in the house or outside, too over a roaring fire.'[92] The wheat would probably have been thrashed with a flail, then thrown in the air from a container to get rid of the chaff, and then ground with a stone.'[93]

Women and children also picked tobacco leaves, beans, and fruits such as raspberries, plums, and crabapples.[94] While women may have shared the reaping of crops with each other, they also set up local market stalls to trade goods. Women walked to surrounding areas in Raleigh Township once or twice a week selling vegetables and fruit. Certainly, Mary Jane Robinson's comment indicates that farming, even on a limited scale, was also directed to local markets: 'Whatever you raise in the ground, you can sell it in Chatham.'[95] Indeed, although itself a farming county town, Chatham was a service centre for the surrounding farming communities.

Women spent a considerable amount of time preparing and cooking food for their families. As a farm woman, Sarah Jane Robinson milked her cow and provided her family with milk. She also churned cream into butter.[96] Women made bread from wheat and corn and most likely provided their families with teas made from plants grown in the area. Women prepared salt pork. Although not all households had livestock, pigs appear to have been plentiful on the settlement.[97]

Women creatively juggled time. As they cleared and worked the land, planted, harvested, shared and sold crops, and fed families, they also made time to plant and enjoy flowers.[98] As Sunday school teachers, Black women in Elgin would have emphasized 'independence, self-reliance, strength and autonomy.'[99] Women would have taught their young daughters and sons 'lullabies, nursery rhymes and children's games' at home.[100] The patriarchal structure set up by the settlement's promoters and led by William King dictated that boys would have a school first. Adults also attended school in the evening. How many adult women attended evening school is not clear. Willema Parker was one of the adults who attended evening school. Girls in the settlement had to wait five years for a school. And, when it came, its curriculum prepared them for housekeeping activities. Unlike their brothers, who were versed in Latin and Greek, girls were instructed in the domestic sciences.[101] In 1856 some of the male students were ready to enter Knox College in Toronto. While Black children were excluded from attending the common schools in the area with white children, white parents could and did exercise their privileged status in choosing to send their sons to the Elgin school because of its curriculum.

As the decade rolled by, the women laboured with a fervour as they collectively developed a community. In 1851, there were 200 to 250 people living in the settlement, representing the 45 families mentioned earlier.[102] Thirty of these families had built houses. By September 1852 there were 74 families, numbering 400 people. By then, 305 acres of land had been cleared, and 204 of these were growing wheat, tobacco, corn, potatoes, and hemp. By the end of 1859, '200 families, each occupying their own house and numbering about 800 people,' were in the settlement. The Elgin Association reported: 'there were 824 acres cleared and under fence, ... of this land already fenced, 354 acres were planted with corn, 200 acres with wheat, 70 acres with oats, 80 acres with potatoes, 120 acres with other crops like beans, peas, turnips and grass.'

Life was particularly difficult at times. Crop failures 'in 1854, 1858 and 1859; weevils and grain rust; and the retarding effect of the panic of 1857, which made money tight,'[103] all had disastrous effects on the settlers. Some men temporarily left the settlement to find employment in the northern United States.[104] Consequently, a number of women were left to manage the homestead. Some 'families were dispossessed of their lands by default in payment of interest and principal and by the failure to carry out the requirements of settlement.'[105]

Mary Jane Robinson's letter to a friend in New York during the mid-nineteenth century provides one of the few glimpses of rural Black life recorded by a Black woman of the time:

I take up my pen to write you a few lines, after so long a delay. I suppose you all thought that we were all dead, but it is not so, I can assure you, although we have been quite sich [sic] since we arrived in Canada. I have been quite ill with the pleurisy, and in the Fall, we all had the dumb ague and fever; but now we are enjoying good health, except my son John; it left him feeble and a pain the side; but he never was strong in health ... We arrive in Chatham of the 13th May, after a pleasant journey. It's really beautiful to travel in the Spring, and to behold the different faces of nature's beauty. In the steamboat we went to Troy; then took the cars to Buffalo, and there we put up until Monday from Friday, and I found Buffalo a very pretty place indeed; then we took the steamboat for Detroit – a beautiful sail across the Lake – Erie – and out of sight of land, it seems to me as on the sea; and then we took the steamboat again for Chatham – then we were done and at our journey's end. Now Chatham is a fine place indeed, a town pleasantly situated on the banks of the Thames; and there we kept house six weeks – we had a small house – much cheaper than to board; and then my husband went to Buxton, to the coloured settlement, a distance of six miles, and purchased a farm of fifty acres, ... O, my dear friend, how I do want to see you again; I do wish you would try and come to Buxton, Canada West. Come to a land of liberty and freedom, where the coloured man is not despised nor a deaf ear turned to them. This is the place to live in peace and to enjoy the comforts of life ... We have all kinds of game, deer, raccoon, ground-hogs, black-squirrels, hens, pheasants, quails, wild turkey, wild duck, woodcock and red-headed woodpeckers, and sapsuckers, wild red raspberries and plumbs, crabapples and wild gooseberries, and all kinds of nuts. Not as cold as I thought ... Do come to Buxton, Canada West.[106]

Mary Jane Robinson's experience, however, was not representative of most of the Elgin women. Having escaped oppressive situations, the majority did not find the journey pleasant. And many more did not come with a family, ready and able to purchase land and livestock.

The women at Elgin built their community around the church. William King established the Buxton Mission, which was supported by the Presbyterian church.[107] Black men and women, however, established Baptist and Methodist churches. Dorothy Shadd Shreve suggests that 'these denominations, appealing to the soul and emotions, had been very popular on the slave plantations, for their services provided a natural outlet for feelings of frustration and despair.'[108] In writing about the Black women in the Baptist church in the United States, Evelyn Brooks Higginbotham points out that 'the Black church represented the realm where individual souls communed intimately with God and where African Americans as a people freely discussed, debated, and devised an agenda for their common good.'[109] The same is true of the Black church in Canada. Black women were the backbone of the church. They planned and ran church activities. They taught Sunday school. They planned and ran church fairs and picnics, and bazaars at harvest time. And while they did not deliver sermons from the pulpit, Black women's spirituality embodied 'the values of sacrifice, nurturance and personal courage – values necessary to an endangered group.'[110] Furthermore, as Higginbotham points out, it is important to look at the 'Multiple discourses – sometimes conflicting, sometimes unifying' within the Black church.'[111]

Women took care of the sick on the settlement. As Robbins points out, 'Carrying her seemingly magic herbs and potions she would appear at the door, take over the sickroom and quite often affect a cure.'[112] Midwives played their part as well: 'there were the tender midwives whose gentle hands eased many a new life into the world. One of the earliest of midwives was Julia Laison and several of the little girls of a hundred years ago born into her capable hands were named after her by their thankful mothers among whom were Julia Watts and Julia Doo.[113]

The establishment of the Elgin Settlement raised many questions. Was the settlement a practical endeavour? (Frederick Douglas, a Black American abolitionist and leader, was critical of the settlement. However, he paid a visit to Elgin, and decided that it was a positive endeavour.) The settlers were given no supplies 'in money, in food, or in clothing.'[114] They were given no agricultural implements. An article in a British newspaper, the *Paisley Herald*, reported that Mr King was of the opinion that 'the negroes are better axe men than European emigrants, and so are better fitted to contend with the difficulties attendant upon clearing a heavily-timbered country.'[115] While men, women, and children worked on the farms in the settlement, as mentioned earlier, William King, William Day, Martin Delany, and Archibald McKellar travelled to England in 1856, attempting to convince British philanthropists of the worthiness of the project. The publicity the settlement received attracted many visitors to Elgin. One visitor commenting on the settlement in the *Toronto Globe* claimed that Rev. Mr King 'is regarded throughout the settlement as the king whom all are bound to obey, and to judge from what I witness, the obedience of the settlers was no less implicit than their confidence and respect were sincere and profound.'[116] The *Provincial Freeman* published an article in response to the one appearing in the *Globe*.

We do not really know, what is meant by such expressions, ... if by it is meant, that men and women are to yield their conscience, and give up their private judgment in obedience to 'the King', then, to us it is clear, the Elgin Settlement will be anything else than a blessing to the colored people. It never can develop an independent and self-respecting people! ... It is also said, 'Enough has been told (of the settlers at Elgin) to prove that under proper management, the Black man is as capable of success, even in agricultural pursuits, as the white one' Etc. That is so much like the slaveholder. It reminds us of a certain Ethnographical Lecture, at a Western College, a laboured effort to prove what every man knows to be true! ... Indeed, is it true that colored people cannot succeed, only as they have some white man to control them? It is anything but true ... They have not succeeded, because WHITE MEN would not allow them to; and especially is that true of our people in Canada. Very true, Bro. King is so far, a noble exception.[117]

As property owners, Black men were entitled to vote. And in 1856 their vote helped to re-elect Archibald McKellar, a supporter of the Settlement.[118] His opponent Larwill led the protest to stop the settlement.

Immediately outside the Elgin Settlement, in Raleigh Township, many Black families lived and farmed: Almira Charleston and her husband Roszeel; Mariah Dyke and her family; Harriet and Abraham Shadd and Absalom Shadd and his family; Elizabeth Shadd Shreve and her husband George; Jane Serena Lewis Rhue and her husband William. These families were part of the Elgin community.

The women at Elgin built their community around the church. In 1855 the Black community in Pittsburgh sent a gift to the settlement of a Liberty Bell, which was placed on St Andrew's church. This bell was used to announce the arrival of a new family, as well as for weddings and the arrival of new babies. Women planned and organized Emancipation Day celebrations in August.

Women's sexuality was kept in check and monitored by the church authorities. The Baptists, B.M.E., and the Presbyterians each had formal and informal mechanisms in place. In 1860 a female member of the Presbyterian church was brought before a church committee accused of ante-nuptial fornication. That King kept a watchful eye on women's sexual activities is revealed in his autobiography.

Chatham

Located on what First Nations peoples called the Eskunisippi River and renamed by white colonials the Thames River,[119] Chatham was viewed by the British as a militarily strategic point. Since water was the primary means of transportation, areas close to rivers and lakes were favoured for defence, and Chatham was one such area.[120] As railroads developed, Chatham became a station, providing links with other areas. It grew from a small village in the eighteenth century, with a small number of settlers, into a county town by the mid-nineteenth century.[121]

When compared to London, Windsor, or Hamilton, Chatham was a rural county town.[122] Chatham was, however, the commercial centre for the surrounding farms in the townships of Kent County. In Chatham, the market was often the centre of local activity, as farm women and men from Raleigh, Harwich, and other townships gathered to sell their produce. During the 1840s, Chatham's waterway provided a steady flow of traffic of white people passing through on their way to the United States. At the time, Chatham's shipbuilding industry was an important part of the town's economy. Steamships like the Brothers operated regularly between Chatham and Detroit; the Western operated between Chatham and Amherstburg.[123] In 1851, Chatham's excursion steamer, the Ploughboy, was launched and ran from Chatham to Detroit and from Chatham to Amherstburg.[124] Black people were, however, often excluded from travelling on these boats. In fact, 'the officers of these boats ... descend to the use of brute force, upon unresisting women to eject them from the cabin or the table.'[125] W. & W. Eberts, Chatham's largest importing, exporting, and merchandising firm, had by 1855 'erected the Eberts Block.' (W. Eberts was one of the protesters trying to stop the Elgin Settlement. Along with others, he formed a vigilante committee in Kent County to keep a watchful eye on Black people.) Described as 'the tallest structure in Chatham, extending from King Street to within a few feet of the river, the four-story brick block was a spectacular undertaking in the Chatham of that period with its rutty mud streets and its population of slightly over 2,000,'[126] With the arrival of the railway in 1854, Chatham's shipbuilding industry began to wane.[127]

Exactly when Black people first arrived in Chatham is not

clear. Sally Ainse 'who was born in Pennslyvania settled along the Thames in 1790. She is said to have brought at least one slave and possibly more.'[128] As well, one Black household was listed among the twenty families recorded there in 1791.[129] Since the first major wave of fugitive slaves from the United States arrived in Ontario between 1817 and 1822, some may have come to Chatham. During the 1830s and 1840s, Black people continued to arrive in Ontario, but at a slower rate than they did at the turn of the century. The largest increase, however, in the Black population occurred between 1850 and 1860.[130] Census figures indicate that in 1851 there were 353 Black people living in Chatham, out of a total population of 2070.[131] By 1856, there were 800 Blacks, out of a total population of 4000.[132] And, by 1861, the Black population totalled 1254.[133] However, other sources identified much larger populations of Black people, thus raising questions about the actual figures. Many Black people who settled in Canada were of mixed racial origin and may not have been included in earlier census figures. The 1852 manuscript census identified race in two separate classifications: 'Colored Persons or Negroes' and 'Indians, if any.' The aggregate census for 1852 notes 'these two Heads are included in other columns.'[134] In 1851 the Voice of the Fugitive reported: 'we are happy to learn through our worthy correspondent at Chatham, Canada West, Rev. S.B. Needham, that four females have just arrived there from New York one of whom is his own sister. He informs us that they were very closely pursue[d] by their owners ... They were in a crowd of other ladies with vails [sic] over their faces and being nearly white they were passed unnoticed even by the slave hunters.'[135] The 1861 manuscript census had a single classification for race: 'Colored Persons, Mulatto or Indian.' What is significant about the classification of people in the census data, is that all other groups were identified by 'country of origin.'

Women in Chatham

In 1851, according to census data, Black women in Chatham numbered 174, or 49 per cent of the total Black population. Of these, women aged 17 to 79 years numbered 84, or 48 per cent of the total female population.[136] Where did these women come from? Eliza Harris, for example, who fled slavery in Kentucky apparently escaped with her baby and somehow made her way to Chatham. Gwendolyn Robinson records that Eliza 'made her escape in the middle of the night carrying only herself and her baby. Upon reaching the Ohio river, she found that it was frozen over and therefore not a viable escape route. She sought refuge at the home of some sympathetic friends where she received a good meal and warmth. The next day, upon hearing that slave catchers were after her, she ran again to the banks of the river. Seeing the river had chunks of floating ice, she decided that she must somehow escape. Panic stricken, she jumped from one cake of ice to another with her child in her arms until she reached the other side of the river, the free soil of Ohio.' Although details about her rescue are not clear, it appears that 'from Cincinnati she was forwarded to Chatham, Ontario, through the Underground Railroad via the Sandusky, Ohio route.'[137] Were women single or married? Were any of them widowed? Did they have children, and if so how many? How did the support themselves and their families?

In 1851, most women living in Chatham had been born in the United States (see table 4). As shown in table 5 most women were married – 76 married women compared to 8 single women who were 17 years and older. Females between the ages of one and 16 years old numbered 82, or 47 per cent of all females during this period. Males one to 16 years old numbered 61, or 34 per cent of the male population.

The figures cited suggest that while some women may have come to Chatham either alone or in the company of other women and children, most came either with a husband or joined one.[138] The number of children born in Canada, shown in table 6, suggests there must have been a sustained Black population in Chatham for some time.

In the 1851 and 1861 census, the occupational classification of most Black women was either not recorded or was listed as housewife. Jonathan Walton points to this in his doctoral thesis 'Black in Buxton and Chatham, Ontario,' and surmises that because Chatham had a large skilled and semi-skilled Black male population, most of whom were married, Black married women did not need to work outside their own households.[139] However, patterns revealed by the census data may underestimate Black women's work in earning income for the family. Census data provide neither 'hard facts' nor 'raw data.'[140] For example, what do census figures reveal about married women whose husbands were absent when the census was taken? Many women worked at more than one occupation, but this is also not reflected in the census. For example, in 1861, Mary Ann Shadd was listed as an 'editress.' Yet there is evidence that she also taught school for some time.[141] During the 1850s, Sarah Grant also taught school, a fact not reflected in the census data.[142]

Even in the absence of these women's diaries, letters, and journals, I offer some general assumptions. Some of Chatham's Black men were artisans, including blacksmiths, shoemakers, watchmakers, wagon-makers, carpenters, and masons. The growth of the manufacturing sector, coupled with the development and growth of the railroads linking Chatham to other areas, helped to fuel business possibilities. As Chatham thrived economically during some of this period, and was in dire need of farm labour, Black men were hired. Certainly, work as farm help was available. There were as well medical doctors. Amelia Shadd and her husband Isaac boarded Dr Amos Aray. Katherine Delany, her husband Martin, and their eight children moved to Chatham from Pittsburgh in 1856. When 'a cholera epidemic hit Chatham in June 1856, Dr. Martin Delany suggested a four-point sanitation program to arrest the epidemic.'[143] A surgeon, Martin Delaney advertised in

TABLE 4
Place of birth for Chatham's Black population, 1851

Place of birth	Number	% of all females	% of total pop-ulation	Number	% of all males	% of total pop-ulation
Canada	58	34	15	42	24	11
United States	115	67	33	137	77	39
Other	1	1	0	–	–	–
Total	174	102	48	179	101	50

SOURCE: Walton, 'Blacks in Buxton and Chatham,' 270; Census of Canada, Chatham, 1851

the *Provincial Freeman* that 'He practices in chronic diseases and the diseases of women and children in particular.'[144] Samuel Watson and R.M. Johnson also practised medicine in Chatham during this period.

Many questions remain. Did artisans and health practitioners work alone? Was the business attached to their home? Who kept records? Were there hired help? It is unlikely that the percentage of Black women who were forced to work for wages in Chatham remained small given the fluctuation in the job market, particularly in 1857–8.[145] In addition, many 'male' jobs were seasonal, which meant the family had to supplement its income. A husband's illness would also have made it necessary for a married woman to find work. As well, children old enough to work would have been contributing in some way to the family economy.

Using selected census data, then, what patterns emerge in Black women's lives over the period? The 1851 and 1861 census lists no occupation for many Black women. However, the 1851 census reveals that, when employed, Black women worked as either servants or labourers. Forty-eight-year-old Mariah Flandy worked as a servant. Since she and her husband both worked as domestics, it is likely that they did day work, as their place of residence is recorded as the east end of Chatham, where the Black population lived, suggesting that they returned home to their young children at the end of the

TABLE 5
Marital status compared with age for all Chatham's Black population,
1851

Age	Number	% of all females	% of group	Number	% of all males	% of group
Single						
1–16 yrs.	82	47	91	61	34	62
17–20	2	1	2	15	8	15
21–29	4	2	4	15	8	15
30–39	1	1	1	6	3	6
40–49	–	–	–	–	–	–
50–59	1	1	1	1	1	1
60–69	–	–	–	–	–	–
70–79	–	–	–	–	–	–
Total	90	52	99	98	54	99
Married						
1–16 yrs.	–	–	–	–	–	–
17–20	6	3	8	–	–	–
21–29	32	18	42	15	8	20
30–39	22	13	30	21	12	28
40–49	6	3	8	24	13	32
50–59	6	3	8	8	4	11
60–69	2	1	3	7	4	9
70–79	2	1	3	–	–	–
Total	76	42	102	75	41	100

SOURCE: Walton, 268; Census of Canada, Chatham, 1851

day.[146] When young single women worked as servants, however, they often lived in white households.

It is likely that women worked on farms as labourers. In 1851, twenty-year-old Nerufsu Harvey, who was born in Ontario, worked as a farm labourer. Her infant son (who had begun teething) had recently died and she was most likely supplementing the family income as a day worker. As a mother of three other young children (aged seven, six, and two), whose husband, William, was a sailor, she had to juggle child-rearing activities, housework, and paid work. So did Harriet Jackson,

TABLE 6
Place of birth compared with age for Chatham's Black population, 1851

Age	Number	% of all females	% of total pop- ulation	Number	% of all males	% of total pop- ulation
Canada						
1 mo.–16 yrs.	46	26	13	33	18	9
17–20	4	2	1	3	2	1
21–29	4	2	1	4	2	1
30–39	1	1	1	–	–	–
40–49	1	1	0	1	1	0
50–59	–	–	–	–	–	–
60–69	1	1	1	1	1	0
70–79	1	1	1	–	–	–
Total	58	34	15	42	24	11
United States						
1 mo.–16 yrs.	35	20	10	28	16	8
17–20	4	2	1	12	7	3
21–29	34	20	10	26	15	7
30–39	23	13	7	31	17	9
40–49	8	5	2	9	5	3
50–59	8	5	2	9	5	3
60–69	2	1	1	6	3	2
70–79	1	1	0	–	–	–
Total	115	67	33	137	77	39

SOURCE: Walton, 271; Census of Canada, Chatham, 1851

mother of three young sons, and Emily Johnson, mother of a three-year-old daughter.[147]

Married women who are listed as housewives may also have done other work. Mary Smith, whose two daughters, ages eleven and ten, and son, aged eight, were all attending school in Chatham in 1852, would have contributed to her husband's blacksmith's shop; so too Emily Stafford, whose husband Henry also had a blacksmith shop and whose two children were attending school.[148]

In addition to keeping livestock and growing vegetables, it

is also likely that housewives may have taken in washing to supplement the family income, very likely one of the few jobs available to Black women. Twenty-year-old Virginia Thomas, who had three young children, may have taken in washing. Her husband, Washington, was a plasterer, but when times were hard Virginia would have had to take what was available. Emeline Carter, whose husband was a carpenter, may have found herself in similar circumstances. With nine-year-old Arthur at school and a younger child at home, she too would have had to take what work she could find. Although washing was physically tiresome, women could work in the privacy of their own homes and away from the watchful eye of an employer. Barbara Cropswhite and Sydney Haynes, both married, worked as washerwomen.[149]

In 1861 thirty-year-old Mary Levere lived with her four daughters and one son. Her husband, whose occupation was listed as a 'Cork' was absent. Mary (12), Susan (10), and Alex (8) attended school, while Lelah (6) and Eliz (4) did not. Did the children attend the 'colored common school'? How often did the children attend school? Did they live in close proximity to it? Most Black people in Chatham lived on the eastern side of the town where the two available schools for their children were located. Consequently, those who lived in other areas found it extremely difficulty, especially during inclement weather, for their children to get to school. Levere, evidently, did some farming, for she and her family lived on three-and-a-quarter acres of land and tended a cow and four pigs. Louise Parker and her husband James and their fifteen-year-old daughter Bertha lived near the Leveres. Unlike the Levere family, whose five children were all born in Upper Canada, Bertha and her parents were born in the United States. James Parker, a shoemaker, was eleven years older than his wife, whose name was not listed in the census. Was she his second wife? The Parkers lived in a one-storey frame house on an eighth of an acre of land with another family. It is not clear whether the two families were related. Were the Whites boarders? They appear to have been living in the same household.

In addition to their own family members, a number of households had young children who did not appear to be related. Three-year-old Matilda Jackson, who was born in Upper Canada, was living with Catharine Horton and her husband Henry. Two-year-old Emma Williams was listed as not being a member of the family she resided with, although she had the same last name. Was this an error on the part of the census taker? In November 1854 Emily Francis married James Monroe Jones, a gunsmith and engraver. How did they meet? Emily may have worked in the business that was attached to their house. She graduated from the University of Michigan with a medical degree in 1885.[150]

While many women were involved in church activities, Sarah Hawkins, as the wife of the pastor of the First Baptist Church, must have had her fair share. Twelve-year-old Mary, ten-year-old Adelaide, and seven-year-old Hendrik were attending school in 1861. A three-year-old boy remained at home. Since Pastor Hawkins also did missionary work throughout the district, Sarah would have had additional duties in maintaining the family while her husband was away. Hill points out that 'Chatham's First Baptist Church on King Street between Prince and Princess Streets, served as a meeting place for the town's Black community. Besides providing Sunday services and weekly prayer-meetings, it became the headquarters of anti-slavery campaigns. It was used during the antislavery campaign of white abolitionist John Brown, when he met with Black men to take immediate action against slavery in the United States.[151] The first organization meeting was held at the B.M.E. church on Wellington Street. Subsequent meetings were held at the First Baptist Church as well as at private homes. Although women were not officially included in the convention held to organize the raid at Harpers Ferry, West Virginia, many supported Brown.[152] Mary Ellen Pleasant and her husband John, who moved to Chatham in 1858, donated funds to John Brown.[153]

By 1861, although a significant number of married women do not have an occupation listed in the census (again, most were noted as 'housewife,') there were Black women artisans.

Martha J. Charity worked as a shoe-binder. Most worked as seamstresses (see appendix 1). Thirty-four-year-old Cath Thomas was a seamstress. She would also have taken care of the livestock she and her labourer husband had on their quarter-acre of land. Forty-year-old Rebecca Wilson was also a seamstress. Her husband was absent from the household in 1861. We are not told whether the couple had separated. Mr Wilson was a cook. Given the economic hardships during the depression of 1857, he may have left the family for some time to look for work. Rebecca's eldest son, eighteen-year-old George, who was married, was listed as absent, suggesting that he too may have been forced to migrate in search of work. We are not told about George's wife. Did two generations share a household? Mary Smith, who had two sets of twins, had a large household. She and her husband Addison, who ran a store on King Street, had twenty-one children. In a recent publication, Saxonia Shadd talked briefly about her grandmother, Mary Smith, who died as a young woman.[154]

In some cases, an adult woman and her daughter might have taken in sewing. Mary Jane Lewis and her two daughters, fifteen-year-old Frances and nine-year-old Norma, were listed as seamstresses. Frances might have assisted her mother or she may have had her own customers. It is likely that Norma also helped her mother. The entry for her in the census may be incorrect. Two other children were in the household, but none appear to have been in school. Mary's husband's occupation is not listed in the census. Is this an oversight? Were she and her two children working together?

We know that Mrs M.A. Sterritt, a 'Dress and Cloak Maker,' ran a 'fashionable' shop at the corner of James and Murray streets in Chatham. Her advertisement in the *Provincial Freeman* in September 1855 reads: 'Respectively solicits the patronage of the Ladies of Chatham and Vicinity. She is prepared to execute the orders of those who may favour her with a call, with neatness and despatch.' Children's clothes were also her specialty. How large was her shop? Did she have apprentices? Were members of her family involved with the business?

Both Lurinda Richardson and Josephine Holden combined domestic activities, child-rearing, and their trade as seamstresses. Jane Spark may have been slightly more privileged than others. She and her family could afford to live in a two-storey frame house. It is likely that her husband, John, kept his business as a watchmaker in a part of the house. As a seamstress, Jane too juggled domestic tasks and child-rearing.

Thirty-two-year-old Sarah Douglas, married to a man twice her age, worked as a tailor. A milliner, thirty-one-year-old Caroline Dunn invested $400 in her business. While not all women could have afforded her hats, she must have carried on a reasonably good business in an era when wearing hats to church was the norm.

There are several questions with no immediate answers. Did seamstresses work alone? What prices did they charge for garments? Who were their customers? In some instances, as many as ten women who appeared to have been neighbours were all seamstresses. Does this mean that they made garments only for members of their own households? How many women could have afforded to pay a seamstress? Was this trade dependable? Did women organize a sewing bee? Quilts were used 'in the underground railroad to provide coded messages – log cabin, evening star/northstar and Jacob's ladder quilts hanging on clotheslines may have served not only as indicators of safe houses but also as maps.'[155]

Whatever the circumstances in which these women practised their craft, whether at home or in a shop, they would have gathered to discuss their families and about their children being denied admission to public schools with white children because of their race. They would have talked, too, about their sisters and brothers in the southern and northern United States. They would have built networks and given advice to someone who needed it. Women's businesses, whether inside or outside the home, would have formed 'an important part of the women's culture.'[156]

At age thirty-seven, Mary Ann Shadd Cary was listed in the 1861 census as an 'Editress' with two children: a girl, Sarah

E. Cary, four years old, and a son, Linton S. Cary, born in 1860. Her husband Thomas was not listed. Since Thomas lived in Toronto, he must have appeared in the census for that city. Because Mary Ann and Thomas lived in different cities, their correspondence provides us with some sense of their relationship. In 1856 Mary Ann contemplated renting out space in the house she lived in for financial reasons. Thomas's letter in the fall of that year to her in this matter indicates how strongly he felt about it. His language and tone suggest that he felt that he should be the one making the final decision: 'It afforded me great satisfaction to here that you and the children was well altho I am in deep distress of mind in Regard to my affairs. You spoke of packing the things in the front Room, up stares and letting it out. Such an a Rangement does not meet my approbation and never would for I am altoghether opposed to any sutch arrangement and if you do you have it all to your self.'[157]

In another letter to Mary Ann, dated 21 May 1857, we get a sense of the respect they had for each other: 'I Received your very long and gratifying letter and was glad to heare that you and children togeather [sic] with Miss F was enjoying good health.' He goes on to inform her of his visit to the legislative council 'to see their doings and here their sayings for a few minutes.' He also informs her that 'I here with forward to you $2. and hope that I will be able to send you some more next weak. I want you to Rite me a long letter So that I will get in on Sunday morning and it will be food for me on that day as I keep in my Shell all of that day boath [sic] Ike (Isaac her brother) and my Self. He pore devil has but one Shirt and I have a half Doz new ones from you.'[158]

In March 1853, while living and teaching in Windsor, Shadd Cary had established the newspaper, the *Provincial Freeman*. Recognizing the obstacles she was likely to encounter, because of her gender, she invited Samuel Ringgold Ward, one of the prominent leaders in the community to act as editor of the newspaper. But as pointed out by Silverman, among others, 'Proclaimed editor of this bold venture, Ward actually lent only his name to the paper to generate interest and subscriptions ... At no time, indeed, did Ward act as editor or invest his own money in the operation.'[159] (Interestingly enough when Ward published his autobiography, he did not mention Shadd Cary.) Shadd Cary moved the paper to Toronto a year later and ran it with her younger sister, Amelia. Amelia got married and moved to St Catharines. By now Ward's name was no longer listed as the editor, and the sisters received no significant support from the men in their community. In 1855 Mary Ann moved with it to Chatham. In Chatham the *Provincial Freeman* was housed in the Charity Building on Queen Street East, which was owned by James Henry Charity. Rebecca Charity worked with her husband in their commercial business. They appear to have had a thriving shoemaker business, for their capital investment was $1850. Martha Charity carried on her shoe-binding business with her husband, Cornelius, brother of James. In 1861 five males and one female were working in the business. Although it is not clear what their respective duties were or the hours worked, female labour was $4 per month while male labour was $24 per month. Martha Charity and her husband had seven children, ranging in age from eleven to one. Four of the children were in school.

The *Provincial Freeman* dealt with anti-slavery and abolitionist activities, racism, temperance, emigration, and women's rights. Shadd Cary, however, had a global vision; as she pointed out, 'we desire, not only that its permanency shall be sure, but that it may be regarded as connected with the soil – a paper for the Canadas, as well as other parts of the world.'[160]

Just as Ida B. Wells decades later in the United States used her pen to educate and bring public awareness to the anti-lynching campaign, Mary Ann Shadd Cary similarly used her pen to educate and bring public awareness to the antislavery campaign both in the United States and in Canada. The *Black Abolitionist Papers* poignantly remind us that by going to Canada, the fugitives made an implicit antislavery statement; each escape attempt gave lie to the 'contented-slave thesis.'[161]

There is not much evidence to show linkages between the

Black women of Buxton and Chatham with white women who were members of the Toronto Ladies Association for the Relief of Destitute Coloured Refugees in April 1851. These women, who included Agnes Willis and Isabel Henning, were married to men who were involved with the Antislavery Society of Canada. These same men were members of the Elgin Association. Referred to as the Ladies Auxiliary – whose founding members included Black woman Ethalinda Lewis, Willis, and Henning – this benevolent society rose in response to the need to assist in 'alleviating the suffering' of large numbers of fugitives who were escaping to Canada following the passage of the Fugitive Slave Bill in the United States.

While helping to settle Black families, with the opportunity to acquire farm land, it must be borne in mind that the white women in the Ladies Auxiliary were also moved to this decision by their concern about the presence of too many Black people in the cities.[162] And while Mary Bibb and Mary Ann Shadd Cary were members of the Windsor Antislavery Society, there is little evidence of networking between Black and white women. Indeed, Shadd Cary expressed some concern in the *Provincial Freeman* that the Ladies Auxiliary was more interested in holding a bazaar to assist Frederick Douglas's antislavery newspaper across the border than it was in supporting the antislavery work of the *Provincial Freeman*.[163] While there has been some question as to whether Shadd Cary was correct in her assessment, it is important to bear in mind that a significant part of the abolitionist activities in which Black women and men in Canada were involved focused on emigration to Canada as one of the solutions for weakening and ultimately breaking the slaveholding class. It is in this regard that the North American Convention organized by Henry Bibb and James Theodore Holly and others was held in Toronto at the St Lawrence Hall on 11 through 13 September 1851. As the *Black Abolitionist Papers* point out, Holly saw Canada as 'a beacon of hope to the slave and a rock of terror to the oppresser.[164] The North American League, which grew out of the above convention, was set up to provide unified action for American and Canadian Black people that would help them to settle in Canada, aid fugitives, and encourage free Black people from the northern states to emigrate to Canada. Shadd Cary was the sole female who attended the convention, and she later wrote and published *A Plea for Emigration to Canada West*.

Just before moving to Chatham, Shadd Cary had turned over the editorship of the newspaper to Rev. William P. Newman, but not without stating, 'In taking leave of our readers, at this time, we do so for the best interests of the enterprise, and with the hope that our absence will be their gain. We want the *Freeman* to prosper and shall labour to that end ... We have worked for it through difficulties such as few females have had to contend against, except the sister [Amelia] who shared our labours for awhile.' Shadd Cary was no doubt responding to the lack of support her paper received. She added, 'To its enemies, we would say, be less captious to him than to us; be more considerate, if you will, it is fit that you should deport your ugliest to a woman ...' She understood and publicly stated that Black men, no less than white, did not want a member of 'the unfortunate sex' as their spokesperson.[165]

In accepting the editorship, Newman referred to Shadd Cary's gender when he said that she was 'one of the best editors our Province ever had,' even if she 'did wear the petticoats instead of the breeches.' He admitted that 'a wrongly developed public sentiment – would crush a woman whenever she attempts to do what had hitherto been assigned to men.'[166]

Shadd Cary's challenge to her sisters to 'go to editing' was a point to be well taken. As publishing agent for the newspaper, she remained involved in its every aspect. She spent a considerable amount of time travelling on a lecture tour in the United States, obtaining subscriptions for the newspaper as well as lecturing. In the Fall of 1855 she addressed the Eleventh Colored National Convention in Philadelphia on emigration to Canada. She was the first woman to address this convention, but only after much objection. It was Frederick Douglass who led the decision for her to speak.[167] She was not bound by the constraints of nineteenth-century travel. She travelled alone both as a single woman and later as a married woman. During the latter stage, she left her young children in Chatham in the care of her sister. Correspondence discovered years later revealed that her sister had written her, pointing out that she, Mary, should spend more time with her children.

By 1858, Shadd Cary's husband, who was twelve years her senior, had joined her in Chatham. He had become too ill, it seems, to stay in Toronto. On one of her many lectures and fundraising tours, she wrote him a letter that enables us to have a glimpse of her concern for him. She expressed anxiety for his health and gave him some advice. Writing from Michigan, she said, 'You smoke an old clay pipe. Some one has said that a Meershaum absorbes the oil in the tobacco and so prevents it from doing smokers so much injury. Do not you think you had better get a Meershaum as you will smoke?' She also tells him to get up and take some walks as 'it will exercise you and help restore your health.' Mary was concerned also about the newspaper, and sent advice to her brother as well: 'Tell Isaac to put in as much reading matter as he can crowd into the *Freeman* as that is the only way to get up an interest in it.'

It was during the Michigan visit that Shadd Cary heard and met Frances Ellen Harper Watkins. Watkins, an abolitionist living in Washington, DC, was also on a lecture tour. Shadd Cary tells Thomas that Watkins is 'the greatest female speaker ever was ... so wisdom obliges me to keep out of the way as with her prepared lectures there would just be no chance of a fabourable [sic] comparison.'[168]

As a newspaperwoman Shadd Cary recognized the potential power of the press. It was crucial, for example, that public knowledge be made of the attempted sexual violation of her body that Chatham resident Sarah Armstrong had suffered[169] at the hands of a white man. Challenging the widely held notion that Black women were sexually loose, Shadd Cary pointed out that Armstrong was 'a very respectable colored lady' who taught in the public school, and that her assailant, J.F. Grady, was an Irish dentist.

Older Black women also helped to build and run family businesses. At age sixty, Martha Barber managed a hotel and tavern with her husband, Sherwood, who apparently came to Chatham in the 1830s. In 1834 he participated in the building of the mud-sill bridge, the first erected in Chatham.[170] They invested $400 in the business, a two-storey frame hotel on half an acre of land. Their daughter, Ardenia, worked as a domestic. Did she work at the family hotel or was she employed elsewhere? What did running a tavern mean during a period when the temperance movement was so strong? At the Elgin Settlement no alcoholic spirits were made or sold. Chatham settlers, however, could buy some alcoholic beverages, while temperance societies worked to keep their members in check. Although Martha Barber is listed in the 1861 census as a 'tavern keeper,' I found no evidence that states when the business started. We do have evidence that John Brown, who came to Chatham in 1856, lodged at Martha and Sherwood's hotel.[171] An editorial in the *Provincial Freeman* of 6 December 1856 read:

A good temperance house of high tone, and fitted up properly and managed by competent persons, would pay well! At the present time, we do not know of a public boarding house that is not also a drinking house. A most unworthy state of morals! and yet such houses, not 'gin palaces either, are blazoned forth as desirable places of resort. We regard them as degrading in their tendency – as calculated to not only corrupt and demoralize the young, but as dangerous to the physical health of the community as the small-pox or cholera ... Some of our Chatham boarding houses make their own liquors and a 'make' they may be supposed to be. While the character of houses here is indifferent so far as we have been informed, the rates for entertainment are enormous. The wants of the travelling community justify better provisions than have been made in this respect, and we sincerely hope some enterprising COLORED Canadian or American will take this matter in hand.

Black women worked diligently in the temperance movement. Spokeswoman Mary Ann Shadd Cary used the newspaper she started to support temperance. Another Chatham newspaper, the *Western Planet*, (a supporter of the Reform party, antislavery, and temperance) called for a law banning the sale of liquor to Blacks based on an incident where an 'inebriated black man has passed the newspaper's office swearing and acting in a disorderly manner,'[172] thus promoting the belief that Blacks are inherently immoral. Shadd Cary responded with an editorial that reads, in part: 'We believe in passing a strictly prohibitory law that will not only prevent Indians and colored men from getting drunk, but will stop white men from drinking as well and not only the "inferior" classes about Chatham, but a drunken Editor ... But the Editor of the *Planet* must be too much of an abolitionist to propose a regulation of the sort in sober earnest, else he must have forgotten that while to see a drunker colored man is of so rare occurrence as to "call him" on the subject. Drunken officers, "limbs of the law," a drunken M.P.P., or a drunken Editor of his class is quite common.'[173]

Mrs E.A. Reyno ran a hotel with her husband Abram Reyno at the corner of King and William streets in Chatham. In an announcement about the opening of the Villa Mansion the owners declared:

Mr. and Mrs. Reyno have purchased and are now residents and active proprietors of the pleasant and commodious mansion on the corner of King and William Streets. Having refitted the house in appeal and elegant manner, they have given it the permanent name of the VILLA MANSION where they will be pleased to receive and accomodate all genteel and respectable persons of any race and none but respectable persons need apply, at this house, as the deportment is required in all of its departments.

An Excellent LIVERY STABLE is a part of the service of this mansion, where the citizens, boarders and strangers generally can be accomodated on the shorter notices with good horses and vehicles.[174]

There are also widows who supported themselves and their families by doing various jobs. The two midwives listed in Chatham were both widows in their sixties.[175] When did Rebecca Scott, aged sixty-five, become a midwife? Had she gained her experience with age or had she been a midwife for a long time? How many children did she deliver? There are no immediate answers. Midwives no doubt had to walk many miles through the woods to deliver and care for newborn babies and their mothers. We can surmise that older women were probably the health-care givers in the community.

Most widows, however, worked as washerwomen. At thirty-eight years old, Papamist Gains, with five children to support, worked as a washerwoman. Mefifa Berry and her sixteen-year-old daughter also worked as washerwomen. Mary Short, who was twenty-four when her husband, William, died in 1860 from consumption, leaving her with a six-year-old son, was a washerwoman.

A widow may have been supported by her adult children, as may have been the case with Julia Burden, whose occupation is unlisted in the census. She received support from her sixteen-year-old daughter, Julia, and two of her oldest sons, all of whom were labourers. Ellen Robinson, another widow, who was thirty-seven years old, in 1860, apparently had nine children, the eldest being twenty-three years old. Both Julia Burden and Ellen Robinson's children were born in Canada, suggesting that both women must have lived in the country for most of their adult lives. Two of Ellen's adult sons worked as labourers while another son was a seaman. Esther Bailey, a widow aged one hundred years, lived with her children.[176]

When working outside their own households, most young Black single women in Chatham worked as servants. In most cases, they lived in white households. Census records indicate these young single women would have been working and living in white areas. Twelve-year-old Maria Burton and thirteen-year-old Matilda Green worked as live-in domestics in white households. Twenty-four-year-old Janie Sanderson worked as a live-in servant. She may have been employed by Walter McCrea, a barrister who lived with his wife and eight children in a two-storey brick house. Nineteen-year-old Fanny Anderson also worked as a live-in servant. What were the working conditions of these young women, confined as they were in white households, knowing that it was their blackness, their imposed subordinate status that all but ruled out the possibility of upward mobility? What went on in the minds and hearts of young Black servant girls who were excluded from attending the common schools with young white girls, some of whom they may have been taking care of?

Black people had fought long and hard to resist the exclusion of their children from the common schools. In the 1830s they petitioned the local government. In 1838 they sent a petition to the Colonial Secretary, and in 1840 they petitioned the International Convention called by the British and Foreign Anti-Slavery Society. In each case they were reminded that education was a local matter.[177] When the Separate School Act was passed in 1850, Egerton Ryerson declared that he 'had exerted all the power I possessed, and employed all the persuasion I could command ... the prejudices and feelings of the people are stronger than law.'[178] Ryerson no doubt saw political expediency as a means of solving the question. In 1838 when he took over as editor of the Wesylean Methodist church's newspaper, the *Guardian*, any reference to antislavery totally disappeared. Ryerson was concerned about proving to the oligarchy in Upper Canada that he and the Wesleyan Methodist congregation were not engaged in subversive activities. He also did not want to offend the slaveholding members of the Wesleyan Methodist church in the United States.[179]

As Jason H. Silverman and Donna J. Gillie point out:

Put simply, white Canadian opposition limited the educational opportunities for fugitive slaves. Governed by locally elected white trustees, school boards across the southwestern portion of the province, where most refugees resided, either excluded black children from common schools or relegated them to inferior separate schools. Consequently, school segregation in Canada West became established even before the Fugitive Slave Law of 1850 propelled thousands of blacks north of the forty-ninth parallel. This latter influx served only to intensify the prejudice and publicize the discrimination. In the end, black/white relations in education during the years 1840–1860 closely resembled the racial environment that many fugitives hoped, and believed, they had escaped.[180]

The philosophy of 'race uplift' ensured that sometime in the 1850s Sarah Grant would make space in her living-room to give Black children the rudiments of an education. She taught at least fifteen students who could not find a place in the Black separate common school in Chatham. The common school,[181] located in a derelict log building on King Street East, registered eighty students. This situation was so oppressive that it led Shadd Cary to publish the following:

The few children of the hundreds of colored people, composing a large portion of our population, must go out of their wards to the 'one horse' school house, there to be taught by the one [coloured] teacher employed at a better salary by the one school committee. The children of the colored school are not promoted to the grammar school, neither are they led to hope that they may be ... the colored people of Chatham must pay taxes and then in order to have their children educated must sustain select schools. It is too bad ... The public school (Negro) should be abandoned and the excellent teacher employed therein sustained as a private teacher, and that disgrace of the place the little colored school house should be left to rot down, or to stand as it is a monument of the injustice the colored people sustain.[182]

In 1850, there were forty-six girls registered at this school and forty-five boys.[183] The average attendance depended on the weather and the harvesting of crops. Did girls attend more regularly than boys? Of the fifteen students who received instruction from Sarah Grant, how many were girls and how many boys? Did Sarah Grant receive any payment for her teaching or was it voluntary? As she was married to James E. Grant, the teacher of the government school, it is possible that the authorities viewed her work as voluntary. In a letter to the *Voice of the Fugitive*, James Grant wrote: 'total number of scholars were 86, and might have numbered 100, or over, had we a school house sufficiently large to have accommodated all who wished to attend, as it was, we were obliged to (during the winter) send some fifteen small scholars to my house, for instruction by my wife.'[184] Indeed some Chatham parents sent their children to the Buxton school. For example, Toussaint L. Delany, eldest son of Katy and Martin Delany, travelled to the Elgin Settlement to attend school.[185]

The 1861 census lists two Black female teachers in Chatham: Sarah Armstrong and Amelia Freeman Shadd. In 1861, Sarah Armstrong taught at the separate common school for Blacks in Chatham. The principal appointed to this school was a Mr Sinclair, a white man who opposed racially integrated schools.[186] Chatham Collegiate Institute, which opened in 1855, did not have any Black girls or boys during the first ten years of its existence. Racism effectively denied their chances of attending. Those Black parents who could afford it enlisted the help of Amelia Freeman. In 1856, U.S.-born and Oberlin College–educated Freeman, at a private school in Chatham, taught painting, drawing, music (voice and piano), and writing.[187] She had been encouraged to move to Chatham from Pittsburgh by the Delanys. The school was well attended, although many parents could barely afford to pay the fees, especially if they were widows. Although it is not indicated in the census records, Shadd Cary, her stepdaughter Ann, as well as Shadd Cary's younger sister, Sarah M. Shadd, also taught at this school.[188] By 1857, the school's curriculum had expanded to include philosophy, algebra, and botany, and in 1861 there were more than 250 students attending day and evening classes. Soon after arriving in Chatham, Amelia Freeman met Issac Shadd, one of the trustees at the mission school where she taught, and they were later married. Amelia and Issac's household also included Issac's sister Sarah, who taught with Amelia, as well as his brother, Garrison.[189]

Community Organizing in Chatham and Buxton

Black women and men organized vigilance committees as part of their anti-slavery activities. Vigilance committees were set up throughout southwestern Ontario to resist slave catchers from the United States. During the 1850s, Shadd Cary was the assistant secretary of the Chatham Vigilance Committee. In 1858, approximately 100 to 150 Black men and women, along with some white male abolitionists, armed with clubs successfully rescued a ten-year-old boy, Sylvanus Damarest, from a train in Chatham. Five members of the committee – three Black men and two white men – were arrested. Shadd Cary ran a circular letter in the *Provincial Freeman* appealing to all abolitionists for financial support. In the letter, she stated: 'As an agent appointed by our Vigilance Committee, established here to conduct the case growing out of the release of the slave ... and as Assistant Secretary of the same, I am authorized, and beg to enlist your pecuniary aid towards defending the suit brought against I.D. Shadd ... One hundred and fifty others are also liable to arrest under a similar charge of riot and (indirectly) abduction.' Charges against the committee had been brought by railroad officials who charged the committee with causing a riot.[190]

The constant tension experienced by Black women and their kin in Chatham was felt elsewhere. Elizabeth Shadd Williamson, who was living in Wilmington, Delaware, at the time of the above rescue, but who was in the process of joining her relatives in Canada, was alarmed. In a letter to her niece she wrote: 'I was struck panic on looking over the *Standard* of last Saturday to see it announced that I.D. Shadd had bin sent to Prison. It made me so sick and so bewildered that I could scaircly attend to my duty. I am much afraid that Canada, is not goint [sic] to prove what it was cracked up to be ... Canada will eventually become hunting ground for the American Blood-hound and when the friends of the fugitive attempts to rescue them the Riot Act will [be] brought against you and Cram you in Prison ... This case of Issac turning out as it has makes me begin to think I had better stay where I am than to go from bad to worse.'[191]

Black women's organizing took place around religious affiliations, as many women were engaged in Sunday school activities. This is not surprising. Higginbotham argues that 'church values and symbols ordered the epistemological and ontological understandings of each individual and gave meaning to the private sphere of family – both as conjugal household and as "household of faith" – church values and symbols helped to spawn the largest number of voluntary associations in the Black community. It follows logically, then, that the church would introduce Black women to public life. The church connected Black women's spirituality integrally with social activism.'[192] It is not surprising, then, that Mary Ann Shadd would choose to deliver a sermon on the equality of women at a Sunday evening service in Chatham in April 1858. She informed her audience, 'We cannot successfully Evade duty because the Suffering fellow woman is only a woman! She too is a neighbor.' In rejecting the generic term 'man' she says, 'in thise [sic] cases particularly was the Sabbath made for man and *woman* if you please as there may be those who will not accept the term man in a generic sense.' And so that there will be no doubt as to her position, she adds, 'Those with whom I am identified, namely the colored people of this country – and the women of the land are in the pit figurat[ively] are cast out.'[193]

By 1846 Chatham's third Black church, the British Episcopal Methodist, was organized; this brought the total membership of the town's three Black congregations to 217 people.[194] Women accounted for a larger percentage of the congregation. In 1859 the brick B.M.E. church, which was located on Princess Street, was large enough to seat over 1000 people. Hill points out that the congregation 'had more than 300 active adult members and a large Sunday School taught by 14 teachers.'[195] As churches were used for anti-slavery meetings and conventions, it was important to have adequate accommodation. Club women were propelled not only by the pressing material wants of the community but by the unrelenting forces of racism expressed by the wider society of all classes. As Nancy Stepan points out, 'A fundamental question about the history of racism in the first half of the nineteenth century is why it was that, just as the battle against slavery was being won by abolitionists, the war against racism was being lost. The Negro was legally freed by the Emancipation of 1833, but in the British mind he was still mentally, morally and physically a slave.'[196] In examining the Black women's club movement in the United States Stephanie Shaw points out that while 'racism was a very important catalyst for the club women's activism,'[197] it is important to bear in mind the internal organizing of these communities. The same has been true for Canada. While not a women's organization, the True Band Society formed in Amherstburg in 1854 is a case in point. Black women and men formed this society, and in two years it had grown to thirteen branches throughout southwestern Ontario, with approximately 1000 members who paid small monthly dues. The society worked to foster economic cooperation among Black people and to provide space for conflict resolution among the population. It also developed strategies for improving schools for Black children. In the 1850s, Chatham's branch of the society had 375 members. It is not clear whether any of its members were from the Elgin Settlement at Buxton. Clearly, the True Band Society 'represented a step in the internal historical process of encouraging and supporting self-determination, self-improvement and community development.'[198]

During the 1850s the Black population was constantly reminded of the fragility of their presence on Canadian soil. In 1855, the *Colonist* reported that 'large numbers of slaves continue to escape into Canada daily from the U.S. One of the

Detroit papers tells us that on the 15th instant no less than 18 of them crossed the river into Canada. We fear they are coming rather too fast for the good of the Province. People may talk about the horrors of slavery as much as they choose; but fugitive slaves are by no means a desirable class of immigrants for Canada, especially when they come in great numbers.'[199] Indeed, white property-holders in Chatham petitioned to stop the immigration of Black people.[200] In 1854 in Raleigh Township, the Tory candidate for member of parliament, Edwin Larwill, defeated the incumbent, Archibald McKellar, on the basis of an anti-Black campaign.[201]

Edmund Head, Canada's governor-general from 1856–65, was himself uncomfortable with any perceived significant increase in the Black population. In official correspondence Head stated his position: 'At any rate as a whole, though they are orderly and well conducted, I do not consider that the accumulation of a colored population in certain portions of this "Peninsula" of Upper Canada is likely to promote its progress: whilst their labour would be most valuable in other British colonies. Any diminution of their numbers here which would cause them to be replaced by other settlers would be most beneficial to Canada.'[202] Decades earlier, Governor-General Charles Metcalfe was of the opinion that, 'solely with a view to the Interests of Canada,' Black people should be encouraged to leave for the West Indies. British Colonial Secretary and abolitionist Lord Grey was also troubled by the growth of the Black population in Canada. By mid-century he was questioning whether 'It is possible to do anything to turn the current to the West Indies.' It was Edmund Head, however, who suggested that providing free passage and land in the Carribean might be an incentive. Head was adamant that 'the land however must be no more than a mere garden or they would rely on it for subsistence instead of depending on their work for wages, and would sink into the normal conditions of the emancipated slaves already there. Under any circumstances perhaps this result would be to be feared.'

In January 1853, women in Chatham formed the Victoria

Reform Benevolent Society for Social Relief. There were thirteen directors including a clergyman. In 1854, H. Cordelia Handsbrow was president, Mrs Bailey was vice-president, Mrs Charlotte Hunter was treasurer, and Mrs Mary Hutton was marshall. These women's lives were similar and different in many ways. Charlotte Hunter was by then forty-eight years old and a widow, with apparently no children in her household; none were listed as absent. In the 1861 census Hunter's occupation is noted as a housekeeper. Considerably younger, Mary Hunton was twenty-two-years old with three young children. By 1861 she had three more children and her occupation was listed also as a housekeeper. Her fifty-year-old husband, Stanton, was listed as a gentleman. This society was opened to all women between the ages of sixteen and forty-five years old who were not 'addicted to intoxication or have a plurality of living husbands.' Like most societies of that period, great emphasis was placed on morality. Although designed to help members who were sick, article 2 of the by-laws stated that 'no member of this society shall be entitled to any relief on account of any disease that she imprudently brought upon herself.'[203] The issue of morality played a significant part in keeping members of the society in strict control. Women were clearly expected to monitor and report any improprieties observed among themselves. Article III, section 2, read in part: 'In case of complaint being made of any member, she shall appoint a committee of five persons to try the accused person. If found guilty for the first offence she shall be removed by the personnel, for the second offence she shall be fined 15 shillings and for the third offence she shall be expelled from the Society.'[204]

The rules and regulations of this particular society provide some insight into the Chatham community. Article 3 reads: 'a member is entitled to benefits as follows: if sickness should prevent her from following her profession, trade or usual employment, and she shall have been sick one week, she shall receive five shillings per week, for the space of three months; after the expiration of three months, shall receive two shillings and six pence per week, for a further three months; and if sickness should still continue, the Society may grant her such a sum weekly as they may think proper, the state of the funds being considered.'[205] Membership dues were seven-and-a-half pence per month, including an initiation fee decided upon at the time of joining. Women in the society also formed a sewing circle.

A Literary Ladies Society, formed in Chatham by Amelia Freeman Shadd, was similar to one organized in Windsor and presided over by Mary Bibb, with members meeting to 'hear speeches and improve their minds.' But despite their titles, these organizations did more than pursue cultural activities. The Windsor Ladies Club, form in 1854 by Mary Bibb, probably heard more than speeches. As shown by Cooper and others, Mary Bibb started a school for Black children in her house, and no doubt members of the Ladies Club organized around the education of Black children. The Ladies Literary Society organized by Amelia Freeman Shadd was involved in a variety of activities ranging from giving financial aid to the *Provincial Freeman* to helping needy women and men.

In its 6 October 1855 issue, the *Provincial Freeman* appealed to its female readers for support. It declared: 'Let our sisters throughout the country go to work on behalf of the defender of their rights ... *The Provincial Freeman.*' This public appeal is full of meaning for the history of Black women and their communities in Canada, and gives a qualitative clue about their lives. It came a year after a meeting was held by the newspaper's editorial board, whose members included its founder and travelling agent, Mary Ann Shadd Cary. The meeting was held to organize the Provincial Union, the goals of which were to promote the social, political, and intellectual interests of Black people not only in Canada but throughout the Americas. These goals were to lead primarily to the assurance of the newspaper's survival as the mouthpiece of the Black communities in Canada. At the formation meeting of the Provincial Union, a women's committee was organized to support and promote 'the people's organ: The *Provincial Freeman.*'

The formation of the Provincial Union as an instrument of the *Provincial Freeman* is hardly surprising. Members of the community were well aware of the significance of the newspaper. Signing her open letter as N.D. Hopewell, a writer introduced herself by asking the editor, 'Will you permit a woman to address a few lines through your very valuable paper to her many friends in the United States?' This letter clearly demonstrates the importance of this medium in providing a means of communication. What is most significant about the letter, however, is the glimpse it provides into the life of this women. Its tone also suggests that the writer felt very strongly about emigrating to Canada and that her views on this topic were very similar to those of Mary Ann Shadd Cary. In fact, Shadd Cary informed her readers that Hopewell was a model citizen. Hopewell informs her readers that she has two reasons for publicly writing to her friends. First, 'I have not time to write to them personally' and, second, 'were I to do so, many of them would not get the letters, for the slaveholders would intecept [sic] them, when they see the Post Mark, CANADA.' We learn that Hopewell is a forty-year-old married woman with two children. She informs her friends as follows:

My dear relations and friends, in keeping with my promise to many of you, when husband and I made up our minds to leave the country of whips and tears – the country of Fugitive Slave Bill and blood hounds, for this the Canaan of the Colored people, I now take my pen to write to you – I say my pen, because I own something, and have learned to write since I left my native state. Here, I own myself, at least, and the pen is mine, and not 'old Mistress's' ... You are aware of the fact, that when we left the States, we had to borrow money to get us to Canada, but God has blest us, and we were able to get here safely, and though very poor, we went right to work, ... I have not space or time to tell you of the turkeys and geese and ducks and guineas. We have raised this season a fine crop of wheat and corn – the hay was first rate, and as for potatoes, I would not count them.
... Our two little children are the sweetest little creatures in the

world! ... God knows I would much sooner follow them to the grave, than the auction-stand! I often think of many of you, who are mothers, in the Slave States, in such connection ...

I may write again to you, should the Editor of the *Provincial Freeman* send you this, through his widely circulated paper. I say his, but it is not really his, but ours. This paper is owned, edited and published entirely by the Colored people of Canada ... The paper talks right out to the white folks, and lets them know we are men and women, and that we are coming right ahead for our rights.

Conclusion

Black women in Buxton and Chatham (like Black men) came to Canada because they believed that British North America was a safe place to escape from slavery. They were firm in this conviction and showed their support by clinging to British institutions. Like the overwhelming majority of settlers, but for fundamentally different reasons, they were concerned about the possibility of republican ideas taking hold in British North America. Unlike other settlers, their allegiance to British institutions was fuelled by the legal protection they achieved and in most cases had to struggle for. As one historian would point out, the universal condemnation of the U.S. 1850 Fugitive Slave Law did not mean that provincial residents were single-mindedly in favour of an antislavery society.[206] And not unlike the conclusions reached by Lieutenant-Governor Edmund Head, one writer in the Toronto *British Colonist* informed readers that Southerners feared emancipation, 'because the Jamaican experience had shown that liberated slaves would work for only three or four days a week, ruining the island's economy.' The writer advised that Canadians should not meddle in the affairs of their neighbours except to provide refugee for those who escape. This was the general feeling among white settlers. Two decades earlier, in response to the formation of the Antislavery Society of Canada, the *Patriot*, a newspaper published by the Tory establishment, had declared that 'it was improper for Canadians to combine against slavery or to desecrate their pulpits with the subject.' Indeed, the paper went on, 'the notion that British North America should entice slaves to leave their masters was vicious and immoral and was rooted in the barest fanaticism.'[207] In commenting on antislavery societies in Canada, Winks observed that such societies were formed 'without any necessary financial or political commitment.'[208] Winks no doubt was referring to antislavery societies in the wider society. Such societies, formed by Black women and men, while lacking financial resources, did not flounder for lack of political commitment. The general comment was always that slavery did not exist in Canada, and it was therefore not good to meddle in the affairs of the United States.

I offer only glimpses into the lives of Black women who lived in Buxton and Chatham. While the lack of much written evidence has made it difficult to provide detailed accounts of most women's lives, these women were active in all aspects of their community. They taught school, ran businesses, raised children, worked as farmers, domestic servants, midwives, and healers, and were political activists.

The two communities differed in that Buxton was an all-Black settlement supported by the Presbyterian church and the government. Promoted as an experiment by King, it ultimately promised to produce a moral citizenry: a 'City of God' as Victor Ullman declared.[209] King himself had written a letter to the children of the Sabbath School to Knox Church in Toronto informing them that it was 'a sad and solemn thought that one hundred million of our fellow creatures are now living in Africa without hearing of Christ and dying without knowing anything of salvation. We are endeavouring at the Buxton Mission to prepare the preachers to go to proclaim it.'[210] Clearly white promoters of the Elgin Settlement saw their experiment as part of a larger mission to Christianize Black people. In his autobiography, King offers the example of young rough white male characters who intruded into the Buxton settlers' log cabins while they were absent to check on their humanity. Who knows what Catherine Riley and her two young children may have felt when they discovered such intruders looking into their window one Sunday morning. Catherine did not attend church services. She may have stayed at home because of an ill child. Since it was in the winter, the weather may have been too severe to go out. Whatever the reasons may have been, the door to their cabin was closed and barred and Catherine was reading the Bible to her children. According to King, 'The young men who had been looking in at the window left the log cabin with their views concerning the moral character of the Elgin Settlement in Raleigh changed.' It was this incident, said King, that raised the moral character of the settlers in the estimation of the whites.[211] This is the most telling statement, for it clearly demonstrates the extent to which white abolitionists held on to beliefs of white supremacy.

Little evidence exists about the international links between Black women in Buxton and Chatham and women in the United States and Britain engaged in antislavery work. Frances Ellen Harper, a Black U.S. abolitionist, visited Toronto, and Mary Ann Shadd Cary met with Harper during one of the former's lecture tours in the United States.[212] Yet little is known about networking activities between the two women.

Through a multiplicity of voices we witness Black women in Buxton and Chatham working for 'self-improvement and racial advancement on a variety of settings.'[213] Antislavery work and the struggle against virulent racism in Canada made their tasks particularly burdensome. Yet, the vibrancy of their communities speaks to us through Mary Jane Robinson, who says, commenting on her farming experiences in Buxton: 'We are to have a log-rolling soon, and then we will have ten acres cleared. They [the people] all will help you to raise and log, and you help them again. Whatever you raise in the ground, you can sell it in Chatham.'[214]

NOTES

This paper is part of a larger work in progress.

1 *The Provincial Freeman*, 30 June 1855, p. 2.
2 Alice Lemmon Keeler wrote for, and then ran, her husband's paper in Brantford in the 1830s; see Lorraine McMullen, ed., *Re(Dis)Covering Our Foremothers: Nineteenth Century Canadian Women Writers* (Ottawa: University of Ottawa Press 1990), 79. However, Mary Ann Shadd is the first woman in Canada to establish and edit a newspaper; see C. Peter Ripley, ed., *The Black Abolitionist Papers*, vol. 2, *Canada, 1830–1865* (Chapel Hill: University of North Carolina Press 1986), 192n. See also Jim Bearden and Linda Jean Butler, *The Life and Times of Mary Shadd Cary* (Toronto: NC Press 1977), 184; Adrienne L. Shadd, 'Black Women's History: Breaking Down the Stereotypes,' speech reprinted in *65th Annual North Buxton Homecoming & Labour Day Celebration, Featuring Women of Buxton*, September 1989, p. 19; Jason H. Silverman, 'Mary Ann Shadd and the Search for Equality,' in Leon Litwack and August Maier, eds, *Black Leaders of the 19th Century* (Urbana: University of Illinois Press 1988), 87; Dorothy Sterling, ed., *We Are Your Sisters: Black Women In the Nineteenth Century* (New York: W.W. Norton 1984), 169.
3 Mary A. Shadd, *A Plea for Emigration to Canada West* (Detroit: George W. Pattison 1852). Shadd strongly believed that emigrating to British North America or Canada West was the solution.
4 Marilyn Richardson, ed., *Maria W. Stewart, America's First Black Woman Political Writer: Essays and Speeches* (Bloomington: Indiana University Press 1987). See also Paula Giddings, *When and Where I Enter: The Impact of Black Women on Race and Sex in Amercia* (New York: William Morrow 1984), 50–1.
5 Jean McMahon Humez, ed., *Gifts of Power: The Writings of Rebecca Jackson, Black Visionary, Shaker Eldress* (University of Massachusetts Press 1981).
6 Angela Davis, *Women, Race and Class* (New York: Random House 1981), 60, 61; Giddings, *When and Where*, 54.
7 Davis, *Women, Race and Class*, 23; Adrienne Shadd, 'Women and the Underground Railroad Movement,' this

collection; Daniel G. Hill, *The Freedom-Seekers: Blacks in Early Canada* (Agincourt: Book Society of Canada 1981), 35; Robin W. Winks, *The Blacks in Canada: A History* (Montreal: McGill-Queen's University Press 1971), 238.

8 Mary Ann Shadd lived in Canada from 1851 to 1862, when she returned to the United States to work as a recruiting officer during the Civil War. She later entered Howard University, where she studied law, and settled in Washington, DC. Harriet Tubman lived in St Catharines, Ontario.

9 Lucille Mathurin, 'Nanny: Rebel, Queen Mother,' in *Women in the Rebel Tradition: The English-Speaking Caribbean* (New York: Women's International Resource Exchange 1987), 5.

10 'Township of Chatham: A History 1850–1953,' on microfilm, Provincial Archives of Ontario (Toronto); Victor Lauriston, *Romantic Kent: The Story of a County 1626–1952* (Chatham: Chamberlain Press 1952), 128.

11 For a discussion on the usefulness and limitations of relying on census data see June Purvis, *Hard Lessons: The Lives and Education of Working-Class Women in Nineteenth-Century England* (Minneapolis: University of Minnesota Press 1989), 13; Margo Anderson, 'The History of Women and the History of Statistics,' *Journal of Women's History* 4, no. 1 (Spring 1992), 14–32.

12 Winks, *Blacks in Canada*, 2.

13 See Linda Carty, 'African Canadian Women and the State,' this collection.

14 Winks, *Blacks in Canada*, 26.

15 Ibid., 26.

16 Ibid., 25.

17 Ibid., 26.

18 S.G. Howe, *Report to the Freedman's Inquiry Commission 1863: The Refugee from Slavery in Canada West* (New York: Arno Press and the New York Times 1969). Whipping posts existed and slaves escaped from Fort Malden (Amherstburg, Ontario) to Ohio (a free state). See also Winks, who claims that Elliot fixed the lashing ring to a tree in front of his

house for apparently psychological effect (*Blacks in Canada*, 51). In an article found in the Hill papers at the national Archives in Ottawa was the following: 'On Matthew Elliot's farm near Amherstburg, however, where there were 50 slaves, a ring was driven into a black locust tree in front of the house. To this ring, now covered over by the tree's natural growth, slaves were tied to be flogged. From 1805, when slavery was abolished in the Michigan Territory, many of Elliot's slaves escaped over the Detroit River to the United States. Other slaves too found freedom across the border. In 1798, Henry Lewis, a slave belonging to William Jarvis at Niagara-on-the-Lake, escaped to Schenectady.'

19 Winks, *Blacks in Canada*, 97.
20 An Official Record of Slavery in Upper Canada by The Honourable William Renwick Riddel, L.L.D., F.R.H.S., Etc.,' in *Ontario History Society Papers* 25 (1929), 395.
21 Letter of Lieutenant Governor Simcoe to Henry Dundas, 16 September 1793, Public Archives of Ontario.
22 Winks, *Blacks in Canada*, 50–1.
23 Reported in 'Slave Days in Canada' by Mrs W.T. Hallman, speech given at the Women's Canadian Historical Society, Toronto, April 1919, 1–14. Mrs Hallman's analysis reveals much about the racist character of the society.
24 Ibid., 4. See also Deed of Sale of Mary, age 25, from Henry Finkle, Ernestown, to Joseph Allan, Marysburgh, for 25 pounds, 7 June 1798. Public Archives of Ontario.
25 'Slave Days in Canada,' 5. See also Hill, *Freedom-Seekers*, 16, and Winks, *Blacks in Canada*, 50.
26 Esmeralda Thornhill, 'Focus on Black Women,' in *Canadian Journal of Women and the Law* 1, no. 1 (1985), 159; Adrienne Shadd, '300 Years of Black Women in Canadian History: circa 1700–1980,' in *Tiger Lily* 1, no. 2 (1987), 4.
27 Hill, *Freedom-Seekers*, 91; Frederick Ivor Case, *Racism and National Consciousness* (Toronto: Plowshare Press 1977), 10; Marcel Trudel, *L'esclavage au Canada Français* (Quebec: Les Presses Universitaires Laval 1960), 226–9.
28 For a discussion on resistance see Angela Davis, *Women,*

Race and Class, and Deborah Gray White, *Ar'n't I a Woman? Female Slaves in the Plantation South* (New York: W.W. Norton 1985), among others.

29 Winks, *Blacks in Canada*, 49–50.

30 Hallman, 'Slave Days in Canada,' 5.

31 Ibid., 5. See also Winks, *Blacks in Canada*, 50. In 1806 Peggy was advertised for sale.

32 Although the proclamation was made in 1833 it was not until 1834 that slavery was abolished in the British Empire. Even so, not all slaves were free throughout British North America in 1834. Black people who settled in Canada included, among others, enslaved people, fugitive slaves from the United States, and Black loyalists.

33 Ripley, ed., *Black Abolitionist Papers*, 4. See also Hill (25) and Winks (142) also *Provincial Freeman*, 6 Oct. 1855, p. 95.

34 *Provincial Freeman*, 25 March 1854.

35 Annual Report of the Elgin Association.

36 Ripley, ed., *Black Abolitionist Papers*, 11.

37 Ibid., 280.

38 Susan E. Houston, 'Social Reform and Education: The Issue of Compulsory Schooling, Toronto 1851–71,' in Neil McDonald and Alf Chaiton, eds, *Egerton Ryerson and His Times: Essays on the History of Education* (Toronto: Macmillan of Canada 1978), 256.

39 Jonathan William Walton, 'Blacks in Buxton and Chatham, Ontario, 1830–1890: Did the 49th Parallel Make a Difference?' Ph.D. thesis, Princeton University, 1979, 40.

40 Both the *Voice of the Fugitive*, started by Henry and Mary Bibb in 1851, and the *Provincial Freeman*, two nineteenth-century newspapers in Canada West, stressed the importance of self-reliance. Howard Law, ' "Self-Reliance Is the True Road to Independence": Ideology and the Ex-Slaves in Buxton and Chatham,' *Ontario History* 77, no. 2 (June 1985), 111.

41 William King, 'Autobiography' (Public Archives of Canada, ca. 1890), 21.

42 Ibid., 48.

43 *Detroit Tribune*, 16 Sept. 1892. This paper ran a series of articles under the headings: 'Personal reminiscences of Rev. William King, an Anti-Slavery Hero,' claiming that he was invested with 'supreme control and authority as residential manager' of the Elgin settlement. When King died, the *Chatham Evening Banner* of 7 January 1895 proclaimed, 'A Mighty Man Has Fallen.' See also the *Paisley Herald*, 26 May 1860.

44 Allen Stouffer, *The Light of Nature and the Law of God: Antislavery in Ontario 1833–1877* (Montreal: McGill-Queen's University Press 1992), 33–6.

45 King, 'Autobiography,' 66. Also quoted in Law, 'Self-Reliance,' 114.

46 Davis, *Women, Race and Class*, 22.

47 Winks, *Blacks in Canada*, 212.

48 Robbins, *Legacy to Buxton*, 35.

49 *Detroit Tribune*, 5 June 1892.

50 *Globe* (Toronto), 25 April 1849; Winks, *Blacks in Canada*, 212.

51 *Examiner* (Toronto), 29 Aug. 1849.

52 *London Free Press*, 12 Aug. 1964.

53 *Detroit Tribune*, 15 May 1892.

54 Ibid.

55 *Detroit Tribune*, 15 May 1892.

56 Ged Martin, 'British Officials and the Attitudes to the Negro Community in Canada, 1833–1861,' *Ontario History* 66, no. 2 (June 1974).

57 Walton, 'Blacks in Buxton,' 47. Black people were concerned about the question of Black settlement in the province. Prior to the establishment of the Elgin Settlement, a number of Black settlements were established by Black people themselves: Wilberforce, Dawn, the Refugee Home Society.

58 See Winks, *Blacks in Canada*, chap. 12, on segregation and schools; also see Hill, *Freedom-Seekers.*, chap. 9.

59 Ripley, ed., *Black Abolitionist Papers*, 19. Beckford Jones and Wilson Abbott were founding members of the Anti Slavery Society; Hill, *Freedom-Seekers*, 77.

60 Walton, 'Blacks in Buxton,' 99.

61 See Walton, 'Blacks in Buxton,' 92.
62 See both the *Provincial Freedom* and the *Voice of the Fugitive*.
63 *Voice of the Fugitive*; see also the *Anti-Slavery Reporter*, London, 1 Feb. 1860, pp. 36–7.
64 Marjorie Griffin Cohen, *Women's Work, Markets and Economic Development in Nineteenth-Century Ontario* (Toronto: University of Toronto Press 1988), 60; Walton, 'Blacks in Buxton,' 92.
65 *Voice of the Fugitive*, February 1852; Walton, 'Blacks in Buxton,' 91–2.
66 Ripley, ed., *Black Abolitionist Papers*, 355.
67 *Voice of the Fugitive*, 5 Nov. 1851.
68 See Joyce Middleton, 'The Women of the Elgin Settlement and Buxton,' in *65th Annual North Buxton Homecoming & Labour Day Celebration* (1989).
69 Gwendolyn Robinson and John W. Robinson, *Seek the Truth: A Story of Chatham's Black Community* (Printed in Canada, 1989), 35.
70 Robbins, *Legacy to Buxton*, 56–7. See also Middleton, 'Women of the Elgin Settlement,' 22–8.
71 Robbins, *Legacy to Buxton*, 58.
72 Middleton, 'Women of the Elgin Settlement,' 22; see also Adrienne Shadd, this collection.
73 Robbins, *Legacy to Buxton*, 80.
74 Ripley, ed., *Black Abolitionist Papers*, 358n; Walton, 'Blacks in Buxton,' 105.
75 Ibid., 279.
76 *Voice of the Fugitive*, 21 May 1851.
77 Ibid., 16 July 1851.
78 Ibid., 2 July 1851.
79 Robbins, *Legacy to Buxton*.
80 Census data, Raleigh Township, 1861.
81 Ibid.
82 John Howison, *Sketches of Upper Canada* (Toronto: Coles Publishing 1970), 249–50.
83 Hill, *Freedom-Seekers*, 80.

84 White, *Ar'n't I A Woman?* 120.
85 Cohen, *Women's Work*, 59.
86 *Voice of the Fugitive*, 21 May 1851.
87 In 1860 women in Windsor participated in the building of the First Baptist Church. They carried water and sand.
88 Joanne M. Braxton, 'Ancestral Presence: The Outraged Mother Figure in Contemporary Afra-American Writing,' in Joanne M. Braxton and Andree Nicola McLaughlin, eds, *Wild Women in the Whirlwind: Afra-American Culture and the Contemporary Literary Renaissance* (New Brunswick, NJ.: Rutgers University Press 1990), 300.
89 Under English common law, women did not have property rights.
90 Benjamin Drew, *The Narratives of Fugitive Slaves in Canada* (Boston: Jewett & Co. 1856), 120.
91 Ripley, ed., *Black Abolitionist Papers*, 280.
92 Hill, *Freedom-Seekers*, 200.
93 Ibid., 212.
94 Ripley, ed., *Black Abolitionist Papers*, 280.
95 Ibid.
96 Ibid.
97 Census data, Raleigh Township, 1861.
98 Hill, *Freedom-Seekers*, 80.
99 Joanne M. Braxton, 'Black Grandmothers: Sources of Artistic Consciousness and Personal Strength,' Working Paper no. 172, Wellesley College (Wellesley, Mass., 1987), 10.
100 Ibid., 300.
101 Hill, *Freedom-Seekers*, 84; Walton, 'Blacks in Buxton,' 96. Stouffer, *The Light of Nature*, 99, tells of a girl at the Elgin School apparently reciting Latin: this calls for further research.
102 *Voice of the Fugitive*, 16 July 1851, p. 3; Walton, 'Blacks in Buxton,' 91.
103 *Elgin Association Report*, 1857.
104 Walton, 'Blacks in Buxton,' 101.
105 Ibid., 100; Ripley, ed., *Black Abolitionist Papers*, 355.
106 Ripley, 279–81.

107 Hill, *Freedom-Seekers*, 80.
108 Dorothy Shadd Shreve, *The AfriCanadian Church: A Stabilizer* (Ontario: Plaideia Press 1983), 42.
109 Evelyn Brooks Higginbotham, *Righteous Discontent: The Women's Movement in the Black Baptist Church, 1880–1920* (Cambridge: Harvard University Press 1993), 16.
110 In her essay 'Nineteenth-Century Black Women's Spiritual Autobiographies, Religious Faith and Self-Empowerment,' Nellie Y. McKay shows how faith in the 'divine' gave expanded meaning to Black women's lived experiences (in *Interpreting Women's Lives: Feminist Theory and Personal Narratives*, ed. Personal Narratives Group [Bloomington: Indiana University Press 1989], 139–52). Joanne Braxton points out that for the former female slave 'her relationship with God is direct and self-authorizing ... she knows that God is on the side of the oppressed' (*Black Women Writing Autobiography: A Tradition Within a Tradition* [Philadelphia: Temple University Press 1989], 16). See also 'Celie,' who writes letters to God in Alice Walker's *The Color Purple.*
111 *Righteous Discontent*, 16.
112 Robbins, *Legacy to Buxton*, 100.
113 Ibid., 100.
114 'The Autobiography of William King,' quoted in Walton, 'Blacks in Buxton,' 36.
115 *Paisley Herald*, 26 May 1860, p. 1.
116 *Globe*, quoted in *Provincial Freeman*, 6 Oct. 1855.
117 *Provincial Freeman*, 6 Oct. 1855.
118 Hill, *Freedom-Seekers*, 86.
119 Lauriston, *Romantic Kent*, 25.
120 Walton, 'Blacks in Buxton,' 4–5.
121 Ibid., 7.
122 Ibid., 62
123 Lauriston, *Romantic Kent*, 26.
124 Ibid.
125 Winks, *Blacks in Canada*, 225.
126 Lauriston, *Romantic Kent*, 26.

127 Ibid.
128 Robinson and Robinson, *Seek the Truth*, 19.
129 Walton, 'Blacks in Buxton,' 20.
130 Winks, Hill (53), Walton.
131 Census data, Town of Chatham, 1851.
132 Ibid.
133 Walton (125), Hill (54).
134 Census data.
135 *Voice of the Fugitive*, 1851, p. 4.
136 See table 5, p. 100.
137 Robinson and Robinson, *Seek the Truth*, 24. This escape
     clearly appears to have been unusual, for as Adrienne Shadd
     points out in her article that women with children tended to
     be more constrained than men in making their escape.
138 Census data, Town of Chatham, 1851.
139 Walton, 'Blacks in Buxton,' 63.
140 Purvis, *Hard Lessons*, 26, 60. She points out that both single
     and married women often worked at a number of casual and
     seasonal jobs that were not recorded.
141 Bearden and Butler, *The Life and Times of Mary Shadd
     Cary*, 191.
142 *Voice of the Fugitive*.
143 Robinson and Robinson, *Seek the Truth*, 23; Hill, *Freedom-
     Seekers*, 209.
144 Robinson and Robinson, *Seek the Truth*, 100.
145 Winks, *Blacks in Canada*, 218.
146 Census data, Town of Chatham, 1851.
147 Ibid.
148 Ibid.
149 Ibid.
150 Robinson and Robinson, *Seek the Truth*, 32.
151 Hill, *Freedom-Seekers*, 143.
152 Robinson and Robinson, *Seek the Truth*, 19.
153 Ripley, ed., *Black Abolitionist Papers*, 398n.
154 Dionne Brand, *No Burden to Carry: Narratives of Black
     Working Women in Ontario, 1920s to 1950s* (Toronto:
     Women's Press 1991), 129.

155 Presentation given by Raymond Dobard at the African-American Quilters Forum on 16 January 1993, reported in Museum of the American Quilter's Society newsletter, April 1993.

156 Lucy Eldersveld Murphy, 'Business Ladies: Midwestern Women and Enterprise, 1850–1880,' *Journal of Women's History* 3, no. 1 (Spring 1991), 67–8. See also Wendy Gamber, 'A Precarious Independence: Milliners and Dressmakers in Boston, 1860–1890,' *Journal of Women's History* 4, no. 1 (Spring 1992). Although both of these articles are written about the United States, their conclusions can be applied in many instances to the Chatham scene.

157 Sterling, ed., *We Are Your Sisters*, 173.

158 Ibid., 173–4.

159 Silverman, 'Mary Ann Shadd,' 92–3.

160 *Provincial Freeman*, 6 Oct. 1855.

161 Ripley, ed., *Black Abolitionist Papers*, 11.

162 Stouffer, *The Light of Nature*, 119–20; Walton, 'Blacks in Buxton,' 81.

163 Winks, *Blacks in Canada*, 266. Winks claims that Shadd was mistaken. He does not adequately show how he arrived at his conclusions. See also Stouffer, *The Light of Nature*, 127; *Provincial Freeman*, 3 June 1854 (reprinted in Ripley, ed., *Black Abolitionist Papers*, 289.

164 Ripley, ed., *Black Abolitionist Papers*, 33.

165 Sterling, ed., *We Are Your Sisters*, 172; Bearden and Butler, *The Life and Times of Mary Shadd Cary*, 164.

166 Ibid., 125.

167 Sterling, ed., *We Are Your Sisters*, 170.

168 Ibid., 174.

169 Ibid., 227.

170 Robinson and Robinson, *Seek the Truth*, 14.

171 Ibid., 21.

172 *Western Planet*, Chatham, reprinted in the *Provincial Freeman*, 6 Oct. 1855.

173 *Provincial Freeman*, 26 July 1856.

174 Robinson and Robinson, *Seek the Truth*, 100.

175 Census data, Town of Chatham, 1861.
176 Ibid.
177 Stouffer, *The Light of Nature*, 61–3.
178 Winks, *Blacks in Canada*, 369.
179 Stouffer, *The Light of Nature*, 54–6.
180 Jason H. Silverman and Donna J. Gillie, ' "The Pursuit of Knowledge under Difficulties": Education and the Fugitive Slave in Canada,' *Ontario History* 74 (1982), 95. See also documents in Alison L. Prentice and Susan E. Houston, eds, *Family, School and Society in Nineteenth-Century Canada* (Toronto: Oxford University Press 1975), 231–40.
181 The Princess Street School was the first public school in the city of Chatham for Black children. Records indicated that Juliana and Israel Williams were involved in the formation of this school. Their six children were denied entrace to the common schools in Chatham. This school operated at the same time as the Canada Mission and the Free Baptist Mission, which had opened for the Black children in Chatham with a Miss Huntingdon as teacher. See Hill, *Freedom-Seekers*, 151; *Voice of the Fugitive*, 9 Apr. 1851; and Robinson and Robinson, *Seek the Truth*, 88.

    In 1854 Aaron Highgate was appointed teacher of the Princess Street School, where he taught until 1856. Alfred Whipper replaced him from 1856 until 1860, when he was replaced by a white teacher, Peter Nicol. Black parents protested and argued that their children needed a Black leader, but the board replied that Nicol, who held a Class A Certificate, was the best-qualified applicant (Hill, *Freedom-Seekers*, 154).
182 *Provincial Freeman*, 6 Oct. 1855.
183 *Voice of the Fugitive*.
184 Ibid.
185 Hill, *Freedom-Seekers*, 209.
186 Ripley, ed., *Black Abolitionist Papers*, 489n.
187 Ibid., 490n.
188 Ibid.
189 Ibid., 166n.

190 Ripley, ed., *Black Abolitionist Papers*, 392.
191 Sterling, *We Are Your Sisters*, 231–2.
192 Higginbotham, *Righteous Discontent*, 16.
193 Ripley, ed., *Black Abolitionist Papers*, 388.
194 Hill, *Freedom-Seekers*, 136.
195 Ibid., 137.
196 Nancy Stepan, quoted in Vron Ware, *Beyond the Pale: White Women, Racism and History* (London: Verso 1992), 108.
197 Stephanie J. Shaw, 'Black Club Women and the Creation of the National Association of Colored Women,' *Journal of Women's History* 3, no. 2 (fall 1991), 10–20.
198 Ibid.
199 *Colonist*, quoted in Walton, 'Blacks in Buxton,' 45.
200 Walton, 'Blacks in Buxton,' 23.
201 Robinson and Robinson, *Seek the Truth*, 23; see also Victor Ullman, *Look to the North Star: A Life of William King* (Boston: Beacon Press 1971), 244. As mentioned earlier in this article, Black property-holders who voted in 1856 successfully contributed to McKellar regaining his seat.
202 Head to Lytton, Official Correspondence, CO 42, Public Record Office, Great Britain.
203 *Provincial Freeman*, 28 Oct. 1854.
204 Ibid.
205 Ibid.
206 Stouffer, *The Light of Nature*, 45.
207 Ibid.
208 Winks, *Blacks in Canada*, 270.
209 Ullman, *Look to the North Star*, 152.
210 Quoted in ibid., 144.
211 Autobiography of Reverend William King,' Public Archives of Canada, Ottawa, 6 Jan. 1892, p. 85.
212 Winks, *Blacks in Canada*, 257; Bearden and Butler, *The Life and Times of Mary Shadd Cary*, 27.
213 Ripley, ed., *Black Abolitionist Papers*, 52.
214 Ibid., 280.

APPENDICES

APPENDIX 1
Recorded occupations for employed females in Chatham for 1861

Category	Number
Seamstress	39
Servant	28
Washerwoman	17
Labourer	14
Cook	7
Nurse/Nurse girl	3
Midwife	2
Teacher	2
Milliner	3
Stewardess	2
Grocer	2
Editress	1
Weaver	1
Shoe-binder	1
Tavern-keeper	1
Innkeeper	1
Farmer	1
Missionary	1
Housewife	175
No occupation listed	361 (276 of which are young females)

SOURCE: Census of Canada, Town of Chatham, 1861

APPENDIX 2
Marital status compared with age for Chatham's Black population, 1861

Age	Number	% of all females	% of group	Number	% of all males	% of group
Single						
1 mo.–						
16 yrs.	284	43	77	245	41	66
17–20	54	8	15	41	7	11
21–29	25	4	7	54	9	15
30–39	5	1	1	19	3	5
40–49	1	0	0	6	1	2
50–59	1	0	0	2	0	1
60–69	–	–	–	3	0	1
70–79	1	0	0	–	–	–
80–100	–	–	–	–	–	–
Total	371	56	100	370	61	101
Married						
1 mo.–						
16 yrs.	–	–	–	1	0	0
17–20	12	2	5	–	–	–
21–29	63	10	28	31	5	14
30–39	73	11	33	62	10	27
40–49	46	7	21	61	10	27
50–59	19	3	8	42	7	19
60–69	11	2	5	22	4	10
70–79	–	–	–	6	1	3
80–89	–	–	–	2	0	1
Total	224	35	100	227	37	101

SOURCE: Walton, 'Blacks in Buxton and Chatham,' 293; Census of
Canada, Town of Chatham, 1861

APPENDIX 3
Marital status for Chatham's Black population, 1861

Female				Male		
Marital status	Number	% of female group	% of total population	Number	% of male group	% of total population
Single	371	56	29	370	61	29
Married	224	35	18	227	37	18
Widowed	59	9	5	7	1	1
Total	654	100	52	604	99	48

SOURCE: Walton, 'Blacks in Buxton and Chatham,' 295; Census of Canada, Town of Chatham, 1861

APPENDIX 4
Place of birth for Chatham's Black population, 1861

Place of birth	Number	% of female group	% of Black population	Number	% of male group	% of Black population
Canada	192	29	15	162	28	13
United States	457	70	36	443	73	35
Other	5	1	0	–	–	–
Total	654	100	51	605	101	48

SOURCE: Walton, 'Blacks in Buxton and Chatham,' 298; Census of Canada, Town of Chatham, 1861

APPENDIX 5
Marital status of all Blacks in Buxton, 1861

Marital status	Number	% of all females	% of total population	Number	% of all males	% of total population
Single	206	59	28	259	65	35
Married	121	36	16	127	32	17
Widowed	15	4	2	6	1	1
Total	342	99	46	392	98	53

SOURCE: Walton, 'Blacks in Buxton and Chatham,' 310; Census of Canada, Raleigh Township, 1861

APPENDIX 6
Marital status for Chatham's Black population, 1851

Marital status	Number	% of female group	% of total population	Number	% of male group	% of total population
Single	98	54	28	90	52	25
Married	75	41	21	76	42	22
Widowed	6	3	2	8	6	2
Total	179	98	51	174	100	49

SOURCE: Walton, 'Blacks in Buxton and Chatham,' 267; Census of Canada, Chatham, 1851

4

Black Women and Work in Nineteenth-Century Canada West: Black Woman Teacher Mary Bibb

AFUA P. COOPER

My decision to do a paper on Mary Bibb came out of my study of the history of women and education in nineteenth-century North America. A study of Black female teachers who taught in Canada West during this period presented itself as a useful task. After discovering several names – including Matilda Nichols, Mary Shadd, Sarah and Mary Anne Titre, and Mary Bibb – I realized that to do a study on all these women would be too great a task at the moment. Therefore, I decided to be less ambitious and study only Mary Bibb. Although she was 'well known,' not much material on her could be found in traditional sources. My quest for her set me on a course for alternative sources, where I discovered compelling and valuable information on her life and on Black education in Canada in general and Canada West in particular.[1]

In the fall of 1850, Mary Bibb, her husband Henry Bibb, and her mother-in-law Mildred Jackson migrated from Boston to Sandwich, Canada West.[2] They had been forced out of the United States by the passage of the Fugitive Slave Law.[3] The Bibbs, as soon as they arrived in Canada, initiated projects to serve the needs of the growing Black community in Sandwich and its environs. (Sandwich was the name of a township in southwestern Ontario – Canada West – that included the villages of Windsor and Sandwich within its borders.) One of these projects was a school set up by Mary Bibb for Black children in the Sandwich area. It was the beginning of a series of schools she would operate to serve the needs of Black children in the areas where she lived.[4]

Mary Bibb was born Mary Elizabeth Miles in 1820, in Rhode Island, to free Black Quaker parents. She was their only child.[5] Further research is necessary to determine exactly where in Rhode Island she was born, and not much is known about her early life or how she got an education in that period. She was probably taught by her parents, attended a Quaker school, or went to a private institution for Black children.[6]

Mary Miles completed her education at the Massachusetts State Normal School at Lexington,[7] which she entered between May and September 1842.[8] Though her residence is given in the school's register as Boston, there is no information about her parents or guardians and their occupations. By 1842, then, she had left Rhode Island and was living in Massachusetts. Who was she living with there? How was she being sponsored at the normal school? Was she already teaching in Massachusetts? These questions, unfortunately, cannot be answered at the moment.

As a resident of Massachusetts, Mary Miles was not required to pay fees. Tuition was free for all residents of the state, while 'for all others it was $10 per term.' At the beginning of each term, each pupil had to pay to the principal $1.25, to meet incidental expenses.[9] If Miles's parents were still alive when she entered normal school, they probably assisted with fees. Since she was already twenty-two years old, it is likely that Mary had already taught before entering the school and hence had some savings. Young women, both Black and white, often began teaching in their teens, and it was a common practice for those who were able to do so, those with experience but without qualifications, to seek training at some professional institution.[10]

The principal of the school, when Mary Miles entered, was the antislavery activist, Reverend Samuel J. May.[11] He was a supporter of women's rights, public education and Black education, and was active in the Underground Railroad. According to William Lloyd Garrison, abolitionist and editor of the newspaper *The Liberator*, May 'helped to educate' Mary Miles.[12] At the normal school, there were three levels of study: Junior, Middle Class, and Senior. The difficulty of study increased with each level. Moreover, all students had to take 'vocal music, drawing, and composition, during the entire year.' Moral philosophy was also taught to the entire school.[13]

Mary Miles graduated in May 1843.[14] According to the register, prior to 1844 a student needed only three terms, or one year, to graduate, and the terms need not have been taken consecutively.[15] Miles spent one year at the institution and fulfilled the requirements to become a teacher. Upon graduation, according to the register, all students were assisted in finding a school to teach: 'graduates of the school are requested to report themselves ... to the principal, and thus enable him to assist them in procuring schools.'[16]

After graduating, with or without the assistance of the principal, Mary Miles found work in a Boston primary school.[17] Two years later, in 1845, she moved to Albany, New York, where she taught at the Wilberforce School for Black children, for a yearly wage of $150.[18] By 1847, however, she had moved to Cincinnati, Ohio, to take a position at the Hiram S. Gilmore High School for Black children, which had a wide and excellent reputation.[19] Wendell P. Dabney, who has written about the Black community of Cincinnati, describes it: 'No expense was spared to make this school a success. Good teachers were employed, and besides the common branches of an English course, latin, greek, music and drawing were taught ... Pupils were prepared for college, and quite a fair proportion of them went from this school to Oberlin and such colleges as drew no color line on matriculation.'[20]

Following her graduation, Mary Miles moved from school to school and from place to place, honing her skills as a teacher. This movement was not uncommon for northern Black teachers at that time. They went where work could be found, where salaries were better, and where they felt they could have a good relationship with the community.[21] Mary Miles's move from Albany to Cincinnati could have been influenced by three factors: a rise in pay, better working conditions, and the reputation of the school. Teaching at a high school suggests that she probably had completed the advance courses at normal school. The length of time Miles spent in Ohio is not known. She left sometime between 1848 and 1849, again for Boston, her permanent home. This move was influenced by her impending marriage.

Mary Miles was not only a teacher but an abolitionist who was known in abolitionist circles in the North. It is not incidental that she operated out of Boston, the centre of abolitionism in the North and North-East. It was at an antislavery meeting in New York City that she met fellow-abolitionist, lecturer, and escaped slave Henry Bibb. Bibb himself described their meeting: 'In the month of May, 1847, I attended the anti-slavery anniversary in the city of New York, where I had the good fortune to be introduced to the favor of Miss Mary E. Miles, of Boston; a lady whom I had frequently heard very highly spoken of, for her activity and devotion to the anti-slavery cause, as well as her talents and learning, and benevolence in the cause of reform generally.'[22]

Bibb started a correspondence with her and soon the couple was engaged. Bibb again noted: 'When I offered myself for matrimony, we mutually engaged ourselves to each other, to marry in one year ... We kept up a regular correspondence during the time, and in June, 1848, we had the happiness to be joined in holy wedlock.'[23]

They were married in Dayton, Ohio.[24] Henry Bibb was pleased with what marriage brought and offered. He declared: 'My beloved wife is a bosom friend, a help-meet, a loving companion in all the social, moral and religious relations of life.'[25] Sometime after the marriage Mary moved from Ohio to Boston, to live with her husband.

Mary Miles married at age twenty-eight; for most of her adult life before marriage she had supported herself as an independent woman. This was not uncommon for free-born Black women teachers of the time.[26] According to the evidence available, Mary Miles Bibb taught for at least seven years in the United States, gaining valuable experience at both the primary and secondary levels.

In the middle decades of the nineteenth century, the tensions inherent in slavery in the United States were clearly manifesting themselves. Numerous slaves had escaped to the northern states and elsewhere. The slaveholding states were pressuring the federal government to act on their behalf. In 1850, a 'compromise' was reached and in September of that year, the dreaded Fugitive Slave Law was passed by the U.S. Congress. Its immediate result was the exodus of thousands of Blacks, both escaped slaves and free, from the United States to Canada and other places. The law granted slave-owners the right to pursue and capture their slaves who had sought refuge in the North. Free Blacks were not safe either; they too could be kidnapped and sold into slavery. The safety of every Black individual was threatened.[27]

In this atmosphere of terror and fear, thousands of Blacks left home, family, possessions, and secure jobs to flee oppression.[28] For Henry Bibb, a known fugitive, the United States was definitely an unsafe place. The Bibbs had no choice but to leave, and they chose to come to Canada.

On arriving in Sandwich, Canada West, they initially sought to 'uplift' the growing Black community in two ways.[29] Henry Bibb was responsible, with the help of his wife, for establishing a newspaper, and Mary, a school.[30] In a letter to white abolitionist and philanthropist Gerrit Smith, with whom the Bibbs had a close relationship, Mary Bibb wrote:

My dear Friend,

Will you aid us by sending as many subscribers as convenience will permit. There are hundreds of slaves coming here daily. My husband & self consider this the field at present. We are about to engage in this. I expect to take a school next week, any aid from the friend will be acceptable. Please let me know what you think of the movement.

In haste,

M.E. Bibb

Sandwich, C. West
Nov. 8th 1850[31]

The newspaper in question was the *Voice of the Fugitive*, edited and published by Mr. Bibb. The first issue appeared on 1 January 1851.[32]

The school Mary Bibb mentions in her letter to Smith began in her home in November or December 1850. It was vital to a community that was denied equal access to public schooling. The same year the Bibbs came to Canada West, the provincial legislature passed an act legalizing separate schooling. The law gave Blacks the *option* to open their own schools. The relevant section of the act reads: '... on the application, in writing, of twelve, or more, resident heads of families, to authorize the establishment of one, or more, Separate Schools for Protestants, Roman Catholics or Coloured People.'[33]

White school supporters interpreted the act to mean that Blacks could and should be denied entry to the local common schools and be required to set up their own. Acting on their interpretation, white school supporters barred many Black children from the common schools, and those Black children who did not have access to a separate school received no schooling at all.[34] Alexander Murray stated: 'Of all the manifestations of Negrophobia the attempt to deny Negroes the equal use of public schools was the most successful. In communities where problems of land sales, voting rights, or jury service never arose, a large number of white inhabitants agreed with efforts to keep Negro children from the schools.'[35]

Separate schooling for Black children in Canada West was a reality well before 1850. As early as the 1830s, white prejudice forced Blacks in several districts in the province to establish their own schools.[36] The act of 1850 gave legitimacy to what was already a common practice. An immediate reaction to the school act by whites was that more and more Black children were driven from the common schools because whites felt they could legally do so. Black parents had no alternative but to set up their own schools.[37] But not enough schools were established, and many of those that were often lacked the necessary support needed to sustain the growing Black school population.

When Mrs Bibb arrived in Sandwich, there was no schooling for Black children in the township. As shown in her letter to Smith, she took action, which was not only influenced by her desire to uplift here community, but was also a loud political statement. Recognizing the racism within the school system and society, she set out with very meagre resources to challenge them.

The *Voice*, in its first issue of 1 January 1851, announced the opening of her school. 'In Sandwich township we have great need of a school. Mrs. M.E. Bibb has commenced with 25 pupils at her residence, with the hope that some suitable place will be provided, and means for carrying out the school properly.' The school had apparently started with fewer than twenty-five scholars, but by the time the *Voice* printed the above quote the number had increased. Later the school grew even larger. As Mrs Bibb, in an article in the *Voice*, disclosed:

No doubt it will be interesting to many to hear something respecting schools in this part of the province. The day school in this place has increased from twelve to forty-six, notwithstanding the embarassing circumstances under which it was started, namely, a dark ill-ventilated room, uncomfortable seats, want of desks, books and all sorts of school apparatus. I would mention with gratitude the assistance from friends in Lenewee county, Michigan ... which enable me to procure a blackboard and the few books with which we commenced.[38]

Obviously, by this time Mrs Bibb had moved the school from her house to a larger place. Teaching for Mary Bibb involved mental stress and physical labour. She was not only the teacher of the school, but the caretaker as well. Daniel Hill notes that she had to carry the firewood used for heating the school herself.[39] She encountered these hardships not only because her school was Black; this was the nature of many schools, especially in rural areas, as the educational enterprise began to expand. However, the problems of the Black schools were compounded, as they received little or no financial support from the educational state.[40]

Mary Bibb's school was purely a self-help effort, as were the schools founded by several of her Black sisters in Canada West.[41] Placed in the broader context of the development of education in Canada West, her action was typical of the pioneering teachers, both Black and white, who started schools. Susan Houston and Alison Prentice, commenting on the drive behind many of the province's early schools, conclude: 'One way or another teachers were at the centre of the Upper Canadian quest for schooling. Theirs was an entrepreneurial spirit. Young and old, married and single, female and male, they were often the creative forces behind their schools.'[42]

Mary Bibb's school suffered from the lack of financial and material resources. She charged each pupil six cents a week, but only a 'very few of those attending the school could afford to pay.'[43] In April 1851, two months after her article in the *Voice*, she wrote to the *Anti-Slavery Bugle*, an American newspaper, informing its readers about the state of her school. The demoralizing effect of not having the means to enable the school to function smoothly was taking its toll. 'My school is not as large as it has been during the winter. Many have hired out to farmers for the season, yet it is now quite large – too large for the room we occupy. I have not yet received a dollar for my labor. I hardly know what is [my] duty in regard to continuing it. I cannot afford to give all my time. A small compensation would satisfy me, but even this has not yet been given.'[44]

By October of that year, the *Bugle* reported that Mrs Bibb 'has received no compensation for all her labors, or not more than ten dollars.'[45] This was after eleven months of teaching. In an 1853 letter to American educator Horace Mann, Mary Bibb explains the financial problems of her school. Parts of the letter also shed much light on the history of this, her first school in Canada West. By the time this letter was written she was involved in another school and was soliciting aid from Mann.

Windsor, Canada West,
January 20th 1853

Sir – The interest you have always manifested in the elevation of the colored people, has encouraged me to acquaint you with my humble effort to establish a school in Sandwich irrespective of color.

We moved to Canada about three years ago, at which time I opened a school (there being none except the French and English Catholic) for the benefit of those who had recently arrived in the province from Republican oppression. Being desirous of doing that which would result in the greater good to this people, I charged each person enjoying its benefits 6 cents per week, thinking there could be none found too poor to pay so small a sum. Experience soon proved that very few of those attending the school did pay.

We then took measures to secure the Government annuity, which amounted to $16.60 for my labor of one year and six weeks. I then felt that duty compeled [sic] me to abandon the school for it required to great a sacrifice of my domestic duties to continue without compensation. My successor was Mr. Jackson, who kept the school six weeks. It was reopened by Mr. Russell who did not collect enough from the people to sustain him although his board and rent was given.

You will perceive that in all, the school was continued near four months during the whole year and that too with two teachers. It was then I resolved on the experiment of starting an Independent School that should be free to all irrespective of *color* at *least*.

The result has more than met my most sanguine hopes; having increased from five on the 13th of Sept. 1852 to fifty-two in January 1853, being just four months.

Should you feel like doing something to promote so humble an effort, please consult,

Rev. Samuel J. May, Syracuse, N.Y.
   ''   Mr. Mumford, Detroit, Mich.
Judge Woodbridge, Sandwich, C. West.

Yours in haste

Mary E. Bibb[46]

The difficulty in teaching and managing the school forced Mrs Bibb to resign as teacher. The school did not simply 'collapse.' It was taken over by two other teachers, Misters Jackson and Russell. The *Voice* confirms the appointment of Mr Jackson and that the school had become a *'government' one* (Mrs Bibb's emphasis). In an article titled 'Colored Settlements and Schools,' the *Voice* notes: 'There is a government school in operation at Sandwich, with from twenty to thirty scholars. It is taught by Mr Jackson, a man of color.'[47] But the meagre support the school received from the government and the parents was not enough to keep it going. It had foundered by April 1852, after a life span of about one year and four months.[48] Its closure meant that Black children in the area were again without formal education.

I would argue that the school was closed for two reasons: the poverty of the pupils' parents and the reluctance of the government to finance its long-term functioning. The parents' inability to pay the fees brings into focus the financial situation of Blacks in Essex County. Many were needy recent arrivals. We must remember that many families and individuals left possessions and properties in their flight from the United States owing to the Fugitive Slave Law. Families also moved away from border towns like Sandwich and settled inland as soon as they became acquainted with the region. This movement led occasionally to the instability of some schools, as their support was sporadic.[49]

The unwillingness of the government to finance Black schools fully reveals the low priority accorded to them by the province. Black children in the Sandwich area could not attend white schools, yet the government would not fully support the only school open to them. The hardships that Mary Bibb endured to keep a school open for Black children were symptomatic of the continued dilemma faced by Black school supporters in making education available to the children of the community.

Canada had styled itself as a haven for the oppressed, those Blacks who had fled the United States because of slavery and virulent racism. But on coming to Canada, many Blacks found that the only difference between the new country and the old was that in the new country the law protected ex-fugitives from re-enslavement. Canada fell short in education, and Black children faced many obstacles in learning the three Rs.

After giving up her first effort, Mary Bibb launched a second school in September 1852. We learn of this endeavour from her letter to Mann. This new school began during the latter part of 1852, after the Bibbs moved to Windsor from Sandwich. However, by the time she wrote to Mann, the new school was thriving. She wanted the school to be open to all 'irrespective of color.' Did she receive some white scholars also?[50] She intended for both Blacks and whites to come to this school and was determined to make it work.

However, the *Black Abolitionist Papers* gives a different account of Mrs Bibb's second school. It states that Bibb's first school foundered sometime in 1852, after which she worked as a dressmaker; then, in the spring of 1853, she 'took charge of a flourishing government-sponsored black school of sixty-nine students.'[51] I believe that the independent school started by Bibb is the same as the one mentioned by the *BAP*; however, the *BAP* is mistaken in that it was a government school. For the 1853 superintendent's report for Sandwich schools, which will be discussed below, clearly states that the Black separate school that was government aided was certainly not in operation in that year.[52]

In January 1853 Bibb appealed to Horace Mann for assistance for her school,[53] in May of the same year we find her writing to George Whipple, field officer of the American Missionary Association soliciting financial aid to hire an assistant. The increase in her school's population made it imperative for her to find help.

Windsor,
May 22nd 1853

Proff. Whipple,

Sir,

The school in which I have been engaged for sometime had increased so much that I have found it necessary to employ an assistant or divide the school. I have now just returned from Oberlin and brought with me a young lady who was recommended to me by Mrs. Dascomb, Principal of the Ladies [sic] department there. Also by Professor Fairchild.

Will the association or missionary society, assist in her salary? I will board her and do all I can to make her home in Canada a pleasant one. I said to her and her friends at Oberlin, I thought it probable you would give $125.00 a year. I only judged of the salary by what was given the other teachers in the province. The Ladies [sic] name is Nichols, her sister taught last winter in St. Catharines and boarded in the family of Hiram Wilson ... Miss Nichols is a member of the Baptist church and will aid in the Sabbath school.

Yours Respectfully,

Mary E. Bibb

My pupils number 69, many of whom walk two and three miles daily, to and from school.[54]

I have not found any evidence that the AMA assisted Mary Bibb with the salary for Nichols. However, it is likely it did, for Nichols had a falling out with Bibb and wrote her sister in Ohio to tell her. The sister then directed the letter to George Whipple.[55] None the less, Matilda Nichols, with or without aid from the AMA, did teach at the school for a brief period.[56]

Mary Bibb's comment in the letter that many of the pupils had to walk quite a distance to the school suggests that children from outside the area also attended the school. It is a reasonable conclusion; many Black children could not attend the common school in their sections, having been barred by the white school supporters.[57]

By the end of 1853 the Sandwich Black separate school, the one taught and founded by Bibb and also taught by Misters Jackson and Russell, had not re-opened. The superintendent of the Sandwich schools, a Mr Vervais, stated in very clear language in his report: 'no school, no meeting for the last two years.'[58] In short the separate school had not functioned for the past two years. In his final remarks about the school, Vervais added: 'they have not the means to keep the school and they do not agree.'[59]

The various school acts passed in Canada West in the mid-nineteenth century provided for the taxation of parents for the maintenance of the common schools. The teacher's salary was to be made up both from the rate bill and property tax and from the provincial grant.[60] However, the effect of this legislation on the provincial grant given to common schools (which included separate schools) was unfair to poor school sections.[61] School grants would now be based on attendance, and many Black and poor white children did not attend school regularly. The grants for their schools would therefore be restricted. Part of the teacher's salary was to come out of the provincial grant; if the grant was small, then the teacher's salary naturally would be cut. Was it the case with the Sandwich separate school that the parents did not or could not pay the rate bill? What was the source of disagreement among the parents? Could Vervais be referring to school segregation, an issue under debate in the Black and wider communities?

This debate in the Black community had class overtones. The more 'enlightened' preached integration and derided those who did not share their opinions.[62] Ultimately, though, even the Black middle class came to realize that their children would have a hard time gaining admission to the common schools run by whites; they became unwilling supporters of separate schooling. Mary Bibb, her husband, and others in the Black community were not on the side of those who supported separate schooling. Mary Bibb taught in a separate school, but she was only facing reality: the education state and the white electorate were powerful enough to force separate schools on those who did not want them. That the Sandwich Black school supporters 'did not agree' could very well have meant that factionalism led to an internecine conflict that contributed to the demise of the school.[63]

Mary Bibb's involvement in education extended to the religious sphere where, along with her husband, she was active in the Sunday school movement. The Sunday school with which they were involved not only held Bible classes but also taught reading and writing. According to Daniel Hill, the Sunday school conducted by the Bibbs was the only schooling available to many youths and adults in the Black community of Essex.[64]

Her efforts to assist members of her race extended beyond teaching. An ardent abolitionist, upon her arrival in Canada, she helped to establish the Windsor Anti-Slavery Society. The society greatly helped many refugees who had fled to Canada from the United States. Her home was sometimes used as a shelter for many of these refugees. Mary and her husband were the Canadian directors of the Refugee Home Society, a colonization scheme established to help Blacks acquire land in the province. Not only did she assist in the establishment of the *Voice*, she also influenced its editorial direction, and during part of 1851, when her husband was on the lecture circuit in Wisconsin and Illinois, she oversaw its production. In addition, she was also involved in the emigrationist movement.[65] She was engaged in several of these undertakings with her husband.[66]

Emancipation day, 1 August 1854, was a turning-point in Mary Bibb's life.[67] Her husband died that day, after an illness. The Black community and the abolitionist movement had lost one of their most dynamic spokespersons and leaders. Mary

Bibb lost a husband, companion, friend, colleague, and 'help-meet.' When Henry Bibb died, he was thirty-nine years old and she was almost thirty-four. They were childless.[68]

Now on her own, Mary Bibb knew she had to draw on whatever resources she had in order to maintain herself. She continued teaching. Boston abolitionist and journalist Benjamin Drew toured Canada West in 1855 to assess the condition of life of the Blacks living there. He found Mrs Bibb teaching: 'Mrs. Mary E. Bibb, widow of the late lamented Henry Bibb, Esq., has devoted herself to teaching a private school in Windsor, and with good success. During the last spring term, she had an attendance of forty-six pupils, seven of whom were white children.'[69]

Teacher training in the nineteenth century was training for life. For many women, Black or white, especially those who were widowed or single, teaching was their only means of support. Mary Bibb was one of these women.

Sometime after 1855, she married Isaac N. Carey (or Cary), brother of Thomas J. Cary, who was married to Mary Shadd, another prominent Black woman teacher in Canada West.[70] In the 1861 census for Windsor, Mary Bibb appeared as Mary E. Carey, aged thirty-nine. Her occupation is not given, though her husband is listed as a 'barber.' There was also a Julia Carey, whose age is not given, living with them. The Careys occupied a two-storey frame house and were Methodists.[71] Since the census-takers did not list the occupations of most married women in that period, we have to turn elsewhere to find out if Mary Bibb Carey was still teaching in 1861.

Well-known abolitionist and writer William Wells Brown provides us with the answer.[72] In his 1861 tour of Canada West he gave an account of the Careys and their activities.

Mr. Cary is one of the most enterprising and intellectual men in Canada, and is deeply interested in the moral, social, and political elevation of all classes. Mrs. Cary, is better known as the beautiful and accomplished Mary E. Miles, afterwards, Mrs. Henry Bibb. Her labours during the lifetime of Mr. Bibb, in connection with him, for the fugitives, and her exertions since, are too well known for me to make mention here. Mrs. Cary has a private school with about 40 pupils, mostly of the better class of Windsor.[73]

I think this is the same school Drew mentioned, which was Mary's second or third educational venture and the most sustained. If this was the private school she started in 1852, it had a life span of at least nine years, a highly unusual situation for an individually run private school in nineteenth century Canada West. Was this longevity due to its patrons, who belonged to the 'better' class of Windsor and were able to pay for an 'accomplished' teacher?

Though Brown's comment about Bibb teaching children of the 'better' class points to a definite class distinction within the Black community, it has to be placed in context. The separate school in Windsor had opened only two years before Brown visited Windsor, and Black parents had needed to find schooling for their children before that time. Bibb's school was the only one prior to 1851 that provided an education for Black children. Perhaps the parents of the pupils in her school had been long established in Windsor and had some means (unlike her first school) to pay the tuition.[74]

In Brown's sketch of Mary Bibb he suggested not only that she had a higher profile when she was Mrs Bibb but that she was also very well known when she was Miss Mary Miles. It would have been worthwhile if he had mentioned her many 'exertions.'

Since her school was private, there is no record of it in the superintendent's report. That report merely acknowledges the existence of private schools in Windsor. The descriptions by Benjamin Drew and William Wells Brown are the only ones available.

Search for information about the school led me to examine the pages of the Dun and Bradstreet business directories. I was treated to a minor shock. In 1865 Mary Bibb appeared in the directories as Mary E. Cary of Windsor, operator and owner of a 'fancy goods' store. Information on this business continued to appear until 1871.[75] Did Mary Bibb Cary give up her private school or did she keep it along with the shop? If she did give up the school, why? Did many of her pupils move away or was she exhausted from teaching.[76]

Mary Bibb's last school was her most successful. Again, because it was a private school, the government had no hand in its affairs. From the time Mary Bibb arrived in Canada she intended to open a private school supported by the parents of her pupils. Her first school did not last. Her experience with the Sandwich government school certainly may have reinforced her desire to have as little as possible to do with the government. The success of her last school suggests her determination to be free and independent from the government.

For the many years that Mary Bibb taught in Canada she was acutely aware that the powers-that-be meant for Blacks to be placed firmly at the bottom of society's ladder. Inferior education was one way to ensure this outcome. Her continued efforts to provide schooling for Black children were battles against racist practices. Maybe one reason that Bibb gave up teaching was because she was tired, physically and mentally. Tired to be constantly fighting a racist society that kept shutting the doors of opportunities in the fact of Black people.

Mary Bibb was one of the few fortunate Black women in nineteenth-century North America who managed to enter normal school, earn qualifications, and become a teacher. She went from school to school, taught at the primary and secondary levels, and moved between the private and public sectors in education.

But being Black and female in nineteenth-century North America had widespread implications. When Mary Bibb was earning her teaching credentials and when she started to teach, most of her people were enslaved. This made her situation rare, but, like many of her sisters with a similar background, she realized that her education meant she had to work for the advancement of her race. She was conscious of her position and of how she had to use it.

She taught first in the northern states, which had sizeable free Black populations and where, in many places, Black children were barred from the common schools.[77] Then she moved to Canada, which had a burgeoning Black population. Black children there, as in the northern United States, faced great obstacles in getting an education. As a Black woman teacher, Mary Bibb persevered in providing an education for them. She did so surmounting many barriers.

Even though Mary Bibb was engaged in other non-teaching efforts to assist her community, I would argue that teaching remained the centre of her 'public' life. Of the twenty-three years or so she lived in Canada, she taught for at least thirteen of them. Her other work revolved around her teaching, and it was only towards the end of her stay in Canada that she went into an undertaking that had nothing to do with teaching.

Mary Bibb was committed in her efforts to bring about the destruction of American slavery and the eradication of the racism faced by the Black community in Canada. She taught school because her skills as a teacher were indispensable to a community that was victimized by racism, a community that was poor and needful of such skills. She taught not only because she was trained to but because she considered it her duty. She believed that with education her race would be 'strengthened and elevated.'[78]

NOTES

1 I have discussed my search for Mary Bibb and the methodological problems encountered in the construction of the story of marginalized peoples in Afua Cooper, 'The Search for Mary Bibb, Black Woman Teacher in Nineteenth-Century Canada West,' *Ontario History* 83, no. 1 (March 1991), 39–54.
2 Henry Bibb's mother, Mildred Jackson, was an ex-slave from Kentucky. Bibb arranged for her to be taken from the South

after she obtained her freedom. She came to live with him in Boston and then later in Canada West. C. Peter Ripley, ed., *The Black Abolitionist Papers*, vol. 2 (Chapel Hill: University of North Carolina Press 1986), 110, 221 (hereafter *BAP*).

3 The Fugitive Slave Law was a 'compromise' bill, passed in the American Congress to appease its slaveholding members and supporters, which granted slaveholders the right to hunt down and capture their escaped slaves. But before 1850 factors other than the FSL were pushing free Blacks out of both the North and South. Discriminatory racial practices made life for free Blacks very difficult. For a discussion of this slave code and its effects on Black people in the United States see Herbert Aptheker, *A Documentary History of the Negro People in the United States, From Colonial Time to the Founding of the NAACP in 1910* (New York: Citadel Press 1951), 220. For conditions of free Blacks by 1850 see Leon F. Litwack's *North of Slavery: The Negro in the Free States, 1790–1860* (Chicago: University of Chicago Press 1961); and Ira Berlin, *Slaves Without Masters: The Free Negro in The Antebellum South* (New York: Pantheon Books 1974).

4 *BAP*, 110–16.

5 Ibid., 110.

6 The *Freedom's Journal*, the first Black newspaper in the United States, co-founded by Black leader John B. Russwurm, in 1827 surveyed the African Free Schools in the North-East and found that in Providence, Rhode Island, there was not one such school. If Mary Miles was born in the vicinity of Providence, she must have had her early training by some other means. See Dorothy Sterling, *We Are Your Sisters* (New York: W.W. Norton 1984), 180. African Free Schools were established by Black communities in the North and North-East to provide education for their children. These schools sprang up as a direct result of Black children being excluded from schools attended by whites. Sometimes the African Free Schools were partially supported by white philanthropy. Charles C. Andrews, *New York Afri-*

can Free Schools (Reprint, New York: Negro Universities Press 1930).

7 It was not easy for aspiring Black women to receive advanced education in the United States, North or South. Even female institutions like Mount Holyhoke and Troy Female Seminary refused to admit Black women. A few normal schools periodically admitted Black female students. Oberlin College was the only school that since its founding was interracial and co-educational; however, very few Black women were able to take advantage of the opportunities there. Blacks, on the whole, never exceeded more that five per cent of Oberlin's student population. The difficulties Black women faced in getting higher education are underscored by the closing of Prudence Crandall's school in Connecticut by the state because Miss Crandall admitted Black female students to her seminary. W.E. Bigglestone, 'Oberlin College and the Negro,' *Journal of Negro History* 56 (1971), 133–9; Frederick Chambers, *Black Higher Education in the United States* (Westport, Conn.: Greenwood Press 1978); Lawrence J. Friedman, 'Racism and Sexism in Ante-bellum America: The Prudence Crandall Episode Reconsidered,' *Societas* 4, no. 3 (Summner 1974), 211–27; Gerda Lerner, ed., *Black Women in White America: A Documentary History* (New York: Vintage Books 1973), 74–7; Ellen NicKenzie Lawson, *The Three Sarahs: Documents of Antebellum Black College Women* (New York and Toronto: Edwin Mellen Press 1984).

8 *Circular and Register of the State Normal School, at Lexington, July, 1839 to Dec. 1846* (Boston: William B. Fowle 1856), 7.

9 Ibid., 18.

10 As mentioned, for Black women this was not easy. Many who taught – Chloe Lee, Ida B. Wells, Emma V. Brown, and others – went to a college or normal school to get better qualifications in order to help their people. Sterling, *We Are Your Sisters*, 180–213; Paula Giddings, *When and Where I Enter* (New York: William Morrow 1984), 20–3.

11 Rev. Samuel J. May was the principal of the Lexington Nor-

mal School from 1842–4. He was asked by Horace Mann, Massachusett's superintendent of education, to take up this position. *BAP*, 198; Thomas James Mumford, ed., *Memoirs of Samuel Joseph May* (Boston 1873), 173.

12 Walter H. Merrill and Louis Ruchames, eds, *The Letters of William Lloyd Garrison, 1850–1860, vol. IV* (Harvard: Belknap Press 1975), no. 73.

13 It is not known if May's abolitionism affected the kind of education he gave to his students. At Oberlin, for example, abolitionism was clearly on the agenda and many Oberlin graduates, both Black and white, were fiery antislavery activists. Regarding the curriculum at Lexington see *Circular and Register*, 18.

14 *General Catalogue of the State Normal School at West Newton, Mass. July, 1850* (Boston: Charles Moody 1850), 8.

15 *Circular and Register*, 18.

16 Ibid., 20.

17 Letter from Carleton Mabee, professor emeritus at SUNY, La Paltz, 9 April 1990. His source was 'God's Chore Boy: Samuel J. May' (unpublished manuscript in the archives at Syracuse University), 153–4. I am indebted to Professor Mabee for providing me with much information on the early teaching life of Mary Miles.

18 Letter from Professor Mabee. Source: *Albany Board of Schools Committee Report*, 1845, 8.

19 Letter from Professor Mabee. Source: Martin Delaney, *The Condition, Elevation, Emigration and Destiny of the Colored People of the United States* (New York: Arno Press 1968), 132, 185. See also *BAP*, 110.

20 Wendell P. Dabney, *Cincinnati's Colored Citizens* (New York: Negro Universities Press 1970), 103.

21 Sterling, *We Are Your Sisters*, 184–200.

22 At the time of their meeting Mary Miles was teaching in Albany, but her permanent address was Boston. For Bibb's statement see Gilbert Osofsky, *Putting' on Ole Massa: The Slave Narratives of Henry Bibb, Williams Wells Brown, and Solomon Northrup* (New York: Harper & Row 1969), 190–1.

23 Ibid., 191.

24 Letter from Professor Mabee.

25 Osofsky, *Puttin' on Ole Massa*, 191.

26 Sterling, *We Are Your Sisters*, 184.

27 See note 3. Well before the FSL, discriminatory laws had pushed many free Blacks from the American republic. However, the FSL exacerbated the already tenuous position of many free Blacks. Thousands chose to leave. Thousands came to Canada.

28 'Two weeks after President Fillmore signed the Fugitive Slave Bill a Pittsburg dispatch to the *Liberator* stated that "nearly all the [Black] waiters in the hotels have fled to Canada ... They went in large bodies, armed with pistols and bowie knives, determined to die rather than being captured." ' 'The members of a Negro community near Sandy Lake in northwestern Pennslyvania, many of whom had farms partly paid for, sold out or gave away their property and went in a body to Canada.' For these and other quotes see Fred Landon, 'The Negro Migration to Canada after the Passing of the Fugitive Slave Act,' *Journal of Negro History*, 1920, 24–5.

29 The 'uplifting' of the race was a nineteenth-century philosophy espoused by the Black middle class. It was felt by members of this class that those Blacks, female and male, who had some money and education, and most assuredly those who were freeborn, should help their less privileged sisters and brothers. Mary Bibb belonged to this Black middle class and she too subscribed to 'race uplift'; therefore, given her beliefs and her relatively privileged origin and position, she was a ready and willing candidate to start a school. For a discussion on 'race uplift' see Linda Perkins, 'Black Women and Race Uplift Prior to Emancipation,' in F.C. Steady, ed., *The Black Woman Cross-Culturally* (Cambridge, Mass.: Schenkman Books 1981), 317–34.

30 Mary Bibb had much more formal education than her husband, and so it can be safely concluded that she was involved in the production of the paper. *BAP*, 110–11.

31 Ibid., 108.

32 The *Voice of the Fugitive* is available on microfilm at the Robarts Library of the University of Toronto, Toronto's Metro Reference Library, the Archives of Ontario (Toronto), and in other locations in the province.

33 J. George Hodgins, *Documentary History of Education in Upper Canada*, vol. 9 (Toronto: L.K. Cameron), 38.

34 Alexander Murray, 'Canada and the Anglo-American Anti-Slavery Movement,' Ph.D. thesis, University of Pennsylvania, 1960, 329.

35 Ibid., 328.

36 *Voice*, 9 April 1851; Daniel Hill, *The Freedom-Seekers, Blacks in Early Canada* (Agincourt, Ont.: Book Society of Canada 1981), 149; Jason H. Silverman, *Unwelcome Guests* (New York: Faculty Press 1985), 130.

37 See 'Petition to the Coloured Inhabitants of Simcoe,' December 1850, to Egerton Ryerson, RG2 C6C, Archives of Ontario; Murray, 'Canada and the Anglo-American ...,' 238–333.

38 *Voice*, 26 Feb. 1851.

39 Hill, *Freedom-Seekers*, 156.

40 Conditions were wretched in many of the province's fledgling schools, but there was hope of improvement as the state began to take education more seriously and to allot more money for the education of its young. However, race was a crucial factor in this process; over time, in many of the Black separate schools conditions worsened. Lack of government financial support was one of the factors responsible. *BAP*, 97–8.

41 Amelia Freeman and Mary Ann Shadd were two other Black women who founded schools for Black children in Canada West. *BAP*, 185–6, 489–90.

42 Susan Houston and Alison Prentice, *Schooling and Scholars in Nineteenth-Century Ontario* (Toronto: University of Toronto Press 1988), 61.

43 Mary Bibb writing to Horace Mann, 20 Jan. 1853, Horace Mann Papers, Massachusetts Historical Society, Boston.

44 The *Anti-Slavery Bugle*, 12 Apr. 1851. The issue of unpaid labour was one that plagued several Black teachers during

their tenure. Teachers Julia Turner and Amelia Freeman sometimes taught for little or no wages during many of their teaching years. This question of unpaid labour should be fitted into the broader subject of women, work, class, and ethnicity in the nineteenth century.

45 *Bugle*, 4 Oct. 1851.
46 Mary Bibb to Horace Mann.
47 *Voice*, 29 Jan. 1852.
48 Bibb to Mann.
49 'The scattering of Negro families in many cases made it more difficult for them to organize and keep a school of their own.' Donald G. Simpson, 'Negroes in Ontario from Early Times to 1870,' Ph.D. thesis, University of Western Ontario, 1971, 377; Mary Ann Shadd, writing to George Whipple about her Windsor school, stated: 'This being very near to the U.S., the fugitive population has been of a transient character, many remaining so long as they can make further arrangements for the interiors so that the school has been somewhat affected by it.' Mary Ann Shadd to George Whipple, 3 Apr. 1852, American Missionary Association Papers, Amistad Research Center (AMA-ARC), Tulane University, New Orleans.
50 See Benjamin Drew, *Narratives of the Fugitive Slaves in Canada* (Boston: Jewett & Company 1856), 321–2.
51 *BAP*, 110–11.
52 Superintendent's report for Sandwich schools, 1853. RG2 F3B, Archives of Ontario.
53 See Bibb's letter to Mann, above.
54 Mary Bibb to George Whipple, 23 May 1853, AMA-ARC.
55 Matilda Nichols to Harriet Fuller, 15 July 1853, Fuller to Whipple, 18 July 1853. AMA-ARC.
56 Bibb's letter to Whipple requesting aid for her assistant was dated May 1853; Nichols's letter to Fuller was dated July of the same year. Nichols therefore spent three months or more at the Sandwich school.
57 Several Black parents, instead of sending their children to a distant separate school, applied for admission to nearby white schools, but in many instances they were refused.

Three of these parents – Dennis Hill, George Stewart, and George Washington – mounted legal challenges to segregated education. *BAP*, 243; Silverman, *Unwelcome Guests*, 135–6; Francis G. Carter, Judicial Decisions on Denominational Schools (Toronto: Ontario Separate School Trustees' Association 1962), 135, 150, 151, 152; W.W. Arthurs, 'Civil Liberties – Public Schools – Segregation of Negro Students,' *Canadian Bar Review* 41 (Sept. 1963), 453–7; 'Washington v School Trustees of Charlotteville,' *Term Book: Court of the King's Bench*, 1854–5, vol. 33, Archives of Ontario.

58 Superintendent Vervais's statement that there was no school for the last two years accords well with Bibb's history of the school as outlined in her letter to Mann. According to the letter, the school continued until April 1852. The superintendent's reports were done in December of each year, hence, in December of both 1852 and 1853, no or limited activity would be reported for the Sandwich Black separate school, since it had ceased operation well before December 1852. Vervais then would be quite correct to note that the school was not kept for two years. Superintendent's report for Sandwich schools, 1853.

59 Ibid.

60 Each school was to be maintained by a government subsidy, the rate bill, and property taxes. Houston and Prentice, *Schooling and Scholars*, 107–17, 131–30.

61 For a detailed discussion of the school laws and how they affected schools and teachers' salaries see Houston and Prentice, *Schooling and Scholars*, chapters 4, 5, and 9.

62 When Henry Bibb, husband of Mary Bibb, found out that several Black families from Windsor had petitioned for a separate school, he stated that the request 'was not made by the intelligent portion of the colored population, but by a lot of ignoramuses who were made tools of and who knew not what they were doing.' It is not known if his wife shared that specific sentiment (*Voice*, 1 Jan. 1852). Mary Ann Shadd, teacher and editor of the *Provincial Freeman*, also felt that Blacks who requested separate schools were misguided. See Mary Shadd (Cary) to George Whipple, 27

Oct. 1851, AMA-ARC. Jason Silverman notes that 'both black and white critics of segregated schools ... may have been blinded by their idealism to the reality of prejudice in Canada West. White Canadians controlled the educational system, and in most cases, tacitly assumed that segregation embodied the only course acceptable to both races. In any event, whites actually needed no justification because, a majority, they easily overruled the desires of the fugitive-slave minority' (*Unwelcome Guests*, 145). A research article by this author (A. Cooper) on the division in the Black community over the issue of separate schooling is forthcoming.

63 Jim Bearden and Linda Jean Butler, in their book *Shadd, the Life and Times of Mary Shadd Cary* (Toronto: NC Press 1977), 34–6, have misrepresented the issue of separate schooling in the controversy between the Bibbs and Mary Shadd. The authors state that the Bibbs advocated separate schooling while Shadd was against it. The Bibbs clearly articulated in several articles in the *Voice* and in letters written by Mary Bibb their support for an integrated school system.

Many Black parents often did not wish to subscribe to segregated schools and withdrew their children from them. Sometimes the schools collapsed as a result. See W.P. Newman of Camden, 'Petition of the Black Residents Against a Separate School,' 13 Jan. 1856, and 'Petition of Colchester Black inhabitants against a Separate School,' 28 November 1857, RG2 C6C, Archives of Ontario.

64 *Freedom-Seekers*, 210; *Voice*, 13 Aug. 1851.

65 Many Blacks in Canada West, given the hostile racial environment they lived in, soon became attracted to Black emigration beyond the North American continent. West Africa and the Caribbean were two favoured places for emigration. Two influential advocates of the emigrationist cause were Martin Delaney and James Theodore Holly. Mary Bibb was an officer at the National Emigration Convention held in 1854 in Cleveland, Ohio. *BAP*, 34–5, 437.

66 For some details on the work that Mary Bibb did with her husband see Floyd Miller, *The Search for a Black Nationality* (Urbana: University of Illinois Press 1975), 145; William

and Jane H. Pease, *Black Utopia* (Madison: Madison State Historical Society of Wisconsin 1963), 109–22; *BAP*, 111; Hill, *Freedom-Seekers*, 179, 210; and Peter Carlesimo, 'The Refugee Home Society: Its Origin, Operations, and Results, 1851–1876,' M.A. thesis, University of Windsor, 1973.

67 Blacks in Canada celebrated 1 August to commemorate the Emancipation Act of 1833. By this act slavery was abolished throughout the British empire. *BAP*, 95.

68 Henry Bibb had a daughter, Frances, from his first marriage with Malinda Bibb.

69 Drew, *Narratives*, 321–2. The question of the precise location of Mary Bibb's second school is ticklish. In her letter to Horace Mann she informs him that the school is in Sandwich (she does not say if she means the village or the general township). Her assistant, Matilda Nichols, in a letter to her sister, revealed that she had to walk four miles from Windsor where she boarded with the Bibbs to Sandwich (the village) where the school was. Yet both Benjamin Drew (1855) and William Wells Brown (1861) in their eyewitness accounts informed us that Mary Bibb's school was in Windsor. Perhaps this vexing issue can be resolved as follows. We can give primacy to Bibb's and Nichols's letters, as they are more authoritative, and infer from them that the school was started and kept for a while in Sandwich; and speculate that, after Nichols's departure in July 1853, Bibb moved the school to Windsor, where her home was. This would match Drew's and Wells Brown's description of the school's location. See also Nichols to Fuller, 15 July 1853, AMA-ARC; and William Wells Brown in *BAP*, 478.

70 *BAP*, 111.

71 Census for Windsor, 1861, Archives of Ontario.

72 William Wells Brown was an escaped slave from Kentucky. After his escape Brown became an ardent abolitionist, travelling and lecturing all over the free states. He is credited as being the first African-American novelist, his two novels, *Clotel* and *St. Domingo*, being written sometime during the 1850s. Brown also wrote his autobiography, which was reprinted in Osofsky, *Puttin' on Ole Massa*. In 1861–2, he undertook a tour of the Black settlements of Canada West. *BAP*, 460.

73 *BAP*, 478.

74 For information on the Windsor separate school see the superintendent's report for Windsor schools, 1859, RG2 F3B, Archives of Ontario.

75 Dun and Bradstreet Reference Books, reels 1–3, Archives of Ontario.

76 In 1863, as the United States army begin to recruit Black men to fight in the Civil War, hundreds of Black men from Canada West took up the call. Many families also returned to the United States to find lost relatives and friends and to help in the reconstruction after the war ended. As a result, many children of school age also left the province (Jonathan W. Waltin, 'Blacks in Buxton and Chatham, Ontario, 1830–1890: Did the 49th Parallel Make a Difference?' Ph.D. thesis, Princeton University, 1979, 164–9). It is also possible that Mary Bibb was burned out from teaching. In 1865 she was forty-five years old and had been a teacher for at least twenty years. The adverse conditions under which many nineteenth-century teachers laboured contributed to their mental and physical fatigue. For Black teachers, given the systemic oppression under which they laboured, their fatigue level would have been even higher than that of white teachers. Mary Ann Shadd (Cary), who was a teacher in and administrator of the private school founded by her sister-in-law, Amelia Freeman, writes of Freeman having 'shattered health from teaching school for almost nothing.' This statement certainly underscores what must have been the common lot of many Black teachers (Shadd Cary to George Whipple, 21 July 1862, AMA-ARC). For teacher burn-out, see also Marta Danylewycz and Alison Prentice, ' "Teachers Work: Changing Patterns and Perceptions in the Emerging School Systems of Nineteenth- and Early Twentieth-Century Central Canada,' *Labour/Le Travail* 17 (Spring 1986), 71–3.

77 For a reading on the condition of education for Black children in the United States, including the northern states, see Walton, 'Blacks in Buxton and Chatham,' 28–35.

78 From an editorial in the *Voice*, 15 Jan. 1851.

5

'We weren't allowed to go into factory work until Hitler started the war': The 1920s to the 1940s

DIONNE BRAND

The purpose of this essay is to review, through oral accounts, the experiences of Black women in Canada between the wars, their location in work outside the home, and the impact of the Second World War on their job opportunities. Using the accounts of several women born between 1900 and 1924, I will examine how race and gender structured life for Black women in this country during the period 1920 to 1946. The oral accounts used here are from the oral history project that I coordinated between 1988 and 1990 – 'Lives of Black Working Women in Ontario' – which was sponsored by the Immigrant Women's Job Placement Centre. Some fifty women were interviewed. These oral accounts can be found in their entirety in my book *No Burden to Carry: Narratives of Black Working Women in Ontario 1920s–1950s* (Toronto: Women's Press 1991).

In order to locate the women who speak in this essay it is necessary to look briefly at the lives of their mothers and grandmothers as described by them. Canadian history and Canadian women's history has given us little if any information of the existence of these women who survived slavery and the Underground Railroad. As a feminist recorder facing the problem of white and biased documentation, I found that oral history opened up that vast and yet untapped well of events, knowledge, and experience that Black women live and have lived in this country. The abolition of slavery, the institution that gave rise to the presence of their great-grand-mothers and grandfathers on Canadian soil, was not one hundred years old when the women in the oral accounts were born.

Still, the abolition of slavery did not eradicate racism as an organizing principle within the social, economic, or political life of Canada and the United States. The mothers and grand-mothers of the women in these accounts worked in fields, tended chickens and hogs, washed, ironed, cooked and cleaned for a wage, and took care of children, grandchildren, and family. For Black women in Canada, however, the availability of work outside the home – long an imperative in their lives – was structured by both their gender and their race. They found themselves in the gender- and race-bound work of their day, which placed them at the lower end of the economic strata. But they had to work, and their place in the economy reflected the prejudices that Canadian society imprinted on their char-acter. Black women of the time had inherited not only the burdensome legacy of a labour force stratified by race and gender but also a social milieu steeped in racial hatred. But if they were burdened, they were not hopeless. Here two women describe life for their grandmother and mother in the late-nineteenth and early-twentieth-century Ontario.

My grandmother didn't talk much about early life, but she talked a little later on about her life as a married woman and as a mother. She talked about the little house that she bought on Lip-pincott Street and how Bathurst Street [in Toronto] was just a cow pasture in those days. To earn a living grandma did sewing, she did all kinds of baking, and she did washing.

She was an ambitious woman, and she felt that Black people should be able to do things like have a restaurant, so she worked hard and she did that – had a restaurant. She was a great person also for buying property. She bought quite a bit of property in the early days; if she was a young woman now, she'd know what to do with it! She was like the young women that we have now that are coming along that are just wonderful –

My mother tells us the story of how when she was quite young they had to deliver the laundry. There were some wealthy people living on Brunswick Avenue and on Huron Street and those streets, and grandma would do the washing. My mother and her youngest brother would have to deliver the washing back to these people.
Gwen Johnston

When my father died my mother kept up a small farm [in North Buxton]. She worked as a housemaid and helped do house cleaning and things of that sort, anything to keep bread in our mouths. We raised tobacco and beans, stuff like that from an early age. We had to go in the field, She did it all, except what help she could get – we had to have somebody come and hoe, come and weed it all.
Saxonia Shadd

In the small Black farming communities of Ontario and in cities like Toronto and Windsor, with their small Black populations, the approach of the Great Depression only compounded the difficulties of daily life. Accounts show more than a passing similarity of experience between rural and urban women as the Depression saw many farm daughters move to the cities to join their urban counterparts seeking work in the twenties and thirties. Addie Aylestock was one such farm daughter. Born near Elmira, Ontario, in 1909, she went on to become the first woman to be ordained in the British Methodist Episcopal Church.

There was four of us – four girls. It seemed like we had the idea in our head to leave. Most of us left home pretty early because our parents were poor and weren't able to look after us.

My sister was doing domestic work, getting her room and board. And there was a friend, in the BME Church, of my mother's and my sister's. When I came to Toronto I used to spend a lot of time at her home, so she sort of was chaperoning us. I was not quite sixteen.

Toronto was like a big city to me then, but not near as big as now. You can't compare: it wasn't built up like it is now. The city was three- or four-storey houses – I thought that was high!

When I worked as a domestic I didn't have much to do. I just got up and got out – got my breakfast and got out in the morning – and back at two o'clock in the afternoon and then I got the dinner ready.

I think they gave me enough for car fare – I really don't remember, but it wasn't very much. I know when I first came to Toronto there weren't many opportunities for Black girls, in those days anyways. And then again, my parents were satisfied that I had a job in housework that I would stay in. I think I got fifteen dollars a month at the start – that was supposed to be enough for your clothes and your car fare. I lived in the west end of Toronto then, on Brighton Avenue.

I guess the Depression started when I came here to Toronto. It didn't really seem like a Depression to me. The reason I knew about the Depression was that I heard mother and dad talking about it. I didn't realise that's what it was, but I knew that sometimes we were getting the same thing to eat, like beans, turnips, maybe something the farmers would give us. My parents didn't have money to go out and buy much.
Addie Aylestock

Depression or not, Black women had to work. Black families, urban and rural, could not survive strictly on the male wage. They survived on the wages of women working in service and of men working as porters on the railroad and in general labour.

Violet Blackman, the only woman of Caribbean descent in these oral histories, came to Toronto in 1920. She describes the city in 1920 and the opportunities for Black women:

That was 1920; then Toronto was just a village. The streetcars had no sidings to them; you could jump on and off, but they always had the motorman and a conductor on them. The Exhibition Ground and Sunnyside, that was all the lake, and the Union Station – all there was nothing but the lake.

You couldn't get any position, regardless who you were and how educated you were, other than housework because even if the employer would employ you, those that you had to work with would not work with you.

Gwen Johnston, whose grandmother was born in Toronto in 1857, outlines the work life of her family:

The women in the family did mainly domestic work. My Aunt Edith was a very excellent cook and had cooking jobs, but they did domestic work – there was no other work that Black people could get in those days. The brother that went to New York worked on the trains and the one known as Uncle Sam, who moved to Montreal, I don't know what he did – I think he worked on trains for a while too. Then Uncle Ernest – he worked in his early years; he worked in the post office, and then he went into the ministry, and he was one of the British Methodist Episcopal ministers.

In her essay 'Domestic Service in Canada 1880–1920,' Genevieve Leslie argues that domestic service changed with industrialization. 'The period 1880–1920 ... was a transitional period which clearly revealed the incompatibility of domestic service and modern industrial trends ... In 1891 domestics accounted for 41 percent of the female work force, and were by far the largest single group of workers; by 1921 domestics represented only 18 percent of all employed women but were still the second largest category of female workers,'[1] Since their arrival in Ontario, first as slaves then as fugitives from slavery, in the early 1800s, Black women had worked on farms, in domestic service, and at home. Indications are that not until 1940 or so did any significant number of them work at industrial labour. Leslie does not talk about Black women in domestic service, and we can assume her statistics reflect only white women working in domestic service, because certainly up to the Second World War at least 80 per cent of Black women in Canadian cities worked in domestic service.[2] Industrialization did not have the overwhelming impact on Black women wage-earners that it did on white women, but race clearly blocked their entrance into industrial labour. Bee Allen, Eleanor Hayes, and Rella Braithwaite, born between 1911 and 1923, recount the difficulties of navigating the race barrier.

I had wanted to be a teacher but when I was young there weren't that many blacks teaching in Toronto.

My first job was, as with many Black girls, in service. I had not been in any kind of work, but I felt I could take care of a child, so I took that job. That's what I did prior to marriage, and not for too long, because I would then be sixteen, maybe seventeen.

In service situations I always asked, 'Do you hire coloured?' because I did not have financial means to go running up to some place up in Rosedale from where I lived and be turned down when I got to the door – that was car fare spent for nothing. Sometimes they would say, 'Well, I'm sorry.' Other times I would phone and they would say, 'Well, are you dark?' and I would say, 'Well, I'm not dark,' and then they might say, 'I'm sorry, the reason I'm asking is because we'd like our coloured help to be unquestionably coloured.' These were domestic jobs; you were going to live in, in many cases, and they did not want to have their friends or relatives wondering at you.

I guess probably some white people lived with the idea that they would live with a coloured person in their home if they were not extremely dark, and that was because they just keep showing up in their face all the time. Others wanted you to be dark because mostly coming from the States they were accustomed to Black help and this is what they wanted.

It was when I was trying to find service jobs that this business about being Black came up. Black women had not really had that long of a life in other jobs because it was the war that opened it. The war brought in the necessity for hiring women.

I lived in for maybe one job, but I didn't stay there very long. In a lot of these service jobs you lived in, and you only had Thursday afternoon off and maybe every other Sunday. Some general domestics were doing everything: they were doing the cooking and they were also serving. They were part of the family, but the mistress didn't want any of your life to keep you from getting up early and getting her breakfast.

I stayed home during the first year of our marriage and then I had the daughter. In '31–'32 – her first year – I was quite ill and spent some five or six weeks in the hospital and came home from that time. Then I got this opportunity to go work in the shoe factory; once I got into working in the shoe factory then I never went back into domestic service. I never did because I felt I had now an opening tool.
Bee Allen

Some of us who have been there ... can talk about it without shame. One woman was saying how much she was getting paid and she was getting five dollars a week in old clothes. If you were lucky – if the lady was nice – five dollars a week and old clothes. Back then I worked for fifteen dollars a month, with car fare. That's nothing! They used to say with car fare or without car fare. A friend of mine was getting twenty dollars a month, but she didn't get car fare. Tokens were four for a quarter.

When I was in high school the girls who wanted to take commercial courses or secretarial courses they weren't encouraged to do so. We were told, 'Well, who would want to hire you?' There were a few businesses that would hire you but very, very, very few! There are women today living here in Toronto who were the first this and the first that: the first Black secretary in the government is living today; the first Black nurse to train in a hospital is living today; the first Black to work in Eaton's is living today.

That's where the openings were – garment factories or knitting mills – anything that wasn't too, too visible. The excuse they had was that the other employees might object. Now you hear them say that there's no discrimination here, but it's beneath the surface. But it wasn't beneath the surface then – they were very, very frank about it.
Eleanor Hayes

I was born in 1923. It must be late, definitely the late 30s, when I came to Toronto. By that time you would take a train, but the connections wouldn't be too good, and the money to get to travel the train – it was hard to get. My older sisters were down in Toronto first and I came down at the age of fifteen. Immediately, my older sister taught me how you could be a mother's helper. I was raring to come to the big city! The first job that you could get, you took. At that time they were advertising for cook generals, and that was the older women. The older women knew how to do all the cooking and look after a household – and that's what my two older sisters were – but when you were young as my age you were a mother's helper.

Thursday was quite the day. It was a very busy day at the hairdressers, that was women's afternoon off. There were some big dances too on Thursday. Special dances, seemed to me, that some of them were, and at that time they also had a midnight show.
Rella Braithwaite

These accounts outline the limitations of Black women's job mobility before the Second World War, as well as the difficult conditions they encountered in the households in which they worked.

The situation of Black women engaged in waged work seems to have been similar in the United States. Jacqueline Jones, in her exhaustive treatment of Black women and work there, points out: 'In 1940 one third of all white, but only 1.3 percent of all black working women had clerical jobs. On the other hand, 60 percent of all black female workers were domestic servants; the figure for white women was only 10 percent.'[3] Ruth Pierson, in her book *'They're Still Women After All': The Second World War and Canadian Women*, states: 'Canada's War effort, rather than any consideration of women's right to work, determined the recruitment of women into the labour force. The recruitment of women was part of a large-scale intervention by Government into the labour market to control allocation of labour for effective prosecution of war.'[4] This was no less true for the women in these accounts. Nor was racial desegregation an objective of the war effort. Ghettoized up to then in domestic work of one sort or another – mother's helpers, housekeeping, laundry work, general help – Black women were released by the war effort from the racialized, segregated, female employment that domestic work was for them, and were given entry into industrial labour and clerical work. 'Things opened up,' many women say.

After Reliable Toy, I worked in a factory down on John Street; they made suits. There was lots of that domestic work, going and cleaning up other people's dirty place. Really and truly, we weren't allowed to go into factory work until Hitler started the war, and then they'd beg you, 'Would you like a job in my factory?' But we weren't allowed in [before]. We were left more or less to clean their dirty houses. Which I never did, I'll tell you that. Then we had a chance to go and work in the ammunition dump.

They called it GICO. That's where Centennial College is now – used to be the war plant. I lasted about a week there. I couldn't stay because I started to haemorrhage. [The work] was filling magazines, little pellets with gunpowder for the soldiers. I kept menstruating – the humidity was too high or something, I couldn't stay. I have pictures of some of us that were out there. There were many Black women out there. I had to go back to other factory work.
Marjorie Lewsey

'Things' also 'opened up' for Black men who were recruited into the armed forces.

The only thing that helped some of the people get an education was the outcome of the war. When the war broke out and the boys went into the army and got their training – some of them did well with that. The war helped in some areas, but then in another area it sort of divided the community.
Eleanor Hayes

The youths would go up to the Hall and report of the troubles Black people were having in getting into the army or getting into the air force. They didn't want you in the army. My own brother – my oldest brother – had to leave Ontario in order to get into the army, and then he was in four years. But they didn't want Black people in the army – it was a white man's war.

Blacks wanted to go into the army because there was no employment. If you didn't go into the army, you'd work on the railroad. Every mother hopes their son would not be a porter. Every mother hopes her daughter would be a nurse.
Esther Hayes

Though the Canadian Army at first rejected Black volunteers, Robin Winks reports that by 1941 it had dropped its most blatant racial policies. Still, the nature of service allowed Black servicemen still reflected the racism of the society.[5] In her narrative one woman recounts trying, as she says, 'to sell my colour to the army,' giving up after getting what she calls the 'runaround.' Robin Winks suggests that racism decreased during the Second World War, stating: 'thus the total impact of World War II was an educational one for white and Black, bettering the status of the Negro worker – in and out of uniform – throughout Canada and The North.'[6] But racism did not so much decrease as mobilization for the war effort made it expedient to do away with some of the more primitive racial restrictions in order to free all the productive forces in the service of winning the war. According to Winks, until 1942 the National Selective Service accepted racial restrictions from employers. In 1942, according to Pierson, the NSS (Women's Division) began a drive to register and recruit much-needed female labour for the war industry and essential services.

As many in these accounts attest, Black women would not have needed much encouragement to flee race-bound domestic work. Most were well within the age group most favoured for recruitment, single and 20–24 years old. Though some were married, by mid-1943 the National Selective Service was recruiting them too.[7] Indeed, given the extent of the labour shortages there was a lot of room for Black women. 'By mid 1943 there were labour shortages in service jobs long dependent on female (*i.e., white*) labour. Women were leaving these for higher paying employment in war industries. Hospitals, restaurants, hotels, laundries, and dry cleaners were clamouring for help, but the labour pool of single women available for full time employment was exhausted.'[8] Then too, as Pierson points out, even non-essential jobs like those in candy, tobacco, and soft-drink companies,[9] were experiencing labour shortages.

The widespread expansion of goods and services that the war occasioned made possible and palatable the employment of Black women in jobs where their employment was once unacceptable, in terms of both their race and their sex. But the nation-wide publicity campaigns undertaken by the NSS to persuade women to sign up for work were not directed towards Black women, nor were their slogans of patriotism instrumental in recruiting Black women. Simply put, Black women needed the work – they needed the money – and waged work had been an essential part of their daily lives. Again, James St G. Walker points out that 'in 1941, 80% of Black adult females in Montreal were employed as domestic servants.'[10] By all accounts, this was also the case in Toronto and other Black communities. And as domestic workers, usually beginning their working lives at fifteen, Black women received wages of from fifteen to thirty dollars a month in conditions of employment that could subject them to such arbitrary demands as forgoing time off, having to work sixteen hour days, and receiving clothing in lieu of wages. Racism created an atmosphere in which Black women's presence was on sufferance. So, the industrial wage (such as it was), the wholesale war recruitment that suggested that one's chances were as good as anyone else's, the anonymity of industrial labourers, and the indications of Black progress that this opportunity signalled were all a boon to Black women and to the Black community as a whole – despite the laissez-faire racism on the job in the war plants and other industries.

There is some evidence that suggests the kind of treatment Black women as a whole experienced in the munitions plants. Grace Fowler refers to working on the 'high explosives side' in one munitions plant.

It was in '44 I went to work at the war plant. November. And so I got a job in the war plant. I worked on what they call the high explosives side, where you got paid a little extra because you were workin' with dangerous powders. We made detonators for torpedoes. And it wasn't a bad job. I learned every job on the line because it was awful boring just to stay in one.
Grace Fowler

Fern Shreve remarks that she felt that another Black women was given a certain dangerous position on the line, making grenades, because of her race.

I remember in the munitions factory – Chatco Steel in Chatham – that was where there were more Blacks than any other job that I think that I worked on. I don't know why, but there were whites there. I guess if I wanted to make a case of it I could probably say that the Blacks were doing the dirtier work, but I can't prove that. There was a lady, an older lady, Mrs. Selby, and they had what they called the oven. These things were dipped in varnish, and then they were cooked, and they'd go around, and poor Mrs. Selby would sit under there and take those things off. Today I would just think that would be the most horrible thing that I could think of. We were also so much younger than she – we should've been doing some of the dirty work. That was really terrible. We worked nights. She'd be sitting there nodding, see the fire burning and go 'Oh!' I think back on it now and think that's just dreadful! Why was she chosen to do that particular job?
Fern Shreve

'Things opened up' also meant that Black women felt freer at least to argue against racism on an equal footing with the white woman they encountered during the war.

When I worked in that war plant, especially on the night shift, when all the machinery breaks down we used to get into some real good discussions. This one night we talked about nursing, and I was saying how they wouldn't let Black girls go into nursing at that time, and she was trying to explain to me why they didn't and was trying to be delicate about it and she was saying, well you know your people have a different odour and somebody sick they don't want somebody around them. I said, 'I work alongside of some of these women. If I smelled as bad as them, I'd shoot myself, so don't talk to me about bad smell.'
Grace Fowler

The narrative of one woman on war work also suggests that she encountered for the first time the unusual circumstance of 'more Blacks in any other jobs that I worked on.' Another left teaching in the Maritimes for service in Ottawa, having been recruited through the Selective Service. Still another became a teacher, recruited through a government war program that offered grade twelve and thirteen students $45 to train as teachers, and another cites the fact that male teachers had been recruited into the armed forces, precipitating the recruitment of women as teachers.

We finished high school at Merlin. That was grade twelve and part of grade thirteen, only part because I took sick. It was during the war. The government offered any grade twelve or thirteen student who would become interested in teaching anywhere in Ontario forty-five dollars. It was a lot of money in that time – just take a six-week teacher training course. I got excited in May when this came through: I'm going to apply and I'm going to be able to make some money for the family, I thought.

Teaching was the last thing I had wanted to do because I had wanted to be a secretary, like my aunt. Norma Brown and I went to London to take this course. Both of us had our jobs before we left. Norma was in Shrewsbury. I had my school in Chatham Township.
Cleata Morris

Though teaching was the other traditional job for a Black woman (there being segregated one-room schoolhouses in Black communities in the Maritimes and Ontario), the Second World War obviously opened up the number of jobs available in the profession.[11] It also changed the make-up of their classrooms from comprising mainly Black students to including white students.

According to Pierson, along with the recruitment of women into industries and services, there was also recruitment of women into agriculture 'to fill some of the gaps in farm power with female labour.' In all provinces farmers' wives and daughters took over farm work in the absence of male relatives and farm workers who had left the land to join the armed forces or to work in industry.[12]

Some Black women, particularly those from south-western Ontario, might have been part of the Women's Land Brigade and Farm Girls Brigade of the Farm Labour Service, as some recount not only working in their own fields but also hiring out as farm help. However, either option would not have been unusual for these women under ordinary circumstances, since some of them had husbands, brothers, and fathers who worked on the railroads as porters, and the women were already carrying the load of farm work. Others already worked planting tobacco or picking tomatoes and cucumbers.

When we worked in Chatham in the Libby's factory, we worked side by side with all the white women. After the war all the country people had to leave all the factories and come back. We did other jobs and then they hired the people from the city of Chatham. A lot of us worked on farms around here. A lot of women went to the fruit orchards out on Highway 3, the fruit farms. We all worked out there. There used to be a great big truck used to come down here. All the bunch came out to the fruit farm. You'd get much more than you'd get for a day's work. It's according to how you picked: if you picked steady all day, you'd make good. But a lot of time a lot of them their legs was tired.

... A lot of women went out to the corn fields. Here in

Chatham they come out in the country and they pick tomatoes, and a lot of them suckered corn in the spring. You go along and take the little riffs that come out in the corn – you break them off so the ears grow. Women worked in the corn; then they worked in the plants in Chatham.
June Robbins

As Pierson[13] has found, despite the recruitment campaigns that stressed patriotic duty, the principal motivation for women in entering the wartime job market was indeed not the need to do patriotic service, but economic necessity. This was perhaps even more true for Black women workers of the time.

After I married, until my son was born I was doing some work on my own, and when the war came on I was doing war work out there. They had a place set up out in Scarborough. There wasn't too many coloured people working there from what I can remember, but there was some.
   I guess if I was thinking about it today maybe I wouldn't have done that with the way you feel about war. But at that time it was good money; we were really filling these shells. When I come to think of it – my goodness, the place could've blown up! You didn't really think too much about it, not when you're younger. When you went in you took a shower; when you went out you took a shower, in case the powder gets on you – and I never did like showers. I always liked baths.
   I don't think the war years was very much different from the way the people'd been feeling, even in other races, all along. I think young men are just eager; I don't think they're thinking about what might happen. Personally, I don't like to think of war because you're just wondering if they'll ever come back. Even now, especially in the States, young men are going for different things, and they're not expecting things to happen, but they're killing people. But the war gave a lot of different work to women. I think maybe that was the part: the women kind of started doing work.
Bertha McAleer

It was quite a traumatic experience for somebody who had lived in the city. Barrie was very small and it was made up of retired farmers. The war had just started, so there were people there from all over living in rented rooms and anything they could get to live in.

   For a while I worked at the tannery. There were a lot of women hired – women had been there for years – and they dyed the skins as they came on the belt. And, of course, I wanted something to do and I wanted more money. So finally with the war on they really needed women: they needed help because the men just weren't there, so finally I got a job there, in the early 40s, over my husband's objections.

   I think the whole thing opened up with the war: more was demanded and consequently they had to have more people in jobs; this was the turning point for Blacks.
Vi Aylestock

When I came back from London in 1945 I went to work in a munitions plant, working with hand grenades. We were preparing these shells – we didn't have anything to do with the explosives – they were dipped and scrapped and stuff like that. We weren't making much money there – they didn't pay money in those days, but you could get work like it was going out of style. It was night work – we worked nights all the time in the munitions plant. I decided that wasn't quite enough money for me, so I'd go out on Saturday and work extra. I went to the unemployment office and they sent me to this lady's house to wash. When I get there she wants me to wash her bathroom, and as slow as I worked I think I made two dollars – and it was something like fifty cents an hour I was being paid. I didn't go to work anymore Saturdays!
Fern Shreve

Black women did see these jobs as a gain for the race, but much to their chagrin, no sooner had they fled domestic work than the retrenchment of women workers began, supposedly back 'into traditionally female occupations,'[14] In their case, 'traditionally female occupations' would mean domestic work, but retrenchment was also accompanied by an infusion of Black Caribbean women recruited by the Department of Immigration for domestic work in Canada.

While no Canadian historian has traced the course, consequences, and significance of Black women's war work in Canada, Jacqueline Jones, in her formidable historical study of Black women and work in the United States, writes of the period: 'From official United States Government posters to short stories in popular women's magazines, recruitment propaganda was aimed exclusively at white women of both the middle and working classes. When Black women were mentioned in connection with the national manpower crises at all, they were exhorted to enter 'war services' by taking jobs that white women most readily abandoned – laundry, cafeteria, and domestic work ... While male workers might absent themselves from the factory as a result of overindulgence the night before, (white) female workers stayed home periodically to catch up on their washing, cleaning, and grocery shopping. Black women thus were supposed to form a behind-the-scenes cadre of support workers for gainfully employed white wives.'[15]

Though the proportion of Black women was smaller in Canada, the same racial and sexual division of labour determined their entry into and location in war work. Black women in the United States had a longer history of factory work than Black women in Canada. While the former had what Jones describes as a 'weak hold on industrial position' from the twenties to the forties (7 per cent of Black women in 1920, 5.5 per cent in 1930, 6 per cent in 1940),[16] Black women in Canada seemed to have had no hold at all. Repeatedly, in these narratives, the women say that Black women could not get any position but that of domestic work before the war.

Their foothold in factory work in the 1940s was, therefore even more precarious than their sisters' to the south. Isolated, in smaller numbers in Toronto, Windsor, Chatham, and smaller communities in Ontario, their chances of collective action were much more slim, though not non-existent. The experiences on the wartime ship floor inspired a militancy that would carry two of the women in these narratives on to union organizing in Barrie and Chatham. The similarities between their experience in war work and that of Black women in the United States is worth noting in a Canada that sees itself as being apart from the legacy of racism at the core of social, political, and economic development in Canada and the United States. Of the experience of Black women in the United States during the war Jones writes: 'often black women found their hard-won jobs in industry were not only segregated but the most dangerous and gruelling ones that a factory had to offer. During the war, certain men's jobs were converted to women's work and in the process down graded to lower pay and status, but others were converted to black women's work of ever greater inferiority. In aeroplane assembly plants, black women stood in stifling "dope rooms" filled with the nauseating fumes of glue, while white women sat on stools in the well ventilated serving room ... Elsewhere black women worked in ammunitions and gunpowder, poisonous plastic and acetone, scaling mud and hazardous equipment ... Furthermore, they were routinely assigned "disengaging" night shifts that imposed additional burdens on them as wives and mothers.'[17]

Albeit dressed up in patriotism, war factory work in the 1940s could not have been a bed of roses for white women either, but racism could be counted on to structure the shop floor and to exact the most harsh penalties from Black women. One example can be cited to show that every step of the way to equality was a fight and that mere entry into industrial labour could not eradicate racism: in 1946, Viola Desmond, a Black woman in New Glasgow, Nova Scotia, was arrested, spent a night in jail, went to trial, and was fined for sitting in the white section of a movie theatre. But as an old Black saying goes, 'you cut your dress to suit your cloth.' So despite the endemic racism in work and social structures, Black women (and men) in Canada grabbed on to the industrial wage and hung on for dear life.

My husband was overseas a couple of years. All of the men remember that they went overseas and gave up jobs or lost out on
education and everything, and when they came back it was very
hard to get a job. He retrained when he came back, along with
the rest of the soldiers, but it was not easy. He remembers the
long line up when they came back: nearly everybody else white
and he was standing in it – he and one other Black soldier. They
pointed right to my husband and they called him up to the front
and they told him right away: 'You! You go to the porters and get
a job there.' They just picked him right out of the line up like
that, but he really didn't want to go there.
Rella Braithwaite

They did not wish to return to the white people's kitchen
where there was isolation, no fair wage, no chance of mobility, nor any recourse for the 'personalized' racism of the employer. In a look at what she calls 'Black Women Workers
Demobilised and Redomesticated,' Jacqueline Jones examines
the impact of the end of the war on Black women workers:
'a government researcher noted that reconversion affected
Negroes more severely than white workers: from July 1945
to April 1946, for example, unemployment rates among non-
whites increased more than twice as much as among whites
... By 1948 most of the gains that blacks had derived from
the wartime boom had been wiped out, and labour analysts
predicted that, given the persistent marginality of black workers, their well being depended almost entirely on a strong
economy.'[18]

Escape as they tried, domestic work stared Black women in
the face once again. Most of the women in these narratives
did escape, but they faced hard times combining part-time
work, child-rearing, and efforts to seek work and careers
outside of domestic work. But if they were reluctant to go
back to domestic work, their Black Caribbean sisters were
not. Fleeing the bust of Caribbean economies in the 1950s,
these women came to Canada to fill the shortages in domestic
workers.

Linda Martin and Kerry Seagrave have examined the state

of domestic work in Canada after the war. 'At the end of the war the Canadian housewife faced the same domestic crisis (as in the U.S.). For Canada the solution lay in immigration, with thousands to be admitted into the country to become domestics. This practice was aided and abetted by the Canadian Government which did the recruiting in Europe. The Senate Committee on Immigration and Labour in an August 1946 report specifically mentioned the desirability of letting experienced foreign servants into the country.'[19] What Martin and Seagrave overlook is that when by 1949 the importation of European servants failed to make up the shortage, Black Caribbean women were imported to do the job. Nowhere do they mention race as a factor in the Canadian 'servant problem.' They do not mention the Caribbean Domestic Worker Scheme of the fifties (some were threatened with deportation in the 1970s), or the undoubtedly dubious but nevertheless racial distinction between European women imported as 'nannies' and Caribbean women as 'domestics.' While European women imported for domestic work would later blend into the white face of Canada, Black Caribbean women brought in as domestic workers would reinforce the stereotype of the Black woman as servant. Well into the sixties and beyond Black women continued to fight for a foothold in non-domestic labour. Even today, a disproportionate number of Black women work in institutionalized domestic work as nursing attendants and health-care aids, and in other service-sector jobs.

NOTES

1 Genevieve Leslie in J. Acton et al., eds, *Women at Work, 1850–1930* (Toronto: Women's Press 1974), 71.
2 James St G. Walker, *A History of Blacks in Canada: A Study Guide* (Ottawa: Ministry of State for Multiculturalism 1981), 132.
3 Jacqueline Jones, *Labor of Love, Labor of Sorrow* (New York: Vintage Books, Random House 1985), 200.

4 Ruth Roach Pierson, *'They're Still Women After All': The Second World War and Canadian Womanhood* (Toronto: McClelland & Stewart 1986), 22.

5 Robin Winks, *The Blacks in Canada* (Montreal: McGill-Queen's University Press 1971), 420–3.

6 Ibid., 423.

7 Pierson, *'They're Still Women'*, 27.

8 Ibid.

9 Ibid.

10 Walker, *History of Blacks*, 132.

11 Winks, *Blacks in Canada*, 388.

12 Pierson, *'They're Still Women'*, 32.

13 Ibid., 47.

14 Ibid., 61.

15 Jones, *Labor of Love*, 236–7.

16 Ibid., 208.

17 Ibid., 240.

18 Ibid., 257.

19 Linda Martin and Kerry Seagrave, *The Servant Problem* (North Carolina and London: McFarland and Co. 1985), 55.

6

African Canadian Women and the State: 'Labour only, please'

LINDA CARTY

Given the terms under which women of African descent in Canada (African Canadian, Black) first arrived in this country, as slaves and later as escaped slaves or newly freed women from the American South, they have long understood that they have been assigned just about the lowest status of any group in Canada at the time. Historically, these women have not had easy access to state services such as education and welfare, and have a long and documented history of working outside the home for wages. The legacy of this combined history has played a key role in defining the place of African Canadian women in contemporary Canada.

This chapter briefly sketches the relationship of African Canadian women to the state from the late eighteenth century and ends with some commentary on that relationship in contemporary Canada. The chapter does not give historical account of Black women's arrival in Canada; nor does it offer historical analysis of the lives of Black women in their early communities; indeed, the sources used here are secondary. The chapter provides an overview of the social context for the early arrivals of Black women in Canada, followed by a charting of the systemic patterns of their relations with the state, and shows that much of their experience has been shaped by their race and class. These relations remain remarkably unchanged today. Towards this end, I analyse the Canadian government's role in structuring the relationship between African Canadian women and the state by looking at Canada's postwar immigration policies and its recruiting of Black women specifically as domestics. That section of the chapter draws heavily on a 1988 Michigan State University doctoral dissertation by Ruth L. Harris. Harris's work is the most recent and most detailed on this topic. That race has long been the major organizing principle shaping opportunities for African Canadian women can best be seen in the development of Canada's settlement policy for the early Blacks from south of the border and in Canada's immigration policy for Blacks from other parts of the world. Since the early part of this century, immigration policy has consistently sought Black women from the Caribbean for the sole purpose of domestic labour in Canada. The social relations of women's labour in Canada have always determined an unequal and inferior place for Black women. It is not accidental that to this day most Black women in the Canadian labour force work in the service sector, though more than a few hold clerical jobs in that sector.

While there is a growing literature on labour priorities in Canadian immigration policy – much of it indicating how Canada has consistently shown a preference for immigrants from the British Isles, Western Europe, and Scandinavia, while practising overt discrimination against Poles, Italians, and Jews, for example, as non-preferred peoples at one time or another – none of this literature critically examines the racialist overtone of Canadian immigration policy as it has affected peoples of African descent.[1] Therefore, for the purposes of my argument, these works are not relevant.

As most of the other chapters in this book point out, the dearth of written records about Black women in Canada makes any attempt to place them in history a formidable task. In academia, the history of African Canadians, a people of an oral tradition, has little legitimacy without written documentation. Yet the patterns of state rule and state influence as these affect Black people in general, and Black women in particular, are evident all around us.

Defining the State

There are perhaps as many notions of what the state is as there are studies of it.[2] There is indeed some difficulty in studying the state,[3] the difficulty revolving around questions such as the following.

What is the state? Is it an idea? Is it the agent of political power in the capitalist social formation? Is the state a political entity that gives neutrality to all political practice? In the case of the Canadian state, how did its formation come about? Did the Canadian state's origin as a settler colony and its eventual evolution into permanence by decimating the First Nations determine its perspective on race? Is the state a system of political practice, government, and the many institutions whose ideological function is to sustain capitalism?

If there is any consensus among today's scholars who study the state, it is that the state is not an instrument that is manipulated by the ruling class.[4] For purposes of my argument, the state is the system of ideological structures within an advanced capitalist social formation that is represented in institutions and agencies of political and administrative control centred in government. Order and domination, for that matter, are maintained through a system of historically specific relations of ruling.[5] And while the state is not an instrument of ruling-class control, the policies and practices implemented in its name more substantially benefit the ruling class than any other.

The workings of the state are manifested as a relation of dominance by a white male ruling élite that is sustained through ideological hegemony, eliminating the need for direct manipulation, force, or conspiracy. These are unnecessary because there is no incongruity between the ideology of hegemony by the ruling élite and the perceptions most people hold of their position in society in relation to that élite. That is, the white male hegemony is accepted by most and that acceptance in some way legitimates the state, albeit as an illusory entity.[6] One author captures the notion of illusion when he states:

> The state is not the reality which stands behind the mask of political practice. It is itself the mask which prevents our seeing political practice as it is. It is, one could almost say, the mind of a mindless world, the purpose of purposeless conditions, the opium of the citizen ... The state comes into being as a structuation within political practice; it starts its life as an implicit construct; it is then reified – as the (res publica), the public reification, no less – and acquires an overt symbolic identity progressively divorced from practice as an illusory account of practice. The ideological function is extended to a point where conservatives and radicals alike believe that their practice is not directed at each other but at the state; the world of illusion prevails.[7]

It is perhaps important that we not conclude that the state seeks to accomplish, or currently enjoys, a sort of unitary relation with the capitalist class, or even with specific fractions of that class, but it is equally important to understand the privileges that capital affords that class in relation to the state.

The Canadian state's early formation came about through France's exploitation of fur trapping, through which First Nations peoples secured their livelihood. This evolved into a well-developed fur trade, with France ultimately securing the region as a settler colony.

The settlement passed between France and Britain through warfare, with the British eventually securing it permanently as a colony. The British relationship with the First Nations peoples evolved into one of the dispossession of these peoples from their lands, their displacement onto reserves, and, in 1867, the formation of the Dominion of Canada, an independent post-colonial state.

There is no work available on the racial formation of the Canadian state. However, when we look at specific state practices – such as the oppression of First Nations peoples, the internment of the Japanese during the Second World War, the call by Prime Minister Mackenzie King in 1947 to exclude Asian immigrants, and, in more recent times, the response by different state officials to a racialist outcry by the dominant society that African Canadians are responsible for rising street crime in some of Canada's metropolitan areas – we see that race has long been a *key* organizing principle of social relations by the state.[8] In May 1992, following some incidents of social unrest in Toronto, Premier Bob Rae of Ontario commissioned Stephen Lewis, as his adviser on race relations, to consult widely across the province and report on the state of race relations. Lewis reported:

What we are dealing with, at root, and fundamentally, is anti-Black racism ... It is Blacks who are being shot, it is Black youth that is unemployed in excessive numbers, it is Black students who are inappropriately streamed in schools, it is Black kids who are disproportionately dropping-out, it is housing communities with large concentrations of Black residents where the sense of vulnerability is most acute, it is Black employees, professional and non-professional, on whom the doors of upward equity slam shut. Just as the soothing balm of 'multiculturalism' cannot mask racism, so racism cannot mask its primary target.[9]

African Canadians have always been in a relationship of social subordination in dealing with the state. It is irrelevant whether the relationship is with the government, the judicial system, the education or social-welfare systems, or any other state-controlled or state-influenced institution. The defining feature of the relationship has been Eurocentrism, that is, an insistence on the centrality of Franco- and Anglo-Canadian concerns to the exclusion of all others. Inherently, it is a relationship of racial superiority.

Early Arrival of Blacks in Canada

As Bristow and Hamilton show in their chapters, Blacks have

been in Canada for well over three hundred years.[10] They were brought first as slaves to New France in the early seventeenth century. Later, in the late eighteenth to early nineteenth centuries, they came as Loyalists after the American War of Independence (1776) and the War of 1812. Finally, they came as fugitives from slavery and, in the case of free Blacks, as fugitives from racism in the United States, fleeing via the Underground Railroad[11] to what they hoped would be a better life.[12]

The provincial parliament in Upper Canada passed an act in 1793 that attempted to do away with slavery gradually, 'without violating private property.'[13] The idea was simultaneously to erase a section of the Imperial Act of 1790, which allowed new settlers to the Americas from the United Kingdom to import into the province 'any Negro, Household Furniture, Utensils of Husbandry, and Clothing, free of Duty.'[14] while not offending those who already had slaves here. The large landowners opposed the Act of 1793, citing their need for slaves as workers in the fields. 'Slavery was clearly supported by the State: the 47th Article of Capitulation of Montreal in 1760 guaranteed slave ownership, and the Peace Treaty of 1763 and the Quebec Act of 1774 upheld this guarantee.'[15]

Blacks who arrived in Canada after 1793 found themselves free to do as they pleased within the constraints governing a people with few legal protections. Like others who came after the complete abolition of slavery in 1833 to the western provinces of Alberta, Saskatchewan, and British Columbia, they immediately settled in and got to work making themselves a new life. This was not an easy task, however, as they encountered many obstacles from whites in general, and even from the government.[16]

After the American Civil War, Blacks who had previously come to Canada because of its reputation for civility began returning to the northern states and even to the South. We can safely conclude that they found little difference in the two countries, and at least they had more relatives and friends in the United States. For most it was 'home.' Canada had made some legal allowances, such as the allocation of land grants, for Blacks to come and stay, but these were not accompanied by social comforts.[17]

In his comprehensive history of Blacks in Canada, Robin Winks provides many examples of what life was like for peoples of African descent by the mid-nineteenth century. He points, for example, to a Toronto city councillor who, in 1864, insisted on referring to Blacks as 'niggers,' until many Black voters in the city protested.[18] A similar case of insensitivity to and disrespect for Blacks is seen in the case of some French Canadians, who, upon being demobilized in Windsor after fighting in the northern army, chose to celebrate their release by staging a raid on a Black 'church during Sunday evening service.'[19]

It seems that while the government and many white people in early Canada were opposed to the practice of slavery by their next-door neighbour, it was more through self-righteousness than a belief in the equality of peoples. This is obvious in the relationship between white settlers and the First Nations people they met in Canada.[20] Euro-Canadians waited with keen interest for U.S. President Lincoln's Emancipation Proclamation, which had been delayed until 1863, to prove the commitment of the North to abolition. Once the proclamation came, many feared it would lead to a massive influx of Blacks into Canada.[21] This irony is not lost on African Canadians today as we witness similar fears by the white population whenever the federal government moves to increase the number of non-white immigrants. It is not accidental that some of Canada's lowest immigration quotas have consistently been for peoples of African descent.[22]

The fears of whites after the passing of the Emancipation Proclamation proved unjustified, but served to intensify the misery of Blacks. In 1850, in an apparent attempt to allay the mounting fears of whites, the Ontario legislature had passed a law that resulted in Black children being prohibited from attending public school. For twenty years before this law, the actions of hostile white parents kept Black children out of the schools. The specific section of the act that 'made legal' this practice read: 'Upon application in writing of five or more heads of families resident in a township, town or village, being coloured people, the council of the township or the board of public school trustees of the city, town or village shall authorize the establishment therin of one or more separate schools for coloured people.'[23] The wording of the act did not specifically deny Blacks the right to attend school, but that is precisely how its ambiguous language was interpreted by white school boards and town councils. The state was not always blatant in instituting discriminatory policies against people of African descent, and may often have voiced Canada's general antislavery sentiment. But its actions were more often than not in support of its overwhelmingly racist white populace. For example, new Black refugees who had arrived post-1850 were refused jobs and many who were already in the country were actively encouraged to return to the United States.[24]

To surmount these obstacles Blacks developed survival skills that made their communities virtually self-sufficient and set up their own organizations: the many abolitionist societies in different towns and provinces, women's support groups such as Mothers Unions, which started in the church, and the African Baptist Association of Nova Scotia, founded in 1854.[25] And, as other chapters of this book point out, there were many qualified teachers, most of them women, in the Black community. Thus, when the children were not allowed in government schools, these women started their own schools so Black children would not be denied formal education. The community also took care of its sick, and those who could work did what they could to earn a wage.

Early free Black arrivals in Canada settled in towns and villages that, in some cases, had few or no whites. Some managed to purchase land, while others took advantage of land grants from the government. For example, Black veterans of the War of 1812 were offered land grants in Ontario's Simcoe

County. In some cases, however, Black Loyalists never received the promised land grants but were encouraged instead to become labourers on white farms. Frequently the land offered to Blacks was extremely remote and proved difficult to settle; nevertheless, the new refugees and immigrants settled wherever they could.[26]

In Ontario, some of the earliest and most well-known Black communities included Oro, Wilberforce, Buxton, Chatham, and Amherstburg. In eastern Canada, mainly Nova Scotia, some three thousand Black Loyalists who arrived shortly after the American War of Independence represented the first large influx of Blacks into that part of the country. As was the practice of the Crown of all Loyalists, they received land grants from the government. Since these lands were grouped together, Blacks were settled in segregated communities. Some of the Nova Scotia communities settled in the late eighteenth century, then, included Birchtown, Shelburne, and the northern part of Preston Township. As in Ontario, many of the plots granted to Blacks were much smaller than those granted to whites and could not be farmed because they were of such poor quality.[27] Not all land grants received by whites were ideal either. Often there were discrepancies between what poor whites had been promised in land grants and what they were given.

Reading Women into These Practices

It is difficult to know what life was like for Black women in these early times. Much of the scant history that has been written about Blacks in Canada has been by and about men. The social relations of gender have traditionally made women subordinate to men and more socially and economically disadvantaged than men. Furthermore, women of the past three centuries – the era of early-to-modern capitalist development spanning the period from when Blacks were brought to Canada – and, indeed, women throughout much of this century, derived their status from men. Regardless of their contributions to the family or community, women were not seen as independent beings. Black women shared slavery with Black men, both having been relegated to similar dehumanizing experiences as slaves,[28] though Black women had the added trauma of rape. The shared suffering of Black women and Black men meant that some measure of shared labour characterized the domestic life of freed Black men and women. Nevertheless, we may safely assume that Black women in early Canada, as part of an evolving capitalist system that depended in part on women's subordination to men for its advancement, found life much more difficult than men did. The degree of difficulty came from the structured gender inequality, compounded by the racism and anti-working-class bias experienced by the Black population in general.

Initially, Black settlements, at least in Upper Canada, were populated by many more men than women, if only because during their early arrivals in Canada as fugitive slaves and refugees, more men could escape than women. As Adrienne Shadd's chapter shows, women who decided to flee north on the Underground Railroad suffered extreme hardship despite their valiant efforts, determination, and incredible strength as individuals. However, they formed much smaller groupings than male runaways.

When they arrived in the North, some of these women picked up their lives with husbands who had left earlier and were now settled in their new country. Countless others, however, married and single, escaped alone because their husbands were afraid or unwilling to take the risks with them, and they were women determined to be free at *any* cost. Harriet Tubman, a married slave women, escaped alone and subsequently devoted all her time before the American Civil War to the abolitionist cause. She was a forerunner of the Underground Railroad and personally led some three hundred slaves to freedom in Canada.[29] After the war, Tubman was involved in women's organizations fighting for the rights of Black women.

For such women, freedom from slavery had everything to

do with determination. History had taught them that Black people needed to be strong and resilient and that, as Black women, their lives were structured so that they could not depend on the male wage. They had to be economically independent. As E. Franklin Frazier states in *The Negro Family in the United States*, Black women, unlike white women, did not learn 'the spirit of subordination to masculine authority by either economic necessity or tradition.'[30] Black women's self-reliance and independence are two of the inevitable results of slavery, and point to a significant difference between Black and white women.

Where white women were socialized to be dependent on their men, Black women could not assume such 'privilege' because of the socially ascribed inferior location of Black men. Indeed, Black women's efforts and work often formed the backbone of slave communities. An Angela Davis points out, because domestic life provided the only opportunities for slave men and women to live as human beings, 'Black women, for this reason – and also because they were workers just like their men – were not debased by their domestic functions in the way that white women came to be. Unlike their white counterparts, they could never be treated as mere 'housewives.'[31] Rape and other forms of exploitation commonly faced by Black women under slavery also effected a significant difference in the social construction of womanhood for Black and white women and further defined the role of housewife as one exclusively for white women.[32] In the sexual exploitation of Black women, Davis asserts,

[it] is important to remember that the punishment inflicted on women exceeded in intensity the punishment suffered by their men, for women were not only whipped and mutilated, they were also *raped*.

It would be a mistake to regard the institutionalized pattern of rape during slavery as an expression of white men's sexual urges, otherwise stifled by the specter of white womanhood's chastity. That would be far too simplistic an explanation. Rape was a weapon of domination, a weapon of repression, whose covert goal was to extinguish slave women's will to resist, and in the process, to demoralize their men.[33]

State Support Services and the Black Population

As noted earlier, the young Canadian state was not very forthcoming with help for new arrivals of African descent. Nor was the Euro-Canadian community at large very welcoming. Many newly arrived whites were given large tracts of good-quality land and were encouraged to settle in areas where they could be relatively close to any support services. Of course, even within white settlements, class sometimes determined status and, therefore, the land grants residents received. So there were odd cases of whites being granted plots that turned out to be rocky and not suitable for farming. There was sometimes a discrepancy between what was promised and what was delivered. But whites often found avenues for redress. Newly arrived Blacks from the United States, by contrast, were not so lucky.[34] Frequently, they were offered land in uninhabited and therefore inaccessible areas. Most eked out an existence and through their determination developed full-fledged communities with churches, homes, and schools.[35] Some went on to do very well. By the mid-nineteenth century, for example, quite a number of the Blacks who had settled in Canada West 'were relatively prosperous. In some areas the Negroes were numerous enough to make their electoral support worth having. Several leading Canadian politicians sympathized with them, and one, the Irish-Canadian leader D'Arcy McGee, seems to have made attempts to include them in his following.'[36]

Blacks may never be institutionally recognized as contributing to Canada's frontier society, but they certainly comprised a significant part of its pioneer communities. Their labour contributed to shaping that early Canada, and despite all the odds, including persistent institutional racial discrimination, they have survived as a people.

Historical Development of Waged Work for African Canadian Women

Since their arrival in Canada, it is the women of the African Canadian communities who have kept the communities going. These women have never had their rightful place in history, even in the history reported by Black men, despite the significant contribution of some works. Black women's economic role means that they have occupied a central and not merely a supporting position.

African Canadian women have managed to keep their families intact when men had to be absent for employment or other reasons. They played a major role in the churches, a focal point of Black communities, and held positions of power in the missionary societies that were the centres for women's work in the church. In education, as some other chapters emphasize, it was the women who turned the schools into a source of strength for African Canadian communities often besieged by racial discrimination. For example, when Blacks were prevented from attending state schools and started their own, most of the teachers in these schools were women. Some dedicated their entire adult lives to teaching without gaining much financial remuneration. They instilled pride and hope into the young African Canadians in their charge,[37] using the school and their knowledge to educate the larger Black community about its role and rights in Canadian society. Thus, from the first arrival of Black people in Canada, many women entered teaching, and Black women continue to be attracted to it today.

In Black women's lives waged work has always been a central feature. However, most of the jobs that they have had access to have been in the service sector. When they hold jobs in the professions, they are in fields that have evolved historically as 'women's work,' and that require domestic labour skills. These fields are primarily nursing and teaching. There is no documented evidence of early African Canadian women entering the formal health-care profession as nurses. But we do know that in early African Canadian communities women worked as nurses, taking care of the sick and assisting as midwives in childbirth, as did white women in their own communities across Canada.

Bernice Redmond was the first Black Canadian registered nurse. She worked in public health. Ms Redmond received her nursing education and training in the United States, graduating in 1945. About one year later, the Nova Scotia Department of Health hired her.[38] We know that prior to the turn of the century, and even as late as the Second World War, Black women were not allowed to work as nurses in clinics or hospitals.[39] Across Canada, they were denied the opportunity to train as nurses, as indicated by Ms Redmond's need to go to the United States for her nurse's training. Many African Canadian organizations worked to help Blacks overcome the obstacles to improving their lives. Often Black women turned to these groups for assistance in getting higher education and in entering the professions. One of the better-known cases in this regard in nursing is that of Vivien Layne, an African Canadian woman in the 1930s in Quebec, who tried unsuccessfully to gain admission to a Montreal hospital to study nursing. At the time, the Universal Negro Improvement Association (UNIA), an organization with a philosophy of encouraging Blacks to help themselves and to help others help themselves, was in its early stages. The UNIA spent a great deal of time and effort trying to find a hospital in Montreal that would accept Vivien Layne. When that turned out to be impossible, they looked to the United States, and she left to study nursing at a hospital in New York. She too returned to Canada, a practice the UNIA always encouraged, and eventually got a nursing job.[40]

The development of nursing in Canada followed a very similar path to that in the United States. Up to the turn of the century, nurses in both countries were part of the same labour union, one that did not accept Blacks as members. In the States, however, Black women could and did attend college and study nursing. Furthermore, they formed their own nursing associations.[41] Today, in Canada, one of the few professions with a high number of Black women is nursing, though most work at the lowest levels.

Historically, in waged work, most Black women have not been employed in nursing or teaching but in service-sector work, that is, primarily in jobs requiring domestic skills: as cleaners, cooks, seamstresses, household help, and so on. A small number have also worked as weavers. This type of employment has shaped Black women's participation in the Canadian labour market.

Canadian feminist analyses of women's role in the labour market have documented gender segregation, showing that being female is the primary indicator for what women work at. There is considerable literature about working women, showing that most of what women do in the workplace bears a great deal of similarity to what they do in the household, that is, work that requires domestic skills. As a result, women's work is not considered of equal value to men's and women frequently do not receive equal pay, even when they are employed in the same job as men.[42] Because capitalism has treated the family as a private not a public institution there is no value attached to domestic skills. Thus, employers use women as part of the reserve army of labour, the last hired and the first fired.

For all the insight these Canadian feminist studies bring to analyzing women's undervalued contribution in the workforce and the gender segregation of the labour market, none of the authors thought it necessary to look at the impact of race on the labour market or to examine how race further segregates the gendered labour force. For example, while labour-force segregation by gender defines all women's labour at a lower value than that of men, race further defines some women's labour as worth less than that of others. To analyse the situation of white women in the labour force as applicable to *all* women, as all these studies have done, is no small oversight. Looking at the history of Black women's struggle in the labour force clearly reveals the manner in which race further compounds the gender discrimination these women encounter in waged work.

Black Women and Domestic Work

Throughout this century in North America, Black women have been employed as domestics. As Adrienne Shadd states in her chapter, the sexual division of labour on the plantation afforded slave men the skilled positions; thus, when they escaped they stood a chance of eventually finding work as artisans or craftsmen. Black women, by contrast, had no such opportunities.[43] In the changing labour market, domestic jobs were the only ones available to them in their flight north. Hence it was their domestic labour that they sold. For six years Harriet Tubman worked the Underground Railroad from a base in St Catharines, Ontario. To finance new arrivals for short periods until they could move on Tubman did cooking and house-cleaning for people in the town. It was the same kind of work she had done when she first moved to the northern states from the South and began her legendary work helping slaves to escape.

Although Black women had no other marketable skills and could only do domestic work immediately after slavery, they were not unique in this regard. Most women of that era, Black or white, were in a similar position, that is, defined by gender and thus by their domestic labour. The difference is that Black's women's race and gender placed them in a position where they could not depend on their husbands' waged work to maintain their families. And though many working-class white women also had to work outside the home – because many if not most working-class men did not earn a 'family wage' – segregation shut Black women out of most working-class jobs. Furthermore, whatever other skills Black women may have had, it is unlikely that these would have made a difference in their hiring. Racism was practised in a much less covert manner then and was endemic in Canadian society. While much may have changed over the years, today's labour market is similarly structured by race and gender, with a systematic pattern of Black women being seen as well suited to domestic work. The Canadian state supports this belief by immigration policies that foster the migration of Black women as part of its foreign domestic program. But more on this later.

The Historical Development of Domestic Work

Domestic work had always played a major role in the lives of women in Canada and in the development of the Canadian economy. Prior to the First World War it was openly said that women's place was in the home; thus, any perception of women working was clearly connected to what women did in the home. In the first decade of the twentieth century there were many changes in the Canadian economy, including the increasing importance of the manufacturing and trade sectors, which led to many new jobs and, combined with an upsurge in immigration, resulted in a sudden increase in the number of women working outside the home.[44]

The development of the manufacturing sector meant that many of the jobs that women previously did in the home – jobs that made up the cottage and craft industry, such as making clothes and preserving and canning fruits and vegetables – had become factory work. Thus, women's waged work primarily consisted of jobs that closely resembled their domestic jobs. Indeed, the Canadian census of 1891 listed dressmakers, servants, teachers, seamstresses, and housekeepers as the five leading occupations for women.[45]

Between 1891 and 1921, the number of domestics as a percentage of the female workforce fell by 23 per cent, that is, from 41 to 18 per cent.[46] This was the beginning of the decline in status of domestic work. As Genevieve Leslie states in her study of domestic work in Canada between 1880 and 1920:

It was not considered an integral part of the economy, and to a large extent was excluded from economic and political discussion. It was

'non-productive' service labour; it took place in the home and depended upon the personal relationship between employer and em-
ployee; it involved no significant outlay of capital and produced no
direct profit. In a society based on the production of commodities
for sale and profit, domestic labour was progressively devalued as
production was removed from the home.[47]

Industrialization brought most white women options. They
could now refuse domestic work because other jobs offered
better wages and working conditions.

Industrialization, did not, however, mean that the need for
domestic work had declined. The increasing urbanization of
the Canadian population and the growth and entrenching of
the middle class, together with the advances in household
technology, meant that housework became more and more
'industrialized' and was relegated to the 'housewife.' It was
logical, then, for households to have fewer domestics. By 1921
there was one domestic for every twenty-one households.[48]
With fewer domestics the demand for those with specialized
skills, those who performed one service only, such as child
care, grew. For these workers Canada turned to immigration
– to England, Ireland, and Scotland – for the immigrant domestic worker. During the first thirteen years of this century
Canada brought in 170,000 domestic workers from these
countries. This became a common practice, and as a result,
before the Second World War, 75 per cent of all domestic
workers in Canada had come from the United Kingdom.[49]

In the meantime, African Canadian women who arrived in
this country centuries earlier still worked largely as domestic
helpers in the cities and towns. They were unable to join the
large numbers of women who could afford to reject domestic
work. No did they get into the relatively privileged sector of
specialized domestic work. Most worked as farm help or in
the household as cleaners, laundresses, and general helpers.
Black women were hired as farm help long before it was common for other women to be doing such work. For example,
as Marjorie Cohen points out in her study on women's work

in nineteenth-century Ontario, women's paid farm labour was quite scarce. She quotes from a Mary O'Brien, writing in 1832 of this scarcity: 'Edward has hired a great tall black girl to take up potatoes with the little Hunts. This is worthy of note because it is the first time we have ever had female Canadians as farm servants, though in my farming days I got some days' work at odd times from some English girls who were living on the farm, but this rather as a freak than anything else.'[50]

Because of the stratification and segmentation of the labour market by race, however, Black women domestics were paid much less than the white women who did these jobs. As indicated in some of the accounts in Dionne Brand's chapter, even as recently as the 1930s and 1940s, some African Canadian domestics got clothing and car fare in lieu of wages.

Before 1920, most of the recruiting of domestics happened through private agencies, less by the state. Similarly, a number of social services, such as welfare and benevolence, were provided by the church and private agencies. But with the onset of industrialization these services were gradually assumed by the state. Although domestic service received little recognition by the state as work of any significant value, domestic labour was becoming increasingly important to Canadian industrialization.

By the third decade of this century, the changing competition of the class structure in Canada that accompanied the advancement of capitalism meant a decline in the number of families that could afford to employ domestic help. But with increasing urbanization and the importance of waged labour, the significance of domestic service to the expanding middle class grew. According to Leslie, the requests to the Department of Immigration at this time for maids came more from small commodity producers, professionals such as engineers and medical officers, and some senior civil servants than previously.[51]

Leslie's study paid no attention to race in the forty-year period covered, leaving the impression that domestic service work was the province solely of white women. More accurately, the state and private recruiting agencies recognized only white women as domestics. But we do know that African Canadian women have always been involved in waged work; it has been essential to their existence. We also know that before the Second World War domestic work was about the only type of work to which they had access. Increasingly since the 1920s, race has played a significant role in the changing face of domestic work in Canada. In his study of Blacks in Canada, James Walker states: 'in 1941, 80% of Black adult females in Montreal were employed as domestic servants.'[52] We have no reason to assume that the situation was not the same across the country. The extremely high percentage was most likely occasioned by the war. As Brand points out in her chapter, white women replaced white men in the labour force. For the first time, Black women were able to enter the labour force in jobs other than domestic service, albeit in marginal positions deemed either unsafe or unsuitable for white women. Similarly, many Black women got domestic-service jobs doing the household chores of the white women who were now employed in waged work.

State Ideology, Immigration Policy, and the Recruiting of Black Women as Domestics

Employment and Immigration Canada, the agency controlling the admission of workers into the country as domestics, is an important federal-government department and a primary institution of the Canadian state. Through its immigration laws the state regulates the selection or rejection of prospective domestic workers as immigrants. State ideology has an important role in determining and defining the needs and demands of the economy, and controls the requirements and human flow to meet those needs. Immigration laws are designed accordingly and coincide with the interests, including those of class and race, of the dominant class, even when such laws carry the appearance of neutrality and are aimed at meeting the needs of what is purported to be, by the state, an equal citizenry. As Karl Marx points out in *The German Ideology*: 'The ideas of the ruling class are in every epoch the ruling ideas: i.e., the class which is the ruling material force of society, is at the same time its ruling intellectual force ... and it is the state's function ... to guarantee the property and interests of the bourgeoisie.'[53] Indeed, Canadian immigration policy plays a central role in fostering the illusion of the state as a neutral entity, whereby the role of the ideology of race and class, concretized in its most negative form as discrimination, is lost.

In 1942, at the beginning of a boom in the Canadian economy, the Canadian director of immigration stated: 'In times of prosperity when there is a scarcity of labour in Canada, there is always a proposal to bring in classes of labour which at other times is neither sought nor welcomed.'[54] As Brand points out in her chapter, the industrial expansion stemming from the war industry in the 1940s brought an increasing consumerism and with it increased labour needs. Further expansion of the Canadian economy in the postwar period necessitated an increase in immigration, which coincided with the recruiting of domestics by the federal government. As immigration increased, the state's concern to monitor who and how many would be allowed to enter Canada led to the government's direct involvement in the recruiting and allocation of domestic workers, as with other labour, to meet the needs of the expanding economy and middle class. Thus, less and less of the task of recruiting domestics fell to private agencies than had been the practice in the past.

Increasingly, domestic work became a race-bound occupation, work synonymous with Black women. The Canadian state played a major role in this designation, yet the state consistently resisted the immigration of Black women to Canada as domestics. In other words, severely curtailing the immigration flow of Black women to Canada was a primary objective of immigration officials, even as they turned to Black women as a last resort to meet an increasing demand for domestic workers. In 1942, the director of immigration was responding to a request for domestics from the Caribbean when he said:

Canada's coloured population has not increased rapidly and while that is to some extent due to our climate it is also due in no small measure to the immigration policy that has been pursued for years. The Immigration regulations reflect the immigration policy and while there is not what one would call a colour line, there is something that comes very close to a racial line, for example, immigration of the Asiatic races has been strictly controlled in recent years ... I did not make the regulations that I have to administer and yet I recognize that these were framed with the purpose of encouraging certain types of immigrants and discouraging others and among the latter is immigration of the negro race.[55]

Immediately following the Second World War, Canadian immigration officials were intent on not expanding immigration.[56] In 1947, responding to the criticism that Canada's immigration policy was discriminatory, then Canadian Prime Minister William Lyon Mackenzie King stated in the House of Commons: 'Canada is perfectly within her rights in selecting the persons whom we regard as desirable future citizens. It is not a "fundamental human right" of any alien to enter Canada. It is a privilege.'[57] This has been the policy of the Canadian state even when Canada needed immigrants because it could not otherwise augment its labour force. From Prime Minister King's and subsequent immigration officials' point of view, however, the argument is presented as Canada not wanting to bring in more immigrants than it has the capacity to absorb.

For African Canadians and for Blacks from other parts of the world wishing to enter Canada as new immigrants, the criticism of Canadian immigration policy has not been that Canada should not exercise its right to choose, but that that right should be exercised fairly. Instead, we have continually seen white immigrants being granted immigrant status much more easily and much more frequently than non-whites, regardless of skills, the number of relatives already in the country, or other so-called necessary criteria.

African Canadians have long been critical of discrimination in Canada in general and of Canadian immigration policy in particular. In the 1940s and 1950s, members of the Brotherhood of Sleeping Car Porters, a predominantly Black union of railway workers across Canada, were outspoken on human-rights issues. Some became vocal members of the Committee for Human Rights of the Canadian Labour Congress, representing the Congress and Black workers. One of these union activists, Stanley G. Grizzle, in the 1950s, 'organized deputations to meet with the provincial and federal governments to discuss antidiscrimination legislation, appeared often on radio and television, and plunged into the controversial area of immigration policy as spokesperson (together with Donald Moore, President of Toronto's new Negro Citizen's Association) for the first delegation of Canadian blacks to meet – on April 27, 1954 – with members of the federal cabinet in order to discuss discrimination against West Indian applicants.'[58] There were mass meetings and a persistent campaign throughout the 1950s by African Canadian organizations in Toronto and Montreal[59] protesting discrimination in Canadian immigration policy against immigrants of West Indian origin. As a result, in 1962 there was a substantial increase in the numbers of immigrants from the Caribbean.

Successive immigration polices have shown that white immigrants are preferred. In the rare instances that the Canadian state has allowed relatively large numbers of non-whites to migrate to Canada, it has been because Canada stood to gain, primarily economically. This is the case with the large numbers of upper- and middle-class immigrants currently being admitted from Hong Kong. Canada has been accused by many, including those representing refugee groups and many others waiting to see if their sponsored relatives will be allowed in, of selling landed-immigrant status. In the face of the evidence,[60] to label Canadian immigration policy as discriminatory is hardly unfair or inaccurate.

By 1948, the total annual number of immigrants allowed into Canada had reached 125,414, but in 1949 the number fell to 95,217.[61] To many, particularly to residents of poor non-white countries that were members of the Commonwealth of Nations like Canada, Canada's immigration policy still seemed discriminatory and was often criticized.

The 1952 Immigration Act was passed specifically to begin a period of intensive foreign labour recruitment for Canada. It marked the first time that Blacks were allowed into the country in any significant numbers, and most came from the Caribbean. By 1970, Black immigrants had moved up in rank, from almost the bottom of the list of ethnic groups entering Canada to third place, just behind immigrants from the United Kingdom and Italy.[62] There were three primary ways that Blacks entered Canada as new immigrants: (1) sponsored by relatives who were Canadian citizens, (2) as unsponsored individuals of exceptional merit, and (3) as employer-sponsored labourers who came through government-instituted work schemes. The latter group included seasonal farm workers, nurses, and domestics who came under bilateral government agreements that allowed them to enter under a special category, bypassing the existing regulations governing permanent immigrants.[63]

The temporary shift in Canadian immigration policy that allowed non-whites into the country did not come about as an act of generosity or benevolence by the Canadian state. Nor was it the result of a new awareness that brought about a change in the government's previous discriminatory policies. Instead, it was the result of pressure from the international community on Canada, which was in an ascendant position in the world community, to modify its position in the arena of 'international relations away from a Eurocentric focus to more interactions with the Third World.'[64] The pressure came largely from the new Commonwealth of Nations, Great Britain, and the newly independent countries of Asia and the Caribbean. Increasingly, then, since the Second World War, more of Canada's immigrants have come from the so-called Third World.

A common practice of many advanced capitalist countries, most notably Britain and the United States, has been to relax immigration policies during economic boom periods, to increase the labour supply. Canada too has engaged in this practice to meet its expanding labour needs. The designated slots in the labour market for many, if not most, of the immigrants from Third World countries have been in the service sector.

The West Indian Domestic Scheme

In 1955, Canada's director of immigration wrote the deputy minister:

It is not by accident that coloured British subjects other than the negligible numbers from the United Kingdom are excluded from Canada. It is from experience, generally speaking, that coloured people in the present state of the white man's thinking are not a tangible community asset, and as a result are more or less ostracized. They do not assimilate readily and pretty much vegetate to a low standard of living. Despite what has been said to the contrary, many cannot adapt themselves to our climatic conditions. To enter into an agreement which would have the effect of increasing coloured immigration to this country would be an act of misguided generosity since it would not have the effect of bringing about a worthwhile solution to the problem of coloured people and would quite likely intensify our own social and economic problem.[65]

In her well-researched study of Canadian immigration policies on the recruiting of foreign labour, specifically Caribbean female domestic workers from the 1950s to 1980s, Ruth L. Harris documents a systematic pattern of racialist beliefs displayed by the Canadian state and of staunch resistance to the immigration of West Indian (Caribbean) nationals, even after prospective employers repeatedly argued their need for

Caribbean immigrants as seasonal farm labourers and domestics.[66] Employers argued that recruiting in the Caribbean would be cheaper owing to its relative proximity to Canada, thus resulting in minimal administrative costs. Furthermore, wages would be lower than those paid to white workers. Caribbean domestics, unlike earlier European domestic workers, would be more likely to remain in their jobs because of the bilateral agreement.

As Harris points out, the government tried to recruit domestics from white countries in the Commonwealth before turning to the Caribbean. 'So reluctant were they to admit black immigrants that the enforcement of Eurocentric immigration became quite expensive and erratic.'[67] State officials justified their reluctance by citing public reaction, the costs of providing social services – particularly medical care – for workers entering the country for an unspecified period, and the problem of marriage with Canadian citizens.[68] Eventually, meetings between Canadian immigration officials and Caribbean officials resulted in a special order allowing groups of women from the Caribbean to come to Canada as domestics, starting in July 1955.

The Canadian state's initial resistance to immigration by Caribbean women was predicated solely on racism. Indeed, the 1955 scheme was not Canada's first attempt to recruit Caribbean women as domestics. Back in 1921 a successful, though short-lived, program brought domestics from Guadeloupe in the French-speaking Caribbean to Quebec. This program was initially quite popular. It was subsequently terminated and all the unmarried women were returned to the Caribbean with children born in Canada.[69] Thus, the Canadian state was very familiar with the potential implications of a successful domestic scheme for Canada and its immigration department would be in charge of the 'stringent controls on the selection, entry and mobility of limited numbers of immigrants.'[70]

The 1955 Domestic Scheme was an employer-sponsored program that brought women from the English-speaking Caribbean, primarily Jamaica, Trinidad, and Barbados. During the seven years[71] that it lasted, hundreds, possibly thousands, of women came to Canada annually to do the work that white women had now refused. Small numbers of white women from Europe were still being sponsored as child-care workers, that is, 'nannies,' a term that carries a higher status than 'domestics,' its signifier being the difference in race. To qualify for the Scheme, Caribbean women were required to have at least a grade eight[72] education – though most had higher and many were qualified nurses and teachers. They also had to be between the ages of eighteen and thirty-five, with no dependents, and had to pass a medical examination. Canadian immigration officials visited Caribbean countries annually to interview final applicants.[73]

The small numbers of women chosen for the Scheme allowed the Caribbean governments to hand-pick the women according to the standards set by Canada's Department of Immigration. Canadian officials argued that the small numbers of women chosen contributed to the success of the Scheme, an advantage they claimed was sure to be jeopardized if a larger volume of such workers were admitted.[74] The Scheme so satisfied Canadian immigration officials that they suggested 'that consideration be given to the philosophy of even sending somebody from Indian Affairs Branch to the British West Indies to study their organization, as it could be very useful in the training of [North American] Indian girls for this type of employment.'[75]

The Scheme as a bilateral agreement gave control over the women to both the home government and the Canadian government. In advertising for recruits, Caribbean governments stated that the women were being admitted to Canada potentially as permanent immigrants, though the numbers were quite small. On the Canadian side, despite some concerns by the state – for example, over possible protests from employers for the loss of a needed and known commodity should the government decide suddenly to end the Scheme – the Canadian government unabashedly stated: 'There is little danger of these girls, once admitted, leaving domestic employment to seek higher wages in industry for there are very limited opportunities for them in Canada in other than domestic service.'[76]

This control was maintained on the Canadian side through yearly follow-up surveys to determine the status of the women who arrived through the Scheme. These surveys showed that while a number of the women changed jobs, 'few left domestic service in their first year. This seemed to verify the assumption that Caribbean women were more inclined to remain in domestic employment than women from other areas.'[77]

Since the West Indian Domestic Scheme, the Canadian state has continued the practice of importing women from the Caribbean as domestic workers. Recently, most domestics are being brought from the Philippines, through the Foreign Domestic Movement program. Domestic work in Canada is perceived as work for women who are not white, for women from poor countries in the Third World. Unlike their sisters who came on the West Indies Scheme and who were required to work in the home of the employer for one year, after which they were allowed to apply for landed-immigrant status, the domestics coming in now are granted employment visas, with a number of stipulations that greatly limit the lives they can lead in Canada. One shared experience for both groups is the drudgery of domestic work and the frequent exploitation by employers.[78]

African Canadian women have been waging an arduous and protracted struggle for some three hundred years to overcome many obstacles. The racialist structure of the Canadian state has given rise to a racially gendered labour market, in which Black women historically have found it difficult to move beyond certain stereotyped roles, primarily involving domestic work, which has long been regarded as Black women's work.

The sexual division of labour is further stratified by race. Together these factors enhance capital accumulation and place Black women virtually at the bottom of the heap of workers. This pattern continues, but African Canadian women have resisted and continue to resist on the job and elsewhere. Their very survival is evidence of this resistance.

NOTES

This work is part of an ongoing project. I thank Multiculturalism and Citizenship Canada and the Ontario Arts Council for financial support.

1 See B. Singh Bolaria and Peter S. Li, *Racial Oppression in Canada*, 2nd ed. (Toronto: Garamond Press 1988); R. Whitaker, *Double Standard: The Secret History of Canadian Immigration* (Toronto: Lester & Orpen Dennys 1987); M. Danys, *DP: Lithuanian Immigration to Canada after the Second World War* (Toronto: Multicultural History Society of Ontario 1986); I. Abella and H. Troper, *None Is Too Many: Canada and the Jews of Europe, 1937–1948* (Toronto: Lester and Orpen Dennys 1982); and D. Avery, *'Dangerous Foreigners': European Immigrant Workers and Labour Radicalism in Canada, 1896–1932* (Toronto: McClelland & Stewart 1979).

2 The concept of the state was first analyzed by the early philosophers of history, including V.I. Lenin, 'The State,' in *Selected Works*, vol. 2 (New York: 1943) and Karl Marx and Frederick Engels, *The German Ideology*, Selected Works, vol. 1 (Moscow: Progress Publishers 1969). Its analysis by contemporary Marxist philosophers includes, most notably, Antonio Gramsci (1934), *Selections from the Prison Notebooks*, Q. Hoare and G. Nowell-Smith (London: Lawrence & Wishart 1971); Nicos Poulantzas, *Classes in Contemporary Capitalism* (London: Verso 1974); Louis Althusser, 'Ideology and Ideological States Apparatuses,' in *Lenin and Philosophy* (London: NLB 1971); and Ralph Miliband, *The State in Capitalist Society* (London: Quartet Books 1969). More recent analyses include Philip Corrigan, *Capitalism, State Formation and Marxist Theory: Historical Investigations* (London: Quartet Books 1980).

3 See Philip Abrams, 'The Difficulty of Studying the State,' *Journal of Historical Sociology* 1, no. 1 (March 1988).

4 See Phillip Corrigan, Harvie Ramsay, and Derek Sayer, 'The State as a Relation of Production,' in Corrigan, ed., *Capital-*

ism, State Formation and Marxist Theory, 1–25. Many contemporary feminist scholars studying the state have also concluded that it is not an instrument that is strictly manipulated by the ruling class. However, unlike most of their male counterparts, they have applied a gender specificity to state relations, indicating that despite the seemingly neutral nature of actions taken by the state, these actions often have a negative impact on women. See, for example, Michele Barrett, *Women's Oppression Today: Problems in Marxist Feminist Analysis* (London: Verso 1980), 227–47; Elizabeth Wilson, *Women and the Welfare State* (London: Tavistock 1977); Mary McIntosh, 'The State and the Oppression of Women,' in Annette Kuhn and AnnMarie Wolpe, eds, *Feminism and Materialism* (London: Routledge & Kegan Paul 1978); Alena Heitlinger, 'Maternity Leaves, Protective Legislation, and Sex Equality: Eastern European and Canadian Perspectives,' in Heather Jon Maroney and Meg Luxton, eds, *Feminism and Political Economy: Women's Work, Women's Struggles* 247–82 (Toronto: Methuen 1987); and Catherine A. MacKinnon, *Toward a Feminist Theory of the State* (Cambridge: Harvard University Press 1989), among others.

5 See Dorothy Smith, *The Everyday World as Problematic: A Feminist Sociology* (Boston: Northeastern University Press 1987). While arguing for a feminist sociology that challenges male hegemony and what is often assumed not to be a determined male standpoint, Smith gives quite a succinct analysis of how rule is carried out in advanced capitalist patriarchies.

6 Marx and Engles were perhaps the first to point to the notion of illusion in relation to the state. In *The German Ideology*, they point out than an important characteristic of the state is that it gives rise to the illusory common interest and free will of a society being exercised (pp. 79–81, 83).

7 Abrams, 'Difficulty,' 83.

8 Two works that look at some of these state practices are Bolaria and Li, *Racial Oppression in Canada* and Robert F. Harney, ' "So Great a Heritage as Ours": Immigration and

the Survival of the Canadian Polity,' *Daedalus* 117, no. 4
(Fall 1988). For an excellent analysis of how race becomes a
key organizing principle in the politics of the state, see Michael Omi and Howard Winant, *Racial Formation in the
United States from the 1960s to the 1980s* (New York: Routledge & Kegan Paul 1986).

9 Report by Stephen Lewis, Adviser on Race Relations, to Premier Bob Rae, 9 June 1992, p. 2.

10 Daniel G. Hill, *The Freedom-Seekers: Blacks in Early Canada* (Agincourt, Ont.: Book Society of Canada 1981), 3–9.
See also Robin W. Winks, *The Blacks in Canada: A History*
(New Haven and London: Yale University Press 1971), chaps
1 and 2.

11 The route that many fugitive slaves took from the American
South to the freedom they had heard so much about in the
North was not a train, per se, but a 'secret operation carried
out by courageous people linked only by their hatred of
slavery and their willingness to hide, feed and help onward
fugitive slaves' (Hill, *Freedom-Seekers*, 25).

12 In addition, just after the American War of Independence,
some Blacks were brought to Canada as slaves, the property
of white Loyalists who migrated to Nova Scotia and Upper
Canada. Here they were kept as slaves until their death or
until slavery was abolished throughout the British Empire
with the Imperial Act of 1833, whichever came first. See
Ontario Archives, Honourable William Renwick Riddell, *An
Official Record of Slavery in Upper Canada* (Osgoode Hall
Toronto, 31 May 1928), 393–7.

13 Ibid., 396.

14 Ibid.

15 Bolaria and Li, *Racial Oppression in Canada*, 189.

16 Winks, *Blacks in Canada*, 114–41, 228–9.

17 See, for example, Winks's insightful recounting of the attempts by Blacks, starting in 1842, to set up a colony named
Dawn in Canada West. This was perhaps the best-supported
effort and, as Winks indicates, its ultimate failure after a
number of years was due largely to Black factionalism.

However, much of the funding came from Britain and from white religious societies and organizations in the United States that were in support of helping newly freed Blacks.

18 *Blacks in Canada*, 288.
19 Ibid., 289.
20 See many of the recent works on Native peoples' experiences in early Canadian history. The treatment of Native Canadian women is now being documented in Canadian women's history. See, for example, Sylvia Van Kirk, 'The Role of Native Women in the Fur Trade Society of Western Canada, 1670–1830,' in V. Strong-Boag and A. Fellman, eds, *Rethinking Canada: The Promise of Women's History* (Toronto: Copp-Clark 196), 59–68.
21 See Winks, *Blacks in Canada*, 289.
22 Immigration statistics, 1980–8, Canada Department of Employment and Immigration. Also, Canadian census reports show Canada's most frequently reported ethnic origins, and here too peoples of non-European origin are least reported; see 1986 Census of Canada.
23 Francis G. Carter, *Judicial Decisions on Denominational Schools* (Toronto: 1962), 118.
24 Winks, *Blacks in Canada*, 289.
25 Ibid., 139.
26 Hill, *Freedom-Seekers*, 62–89.
27 Winks, *Blacks in Canada*, 35–9; Hill, *Freedom-Seekers*, 63.
28 Angela Y. Davis, *Women, Race and Class* (New York: Random House 1981), chap. 1. In this extraordinary work about the location of Black women in American history, which has always set them apart from white women in any women's rights campaign – even in the contemporary women's movement – Davis points out that Blacks took the negative equality they experienced during slavery, that is, whereby both women and men were treated as means of production, and transformed it into positive equality in their social and domestic life in the post-slavery period.
29 Paula Giddings, *When and Where I Enter: The Impact of Black Women on Race and Sex in America* (Toronto, New

York: Bantam Books 1984), 73, 94. See also Hill, *Freedom-Seekers*, 35–9.

30 E. Franklin Frazier, *The Negro Family in the United States* (Chicago: University of Chicago Press 1939), 102. The comments are as applicable to all classes of Black women today as they were under slavery. See also Davis, *Women, Race, and Class*, chap. 1, and Giddings, *When and Where I Enter*, chap. 3.

31 *Women, Race, and Class*, 17.

32 Ibid., 16–17.

33 Ibid., 23–4 (author's emphasis).

34 See Ged Martin, 'British Officials and Their Attitudes to the Negro Community in Canada, 1833–1861,' *Ontario History* 66, no. 2 (June 1974). Also Hill, *Freedom-Seekers*, chap. 4.

35 Hill, *Freedom-Seekers*, 48–61.

36 Martin, 'British Officials,' 88.

37 See Winks, *Blacks in Canada*, chap. 12.

38 Rella Braithwaite, *The Black Woman in Canada* (Toronto: OISE 1975), 42.

39 See Colin Thompson, *Born With a Call: A Biography of Dr William Pearly Oliver* (Halifax: Black Cultural Centre for Nova Scotia 1975).

40 Joan Bertley, 'The Role of the Black Community in Educating Blacks in Montreal, from 1910 to 1940, with special reference to Reverend Dr Charles Humphrey Este,' unpublished M.A. thesis, McGill University, Montreal, 1982, 80.

41 For an analysis of the development of the nursing profession in the United States and some insight into how racism has manifested itself there, see Darlene Clark Hine, *Black Women in White: Racial Conflict and Cooperation in the Nursing Profession 1890–1950* (Bloomington and Indianapolis: Indiana University Press 1989).

42 The better-known studies include P. Armstrong and H. Armstrong, 'Lessons from Pay Equity,' *Studies in Political Economy*, no. 32 (Summer 1990); C. Cuneo, *Pay Equity: The Labour-Feminist Challenge* (Toronto: Oxford University

Press 1990); Pat Armstrong and Hugh Armstrong, *The Double Ghetto: Canadian Women and Their Segregated Work* (Toronto: McClelland & Stewart 1978; rev. 1984) and *A Working Majority: What Women Must Do for Pay* (Ottawa: Canadian Advisory Council on the Status of Women 1983); Patricia Connelly, *Last Hired, First Fired* (Toronto: Women's Press 1978); Paul Phillips and Erin Phillips, *Women and Work: Inequality in the Labour Market* (Toronto: James Lorimer 1983); Patricia M. Marchak, 'The Canadian Labour Force: Jobs for Women,' in Marylee Stephenson, ed., *Women in Canada*, 202–12 (Toronto: General Publishing 1977); Heather Jon Maroney and Meg Luxton, eds, *Feminism and Political Economy: Women's Work, Women's Struggles* (Toronto, New York, London: Methuen 1987); Marjorie Griffin Cohen, *Women's Work, Markets, and Economic Development in Nineteenth-Century Ontario* (Toronto: University of Toronto Press 1988).

43 This lack of opportunities also has to do with the undervaluing of women's work. At the time, many of these women would also have had skills as artisans – weaving, sewing, dyeing, etc., but these skills would not have been recognized by potential employers.

44 Leo A. Johnson, 'The Development of Class in Canada in the Twentieth Century,' in G. Teeple, ed., *Capitalism and the National Question in Canada* (Toronto: University of Toronto Press 1972), 169.

45 *Women at Work in Canada* (Ottawa: Department of Labour, Queen's Printer, 1957 and 1964), 1, quoted in Genevieve Leslie, 'Domestic Service in Canada, 1880–1920,' in Janice Acton et al., eds, *Women at Work: Ontario, 1850–1930* (Toronto: Canadian Women's Educational Press 1974), 71–125.

46 Leslie, 'Domestic Service,' 71.

47 Ibid., 73. Though Leslie's work is dated, I rely heavily on it in this section because it gives a good historical analysis of domestic work in Canada for the crucial forty-year period ending in 1920. At about this time, in the early twentieth century, the Canadian government became the main recrui-

ter for domestic workers, and immigration officials became
convinced that the supply of domestics from more 'preferred' sources (i.e., Europe and Scandinavia) had been exhausted. Only then did they turn to 'non-preferred'
countries and regions such as the Caribbean as a last resort.
Other works that deal with domestic service in Canada,
though less relevant for the argument being presented here,
include those of Jean Burnet, Irving Abella, and Harold Troper.

48 *Census of Canada, 1921, Volume I – Population.*
49 Agnes Calliste, 'Canada's Immigration Policy and Domestics
from the Caribbean: the Second Domestic Scheme,' in Jesse
Vorst et al., eds, *Race, Class, Gender: Bonds and Barriers*
(Toronto: Between the Lines 1989).
50 A.S. Miller, ed., *The Journals of Mary O'Brien 1828–1838*,
quoted in Cohen, *Women's Work*, 86.
51 Leslie, 'Domestic Service,' 76.
52 James W. St G. Walker, *A History of Blacks in Canada*
(Hull, Que.: Minister of Supply and Services 1980), 132.
53 Karl Marx, 'Feuerbach: Opposition of the Materialistic and
Idealistic Outlook' in Karl Marx and Frederick Engels, *Selected Works*, vol. 1 (Moscow: Progress Publishers 1977),
47.
54 Correspondence from Director, Immigration, Hon. Mr
Crerar, Re: Coloured Domestics from British West Indies.
Ottawa, 17 Apr. 1942, 2 pp. NAC, RG 76, vol. 83–4/346,
Box 18, File 58506-6-4 533, part 1. Quoted in Ruth L. Harris, 'The Transformation of Canadian Policies and Programs
to Recruit Foreign Labor: The Case of Caribbean Female
Domestic Workers, 1950's–1980's,' unpublished Ph.D. dissertation, Michigan State University, 1988, 106.
55 Correspondence, Department of Mines and Resources Mr
Birks, from Director, Immigration, Re: Movement of Coloured Servants from the West Indies. Ottawa, 8 Apr. 1942.
Quoted in Harris, 'Transformation,' 106.
56 See note 1, above, on labour priorities in Canadian immigration policy and Robert F. Harney, ' "So Great a Heritage as

Ours'': Immigration and the Survival of the Canadian Policy,' in *Daedalus* 117, no. 4 (fall 1988).

57　Canada, *House of Commons Debates, 1974,* 1 May, quoted
in Winks, *Blacks in Canada,* 435.

58　Ibid., 425.

59　See H. Tulloch, *Black Canadians: A Long Line of Fighters*
(Toronto: NC Press 1975).

60　The practice of executing immigration policy on racialist
lines and of stereotyping by officials continues. See Immi-
gration Canada, 'Annual Report to Parliament on Future Im-
migration Levels,' Employment and Immigration Canada,
IM-052/10/89, 1989, and Immigration Canada, *Canada's
Immigration Law,* Government publication IM008/7/90,
MP23-65/1990 (Ottawa: Minister of Supply and Services
Canada 1990).

61　Harris, 'Transformation,' 76.

62　Grace Anderson, 'Immigration and Social Policy,' in Shankar
A. Yelaja, ed., *Canadian Social Policy,* 115 (Waterloo: Wil-
frid Laurier University Press 1978).

63　Harris, 'Transformation,' 72.

64　Ibid.

65　Memo from the Director of Immigration to the Deputy
Minister, Re: A Review of Immigration from the British
West Indies. Ottawa, 14 Jan. 1955. NAC, TG 26, vol. 24,
File 333-6, Part 1. Quoted in Harris, 'Transformation,' 110.

66　Harris, esp. chap. 4.

67　Ibid., 78.

68　Ibid., 79.

69　Ibid., 80.

70　Hill, *Freedom-Seekers,* 80.

71　The Scheme came to an end when the West Indies Federa-
tion, an attempt at unitary government by the British-con-
trolled Caribbean countries that began in 1958, ended in
1962. The West Indies governments' preoccupation with ne-
gotiations for this experiment result in a decline in enthusi-
asm for the Scheme. See Harris, chap. 4.

72　It is quite possible, indeed probable, that this low requirement was meant to ensure that these women remained in domestic work once in Canada. However, in their zeal to please Canadian officials, the Caribbean officials who were hand-picking the applicants would choose the most highly educated. The requirement was later changed to some high school education in 1961. One author has suggested that the change not only reflected the general educational upgrading of the Canadian labour force, but also recognized the likelihood that Caribbean domestic workers might leave domestic work. See Calliste, 'Canada's Immigration Policy,' 141.

73 See Frances Henry, 'The West Indian Domestic Scheme in Canada,' *Social and Economic Studies* 17, no. 1 (March 1968), 83–91, and Makeda Silvera, *Silenced* (Toronto: Williams-Wallace 1983).

74 Harris, 'Transformation,' 82.

75 Memorandum from Laval Fortier, Deputy Minister of Citizenship and Immigration, to the Minister, Re: Training School for Domestics in Barbados and Jamaica. Ottawa, 29 May 1956. NAC, RG 26, vol. 124, File 333-6, Part I. Quoted in Harris, 'Transformation,' 82.

76 Draft Memorandum to Cabinet from Department of Citizenship and Immigration to Department of Labour, Re: Admission of Domestics from B.W.I. Ottawa, May 1955. NAC, RG 27, vol. 292, File 1-26-69-2, Part I. Quoted in Harris, 'Transformation,' 81.

77 Harris, 'Transformation,' 82.

78 See Makeda Silvera, *Silenced*, for the stories of Caribbean domestics; Ronnie Leah and Gwen Morgan, 'Immigrant Women Fight Back: The Case of Seven Jamaican Women,' in *Resources for Feminist Research* 8, no. 3 (1982); and numerous reports by the Toronto Organization of Domestics Workers' Rights (INTERCEDE), including Sedef Arat-Koc and Fely Villasin, 'Report and Recommendations on the Foreign Domestic Movement Program,' October 1990, for analyses of domestics in general.

Picture Credits

Selected Bibliography

Primary Sources

Archival Material

Note: All documents are used with permission.
Archives of Ontario, Agricultural Census for the Township of Raleigh, 1851, 1861.
- Census of the Canadas, Town of Amherstburg, 1851, 1861.
- Census of the Canadas, Town of Chatham, 1851, 1861.
- Census of the Canadas, Township of Raleigh, 1851, 1861.
- Census of the Canadas, Town of Windsor, 1851, 1861, 1871.
- Diary of John Symons.
- Dun and Bradstreet Directories, 1865–73.
- Education Department, Annual Reports of the Local Superintendents of Common Schools.
- Education Department, Egerton Ryerson Papers.
- Education Department, Register of Students for the Toronto Normal School, vols. 10, 11.
- Marriage Registers for Essex and Kent Counties.
- McCurdy Papers, Minute Book of the Trustees of the Amherstburg Black Separate School, 1851–82.
Black Abolitionist Papers, University Microfilms International, Ann Arbor, Michigan.
Boston Public Library, Horace Mann Papers.
Brock University, Special Collections, 1858 Assessment Roll for the Town of St Catharines.

Census of Canada, 1921, vol. 1 – Population. Ottawa: King's Printer.

Framingham State College Archives, Circular and Register of the State Normal School from Its Commencement at Lexington, July 1839, to Dec. 1846.

National Archives of Canada (Ottawa), Colonial Church and School Society Papers.

– Diary of the Reverend William King.

– Mary Shadd Cary Papers.

Oberlin College Archives, General Catalogue of Oberlin College, 1833–1908.

Public Archives of Nova Scotia, Census Returns for Nova Scotia, 1767 and 1881.

– General Sessions of the Peace, Shelburne, 1786, 1787, 1791. MG 4, vol. 141.

– Muster Book of Free Blacks at Birchtown, 1784. MG 100, vol. 220, no. 4.

Public Record Office (London, Eng.), Colonial Office Records, 217/269.

Raleigh Centennial Museum (North Buxton, Ont.), Rapier Family Papers.

Syracuse University (New York), Gerritt Smith Papers.

Tulane University (New Orleans), Amistad Research Center, American Missionary Association Papers (Canadian Files).

Newspapers

American Baptist

Anti-Slavery Bugle

Anti-Slavery Reporter

Baptist Annual Register

Chatham Evening Banner

Chatham Gleaner

Chatham Tri-Weekly Planet

Chatham Weekly Planet

Chronicle Herald

Detroit Tribune

Examiner, Toronto

Globe

Halifax Mail Star

Liberator

London Free Press

Missionary

Paisley Herald

Pennsylvania Freeman

Provincial Freeman

Sunday Leader

Toronto Globe   *Voice of the Fugitive*
Toronto Star

Secondary Sources

Theses and Dissertations

Althouse, J.G. 'The Ontario Teacher: An Historical Account of
  Progress, 1800–1910.' University of Toronto, Doctor of Peda-
  gogy, 1929.
Bertley, Joan. 'The Role of the Black Community in Educating
  Blacks in Montreal, from 1910 to 1940, with special reference
  to Reverend Dr. Charles Humphrey Este.' McGill University,
  Master's, 1982.
Carlesimo, Peter. 'The Refugee Home Society: Its Origin, Opera-
  tions, and Results.' University of Windsor, Master's, 1973.
Chatters, Harriet. 'Negro Education in Kent County.' Howard
  University, Master's, 1956.
Farrell, John. 'The History of the Negro Community in Chatham,
  Ontario, 1787–1865.' University of Ottawa, Ph.D., 1955.
Harris, Ruth L. 'The Transformation of Canadian Policies and
  Programs to Recruit Foreign Labor: The Case of Caribbean
  Female Domestic Workers, 1950's–1980's.' Michigan State
  University, Ph.D., 1988.
Hill, Daniel, 'Negroes in Toronto: A Sociological Study of a Mi-
  nority Group.' University of Toronto, Ph.D., 1960.
Jensen, Carole. 'History of the Negro Community in Essex
  County, 1850–1860.' University of Windsor, Master's, 1966.
Murray, Alexander. 'Canada and the Anglo-American Anti-Slav-
  ery Movement.' University of Pennsylvania, Ph.D., 1960.
Pemberton, I.C. 'The Anti-Slavery Society of Canada.' University
  of Toronto, Master's, 1967.
Simpson, Donald. 'Negroes in Ontario from Early Times to
  1870.' University of Western Ontario, Ph.D., 1971.
Spencer, Hildreth H. 'To Nestle in the Mane of the British Lion:
  A History of Canadian Black Education, 1820–1870.' North-
  western University, Ph.D., 1970.

Walton, Jonathan. 'Blacks in Buxton and Chatham, Ontario, 1830–1890: Did the 49th Parallel Make a Difference?' Princeton University, Ph.D., 1979.

Books

Acton Janice, ed. *Women at Work, Ontario, 1850–1930.* Toronto: Canadian Women's Educational Press 1974.

Anderson, James D. *The Education of Blacks in the South, 1860–1935.* Chapel Hill: University of North Carolina Press 1988.

Andrew, Williams L. *Six Women's Slave Narratives.* New York: Oxford University Press 1988.

Andrews, Charles C. *New York African Free Schools.* Reprint. New York: Negro Universities Press 1930.

Aptheker, Herbert. *A Documentary History of the Negro People in the United States, From Colonial Times to the Founding of the NAACP in 1910.* New York: The Citadel Press 1951.

Armstrong, Pat and Hugh. *The Double Ghetto: Canadian Women and Their Segregated Work.* Toronto: McClelland and Stewart 1978.

Bearden, Jim, and Linda Jean Butler. *Shadd: The Life and Times of Mary Shadd Cary.* Toronto: NC Press 1977.

Beddoe, Deirdre. *Discovering Women's History.* London, Eng.: Pandora Press 1983.

Berlin, Ira. *Slaves without Masters: The Free Negro in the Ante-Bellum South.* New York: Pantheon Books 1974.

Best, Carrie. *That Lonesome Road: The Autobiography of Carrie M. Best.* New Glasgow, NS: Clarion Publishing 1977.

Black, Clinton V. *The Story of Jamaica.* London: Collins 1965.

Blassingame, John W., ed. *Slave Testimonies: Two Centuries of Letters, Speeches, Interviews, and Autobiographies.* Baton Rouge: Louisiana State University Press 1977.

Blockson, Charles. *The Underground Railroad.* New York: Prentice Hall 1987.

Bolaria, Singh B., and Peter S. Li. *Racial Oppression in Canada.* 2d ed. Toronto: Garamond Press 1988.

Bond, Horace Mann. *The Education of the Negro in the American Social Order.* New York: Octagon Books, 1966.

Bradforn, Sarah. *Harriet Tubman, The Moses of Her People.* Secaucus, NJ: Citadel Press, 1961.

Braithwaite, Rella. *The Black Woman in Canada.* West Hill, Ont., 1977.

Braithwaite, Rella, and Tessa Benn-Ireland. *Some Black Women, Profiles of Black Women in Canada.* Toronto: Sister Vision Press 1993.

Brand, Dionne. *No Burden to Carry: Narratives of Black Working Women in Ontario, 1920s to 1950s.* Toronto: Women's Press 1991.

Braxton, Joanne M., and Andree N. McLaughlin, eds. *Wild Women in the Whirlwind: Afro-American Culture and the Contemporary Literary Renaissance.* New Brunswick, NJ: Rutgers University Press 1990.

Brooks Higginbotham, Evelyn. *Righteous Discontent: The Women's Movement in the Black Baptist Church, 1880–1920.* Cambridge: Harvard University Press 1993.

Bullock, Henry Allen. *A Study of Negro Education in the South from 1619 to the Present.* Cambridge: Harvard University Press 1967.

Butchart, Ronald E. *Northern Schools, Southern Blacks, and Reconstruction: Freedmen's Education, 1862–1875.* Connecticut: Greenwood Press 1980.

Campbell, Mavis, ed. *The Maroons of Jamaica 1655–1796: A History of Resistance, Collaboration and Betrayal.* Granby, Mass.: Bergin & Garvey 1988.

– *Nova Scotia and the Fighting Maroons: A Documentary History.* Williamsburg, Va., 1990.

Carroll, Bernice. *Liberating Women's History.* Chicago: University of Illinois Press 1972.

Carter, Francis G. *Judicial Decisions on Denominational Schools.* Toronto, 1962.

Carter, Velma. *The Black Canadians: Their History and Contributions.* Edmonton: Reidmore Books 1989.

Case, Frederick Ivor. *Racism and National Consciousness.* Toronto: Ploughshare Press 1977.

Chambers, Frederick. *Black Higher Education in the United States.* Connecticut: Greenwood Press 1978.

Coffin, Levi. *Reminiscences of Levi Coffin.* London, 1896.

Cohen, Majorie. *Women's Work, Markets, and Economic Development in Nineteenth Century Ontario.* Toronto: University of Toronto Press 1988.

Coleman, Peter J. *The Transformation of Rhode Island, 1790–1860.* Providence: Brown University Press 1963.

Cooper, Anna Julia. *A Voice from the South.* Reprint. New York: Oxford University Press 1988.

Corrigan, Philip. *Capitalism, State Formation and Marxist Theory: Historical Investigations.* London: Quartet Books 1980.

Cottrol, Robert J. *The Afro-Yankees, Providence's Black Community in the Antebellum Era.* Connecticut: Greenwood Press 1981.

Craft, William and Ellen. *Running a Thousand Miles for Freedom.* New York: Arno Press and New York Times 1969.

Crow, Jeffrey J., and Flora J. Hatley, eds. *Black Americans in North Carolina and the South.* Chapel Hill: University of North Carolina Press 1984.

Curtis, Bruce. *Building the Educational State in Canada West, 1836–1871.* London, Ont.: Althouse Press 1988.

Dabney, Wendell P. *Cincinnati Colored Citizens.* New York: Negro Universities Press 1970.

Davis, Angela. *Women, Race and Class.* New York: Random House 1981.

Dictionary of Canadian Biography, vol. I. George W. Brown, ed. Toronto and Quebec: University of Toronto Press / Les Presses de l'Université Laval 1966.

Drew, Benjamin. *The Narratives of Fugitive Slaves in Canada.* Boston: Jewett & Co. 1856.

– *The Refugee: A North-side View of Slavery.* Reading, Mass.: Addison-Wesley 1969.

Dyer, Thomas, ed. *To Raise Myself a Little: The Diaries and Let-*

ters of Jennie, a Georgia Teacher, 1851–1866, Amelia Akehurst Line. Athens: University of Georgia Press 1982.

Fairchild, James H. *Oberlin: The Colony and the College, 1833–1883.* Oberlin, Ohio: E.J. Goodrich 1883.

Ferguson, Charles B. *Clarkson's Mission to America, 1791–1792.* Public Archives of Nova Scotia, Halifax, 1971.

Fleming, Alice. *Great Women Teachers.* Philadelphia: J.B. Lippincott 1965.

Franklin, John Hope. *From Slavery to Freedom: A History of Negro Americans.* 3d ed. New York: Vintage Books 1979.

Fyfe, Christopher. *A History of Sierra Leone.* London, 1962.

Gagan, David. *Hopeful Travellers: Families, Land, and Social Change in Mid-Victorian Peel County, Canada West.* Toronto: University of Toronto Press 1981.

Gara, Larry. *The Liberty Line: The Legend of the Underground Railroad.* Lexington: University of Kentucky Press 1967.

Giddings, Paula. *When and Where I Enter: The Impact of Black Women on Race and Sex in America.* New York: William Morrow & Co. 1984.

Gilkeson, John S. *Middle Class Providence, 1820–1940.* Princeton: Princeton University Press 1986.

Grant, John. *The Immigration and Settlement of the Black Refugees of the War of 1812 in Nova Scotia and New Brunswick.* Hantsport, NS: Lancelot Press 1990.

Greene, Lorenzo Johnston. *The Negro in Colonial New England.* New York: Atheneum 1969.

Gutman, Herbert G. *The Black Family in Slavery and Freedom, 1750–1925.* New York: Vintage Books 1976.

Hamil, Frederick Coyne. *The Valley of the Lower Thames, 1640–1850.* Toronto, 1951.

Haviland, Laura S. *A Woman's Life-Work: Labors and Experiences of Laura S. Haviland.* Chicago: C.V. Waite & Co. 1887.

Henson, Josiah. *An Autobiography of Rev. Josiah Henson.* Reprint. Reading, Mass.: Addison-Wesley 1969.

Hill, Daniel G. *The Freedom-Seekers: Blacks in Early Canada.* Agincourt, Ont.: Book Society of Canada 1980.

Hodgins, George J. *Documentary History of Education in Upper Canada*. Toronto: L.K. Cameron 1883.

Hooks, Bell. *Ain't I a Woman: Black Women and Feminism*. Boston: South End Press 1981.

Houston, Susan, and Alison Prentice. *Schooling and Scholars in Nineteenth Century Ontario*. Toronto: University of Toronto Press 1988.

Howe, Samuel Gridley. *Report to the Freedmen's Inquiry Commission, 1864. The Refugees from Slavery in Canada West*. Reprint. New York: Arno Press 1969.

Howison, John. *Sketches of Upper Canada*. Toronto: Coles Book Publishing 1970.

Humez, Jean McMahon. *Gifts of Power: The Writings of Rebecca Jackson, Black Visionary, Shaker Eldress*. Amherst: University of Massachusetts Press 1981.

Jacobs, Harriet. *Incidents in the Life of a Slave Girl*. Reprinted in *The Classic Slave Narratives*. Henry Louis Gates, ed. New York: Mentor Books, New American Library 1987.

Johnson, Charles. *The Negro College Graduate*. Maryland, 1938.

Jones, Jacqueline. *Labor of Love, Labor of Sorrow*. New York: Random House 1985.

Jones, Thomas Jesse, ed. *A Study of the Private and Higher Schools for Colored People in the United States*. New York: Arno Press 1969.

Katz, Michael B. *The Irony of Early School Reform: Educational Innovation in Mid-Nineteenth Century Massachusetts*. Boston: Beacon Press 1968.

Keane, David, and Colin Read, eds. *Old Ontario: Essays in Honour of J.M.S. Careless*. Toronto: Dundurn Press 1990.

Lauriston, Victor. *Romantic Kent: The Story of a County, 1626–1952*. Wallaceburg, Ont.: Standard Press 1952.

Lawson, Ellen NicKenzie. *The Three Sarahs: Documents of Antebellum Black College Women*. New York: Edwin Mellen Press 1984.

Lenin, V.I. *Selected Works*, vol. 2. New York, 1943.

Lerner, Gerda, ed. *Black Women in White America*. New York: Vintage Books 1973.

Light, Beth, and Alison Prentice, eds. *Pioneers and Gentle-Women of British North America, 1713–1867.* Toronto: New Hogtown Press 1980.

Litwack, Leon. *North of Slavery: The Negro in the Free States, 1790–1860.* Chicago: University of Chicago Press 1961.

– and August Meier, eds. *Black Leaders of the Nineteenth Century.* Urbana: University of Illinois Press 1988.

Loewenberg, Bert James, and Ruth Bogin, eds. *Black Women in Nineteenth-Century American Life: Their Words, Their Thoughts, Their Feelings.* University Park: Pennsylvania State University Press 1976.

Mabee, Carleton. *Black Education in New York State, From Colonial to Modern Times.* New York: Syracuse University Press 1979.

Maroney, Heather Jon, and Meg Luxton. *Feminism and Political Economy: Women's Work, Women's Struggles.* Toronto: Methuen 1987.

McCullough, A.B. *Money and Exchange in Canada to 1900.* Toronto: Dundurn Press 1984.

McKerrow, P.E. *A Brief History of the Coloured Baptists of Nova Scotia and Their First Organisation as Churches A.D. 1832.* Dartmouth: Afro-Nova Scotian Enterprises 1975.

McMullen, Lorraine, ed. *Re(Dis)Covering Our Foremothers: Nineteenth Century Canadian Women Writers.* Ottawa: University of Ottawa Press 1990.

Martin, Linda, and Kerry Seagrave. *The Servant Problem.* North Carolina: McFarland & Co. 1985.

Merrill, Walter H., and Louis Ruchames, eds. *The Letters of William Lloyd Garrison,* vol. 4, 1850–1860. Cambridge: Harvard University Press 1975.

Miller, Floyd. *The Search for a Black Nationality, Black Emigration and Colonization.* Urbana: University of Illinois Press 1973.

Oliver, Pearleen. *A Brief History of the Coloured Baptists of Nova Scotia, 1782–1953.* Halifax, 1953.

Osofsky, Gilbert, ed. *Puttin' on Ole Massa: The Slave Narratives of Henry Bibb, William Wells Brown, and Solomon Northup.* New York: Harper & Row 1969.

Pachai, Bridglal. *Beneath the Clouds of the Promised Land: The Survival of Nova Scotia's Blacks*, vol. 2, 1800–1989. Halifax, 1991.

Pease, William, and Jane H. Pease. *Black Utopia: Negro Communal Experiments in America*. Historical Society of Wisconsin, 1963.

Perry, Charlotte Bronte. *The Long Road: A History of the Coloured Canadian in Windsor, Ontario 1867–1967*. Windsor, 1967.

Personal Narratives Group, *Interpreting Women's Lives: Feminist Theory and Personal Narratives*. Bloomington: Indiana University Press 1989.

Piersen, William D. *Black Yankees*. Amherst: University of Massachusetts Press 1988.

Pierson, Ruth Roach. *'They're Still Women After All': The Second World War and Canadian Womanhood*. Toronto: McClelland & Stewart 1986.

Prentice, Alison, and Susan Houston, eds. *Family, School and Society in Nineteenth Century Canada*. Toronto: Oxford University Press 1975.

Quarles, Benjamin. *The Black Abolitionist*. New York: Oxford University Press 1969.

– *Black Mosaic: Essays in Afro-American History and Historiography*. Amherst: University of Massachusetts Press 1988.

Reilly, Wayne E., ed. *Sarah Jane Foster, Teacher of the Freedmen: A Diary and Letters*. University Press of Virginia, 1990.

Rice, C. Duncan. *The Rise and Fall of Black Slavery*. London, Eng.: MacMillan Press 1975.

Richardson, Marilyn, ed. *Maria W. Stewart, America's First Black Woman Political Writer: Essays and Speeches*. Bloomington: Indiana University Press 1987.

Ripley, C. Peter. *The Black Abolitionist Papers*, vol. 2, Canada, 1830–1865. Chapel Hill: University of North Carolina Press 1986.

Robbins, Arlie C. *Legacy to Buxton*. Chatham, Ont. 1983.

Robinson, Gwendolyn and John W. *Seek the Truth: A Story of Chatham's Black Community*. Printed in Canada, 1985.

Shadd, Mary Ann. *A Plea for Emigration or Notes of Canada West, in Its Moral, Social and Political Aspect: With Questions Respecting Mexico, W. Indies and Vancouver's Island for the Information of Colored Emigrants*. Detroit: George W. Pattison 1852.

Shadd Shreve, Dorothy. *The AfriCanadian Church: A Stabilizer*. Ontario: Plaideia 1983.

Silvera, Makeda. *Silenced*. Toronto: Williams-Wallace 1983.

Silverman, Jason H. *Unwelcome Guests: Canada West's Response to American Fugitive Slaves, 1800–1863*. New York: Faculty Press 1985.

Sklar, Kathryn Kish. *Catherine Beecher: A Study in Domesticity*. New Haven: Yale University Press 1984.

Smith, Dorothy. *The Everyday World as Problematic: A Feminist Sociology*. Boston: Northeastern University Press 1987.

Steady, Filomina Chioma, ed. *The Black Woman Cross-Culturally*. Massachusetts: Schenkman Books 1985.

Sterling, Dorothy, ed. *We Are Your Sisters: Black Women in the Nineteenth Century*. New York: W.W. Norton & Company 1984.

Stevenson, Brenda, ed. *The Journals of Charlotte Forten Grimke*. New York: Oxford University Press 1988.

Steward, Austin. *Twenty-Two Years a Slave, and Forty Years a Freeman*. New York: Canandaiga 1869.

Still, William. *The Underground Railroad: A Record of Facts, Authentic Narratives, Letters etc*. Philadelphia: Porter & Coates 1872.

Stouffer, Allen. *The Light of Nature and the Law of God: Anti-Slavery in Ontario 1833–1877*. Montreal: McGill-Queen's University Press 1992.

Strong-Boag, Veronica, and A. Fellman. *Rethinking Canada: The Promise of Women's History*. Toronto: Copp-Clark 1986.

Taylor, Susan King. *Reminiscences of My Life in Camp*. New York: Arno Press 1969.

Teeple, G. *Capitalism and the National Question in Canada*. Toronto: University of Toronto Press 1972.

Tisdall, Alice Constance Muriel. *Forerunners: The Saga of a Family of Teachers*. Melbourne: Cheshire 1961.

Tremaine, Marie. *A Bibliography of Canadian Imprints, 1751–1800*. Toronto: University of Toronto Press 1952.

Trudel, Marcel. *L'esclavage au Canada Français*. Quebec: Les Presses Universitaires 1960.

Tulloch, Headley. *Black Canadians: A Long Line of Fighters*. Toronto: NC Press 1975.

Tyack, David B. *The One Best System: A History of American Urban Education*. Cambridge: Harvard University Press 1974.

Ullman, Victor. *Martin R. Delaney, The Beginnings of a Black Nationalism*. Boston: Beacon Press 1971.

– *Look to the North Star: The Life of William King*. Boston: Beacon Press 1971.

Vorst, Jesse, ed., *Race, Class, Gender: Bonds and Barriers*. Toronto: Between the Lines 1989.

Walker, James W. St G. *A History of Blacks in Canada*. Quebec: Government Publications 1980.

– *The Black Loyalists: The Search for a Promised Land in Nova Scotia and Sierra Leone, 1783–1870*. London, 1976.

Ward, Samuel Ringgold. *His Anti-Slavery Labours in the United States, Canada and England*. Reprint, 1970.

Ware, Vron. *Beyond the Pale: White Women, Racism and History*. London: Verso 1992

White, Deborah Gray. *Ar'n't I a Woman: Female Slaves in the Plantation South*. New York: W.W. Norton & Co. 1985.

Wilson, Ellen G. *The Loyal Blacks*. New York, 1976.

Wilson, J. Donald, ed. *Canadian Education: A History*. Prentice-Hall of Canada 1970.

Winks, Robin. *The Blacks in Canada*. New Haven: Yale University Press 1971.

– *The Historian as Detective*. New York: Harper & Row 1986.

Woodson, Cater G. *A Century of Negro Migration*. Washington: Association for the Study of Negro Life and History 1918.

– *The Education of the Negro Prior to 1861.* New York: Arno Press 1968.
– *The Mind of the Negro as Reflected in Letters Written During the Crisis, 1800–1860.* New York: Negro Universities Press 1969.

Articles

Abrams, Philip. 'The Difficulty of Studying the State.' *Journal of Historical Sociology* 1, no. 1 (March 1988).

Armstrong, P., and Armstrong, H. 'Lessons from Pay Equity.' *Studies in Political Economy* 32 (Summer 1990).

Arthurs, W.W. 'Civil Liberties – Public Schools – Segregation of Negro Students.' *Canadian Bar Review* 41 (September 1963), 453–7.

Benjafield, Gail. 'St. Catharines: The Open Door.' *The Downtowner* 6, no. 3 (May–June 1990), 2.

Bigglestone, W.E. 'Oberlin College and The Negro.' *Journal of Negro History* 56 (1971), 133–9.

Bond, Horace Mann. 'A Century of Negro Higher Education.' In William Brickman and Stanley Leher, eds, *A Century of Higher Education*, 182–96. New York, 1962.

Butchart, Ronald E. ' "We Best Can Instruct Our Own People": New York African Americans in the Freedmen's Schools, 1861–1875.' *Afro-Americans in New York Life and History*, January 1988.

– ' "Outthinking and Outflanking the Owners of the World": A Historiography of the African American Struggle for Education.' *History of Education Quarterly* 28, no. 3 (Fall 1988), 333–66.

Carnochan, Janet. 'A Slave Rescue in Niagara Sixty Years Ago.' *Niagara Historical Society Papers* 2 (1897), 14–16.

Clearly, Francis. 'Notes on the Early History of the County of Essex.' *Ontario History* 6 (1905), 66–75.

Collier-Thomas, Bettye. 'The Impact of Black Women in Education: An Historical Overview.' *Journal of Negro Education* 51, no. 3 (1982), 173–80.

Cooper, Afua. 'The Search for Mary Bibb, Black Woman Teacher in Nineteenth-Century Canada West.' *Ontario History* 83, no. 1 (March 1991).

Cooper, J.I. 'The Mission to the Fugitive Slaves at London.' *Ontario History* 46 (April 1954), 133–9.

Danylewycz, Marta, et al. 'The Evolution of the Sexual Division of Labour in Teaching: A Nineteenth-Century Ontario and Quebec Case Study.' *Histoire Sociale / Social History* 16, no. 31 (May 1983), 81–109.

Danylewycz, Marta, and Alison Prentice. 'Teachers' Work: Changing Patterns and Perceptions in the Emerging School Systems of Nineteenth- and Early Twentieth-Century Central Canada.' *Labour/Le Travail* 17 (Spring 1986), 59–80; reprinted in Jenny Ozga, ed., *Schoolwork: Approaches to the Labour Process of Teaching*. Open University Press 1988.

Eames, Frank. 'Pioneer Schools of Upper Canada.' *Ontario History* 18 (1920).

Farrell, John. 'Schemes for the Transplanting of Refugee American Negroes from Upper Canada.' *Ontario History* 52 (December 1960), 245–9.

Friedman, Lawrence J. 'Racism and Sexism in Ante-bellum America: The Prudence Crandall Episode Reconsidered.' *Societas* 4, no. 3 (Summer 1974), 211–27.

Ginzberg, Lori D. 'The "Joint Education of the Sexes": Oberlin's Original Vision.' In Carol Laser, ed., *Educating Men and Women Together: Coeducation in a Changing World*, 67–80. Urbana: University of Illinois Press 1987.

Hamilton, Sylvia. 'Our Mothers Grand and Great: Black Women of Nova Scotia.' *Canadian Women Studies / Les Cahiers de la Femme* 4, no. 2 (1982).

Harley, Sharon. 'Beyond the Classroom: The Organizational Lives of Black Female Educators in the District of Columbia, 1890–1930.' *Journal of Negro Education* 51, no. 3 (1982), 254–65.

Harney, Robert F. ' "So Great a Heritage as Ours": Immigration and the Survival of the Canadian Polity.' *Daedalus* 117, no. 4 (Fall 1988).

Henry, Frances. 'The West Indian Domestic Scheme in Canada.' *Social and Economic Studies* 17, no. 1 (March 1968), 83–91.

Hill, Daniel G. 'Negroes in Toronto, 1793–1865.' *Ontario History* 55 (June 1963), 73–91.

Hite, Roger W. 'Voice of the Fugitive, Henry Bibb and Antebellum Black Separatism.' *Journal of Black Studies*, March 1974, 269–83.

Jacobs, Donald M. 'The Nineteenth Century Struggle over Segregated Education in the Boston Schools.' *Journal of Negro Education* 39 (1970), 76–85.

Jensen, Joan M. 'Not Only Ours but Others: The Quaker Teaching Daughters of the Mid-Atlantic, 1790–1850.' *History of Education Quarterly*, Spring 1974, 3–19.

Landon, Fred. 'The Buxton Settlement in Canada.' *Journal of Negro History* 4 (October 1918), 360–7.

– 'Fugitive Slaves in London Before 1860.' *London and Middlesex Historical Society*, January 1919, 25–37.

– 'The Negro Migration to Canada after the Passing of the Fugitive Slave Act.' *Journal of Negro History* 3 (1920), 22–36.

– 'Henry Bibb, A Colonizer.' *Journal of Negro History* 5 (1920), 437–47.

– 'The Diary of Benjamin Lundy, Written During His Journey through Upper Canada, January 1832.' *Ontario History* 19 (1921), 110–33.

– 'The Work of the American Missionary Association Among the Negro Refugees in Canada West, 1858–1864.' *Ontario History* 21 (1924), 198–205.

– 'Amherstburg, Terminus of the Underground Railroad.' *Journal of Negro History* 10 (January 1925), 1–11.

– 'Social Conditions Among the Negroes in Upper Canada Before 1865.' *Ontario History* 12 (1925), 144–61.

– 'The Anti-Slavery Society of Canada.' *Ontario History* 47–49 (1953–57), 125–31.

Laskin, Susan, et al. 'Studying the History of an Occupation: Quantitative Sources on Canadian Teachers in the Nineteenth Century.' *Archivaria* 14 (Summer 1982), 75–92.

Law, Howard. 'Self-Reliance Is the True Road to Independence:

Ideology and the Ex-Slaves in Buxton and Chatham.' *Ontario History* 77 (June 1985), 107–21.

Lawr, D.A., and R.D. Gidney. 'Who Ran the Schools? Local Influence on Education Policy in Nineteenth-Century Ontario.' *Ontario History* 72, no. 2 (June 1980), 131–43.

Leah, Ronnie, and Morgan, Gwen. 'Immigrant Women Fight Back: The Case of Seven Jamaican Women.' *Resources for Feminist Research / Documentation sur la recherche du féministe* 8, no. 3 (1982).

Mabee, Carleton. 'A Negro Boycott to Integrate Boston Schools.' *New England Quarterly* 41 (1968), 341–61.

McCormick, Richard P. 'William Whipper: Moral Reformer.' *Pennsylvania History* 43 (1976), 23–46.

MacDonald, Cheryl. 'Mary Ann Shadd in Canada, Last Stop on the Underground Railroad.' *Beaver*, February–March 1990, 32–8.

Martin, Ged. 'British Officials and Their Attitudes to the Negro Community in Canada, 1833–1861.' *Ontario History* 66, no. 2 (June 1974), 79–88.

Middleton, Joyce. 'The Women of the Elgin Settlement and Buxton.' In *65th Annual North Buxton Homecoming & Labour Day Celebrations.* North Buxton, September 1989.

Monaghan, E. Jennifer. 'Literacy Instruction and Gender in Colonial New England.' *American Quarterly* 40, no. 1 (1988).

Murray, Alexander L. 'The Provincial Freeman: A New Source for the History of the Negro in Canada.' *Ontario History* 51, no. 1 (1959), 25–31.

Pease, William, and Jane H. Pease. 'Opposition to the Founding of the Elgin Settlement.' *Canadian Historical Review* 28 (September 1957), 202–18.

Perkins, Linda. 'Heed Life's Demands: The Educational Philosophy of Fanny Jackson Coppin.' *Journal of Negro History* 51, no. 3 (1982), 181–90.

– 'The Impact of the "Cult of True Womanhood" on the Education of Black Women.' *Journal of Social Issues* 39 (1983), 17–28.

– 'The Black Female American Missionary Association Teacher

in the South, 1861–1870.' In Jeffrey J. Crow and Flora J. Hatley, eds, *Black Americans in North Carolina and the South*, 123–36. Chapel Hill: University of North Carolina Press 1984.
– 'Black Women and Racial "Uplift" Prior to Emancipation.' In F.C. Steady, ed., *The Black Woman Cross-Culturally*, 317–34. Massachusetts: Schenkman Books 1985.
Perlman, Daniel. 'Organizations of the Free Negro in New York City, 1800–1860.' *Journal of Negro History* 56 (1971), 181–97.
Prentice, Alison. 'The Feminization of Teaching in British North America and Canada, 1845–1875.' *Histoire Sociale / Social History* 8, no. 15 (May 1975), 5–20; reprinted as 'The Feminization of Teaching,' in Susan Mann Trofimenoff and Alison Prentice, eds, *The Neglected Majority: Essays in Canadian Women's History*, 49–65. Toronto: McClelland and Stewart 1977.
– 'From Household to School House: The Emergence of the Teacher as Servant of the State.' *Material History Bulletin* 20 (Fall 1984), 19–29.
Public Archives of Nova Scotia. 'Opinions of Several Gentlemen of the Law on the Subject of Negro Servitude in the Province of Nova Scotia.' Halifax, 1802.
Rammelkamp, Julian. 'The Providence Negro Community, 1820–1842.' *Rhode Island History* 6 (1947–53), 20–33.
Rector, Theresa A. 'Black Nuns as Educators.' *Journal of Negro Education* 51, no. 3 (1982), 238–53.
Riddell, William. 'The Slave in Canada. *Journal of Negro History* 5 (1920), 261–377.
Schwager, Sally. 'Educating Women in America.' *Signs* 12 (Winter 1987), 333–73.
Schweninger, Loren. 'A Fugitive Negro in the Promised Land: James Rapier in Canada, 1856–1864.' *Ontario History* 67 (1975), 91–104.
– 'A Slave Family in the Ante Bellum South.' *Journal of Negro History* 60 (January 1975), 29–44.
Silcox, Harry C. 'Nineteenth Century Philadelphia Black Militant: Octavius V. Catto (1839–1871).' *Pennsylvania History* 44 (1977), 53–76.

Silverman, Jason. 'Mary Ann Shadd and the Struggle for Equality.' In Leon Litwack and August Meier, eds, *Black Leaders of the Nineteenth Century*, 87–100. Urbana: University of Illinois Press 1988.

– and Donna J. Silverman. ' "The Pursuit of Knowledge Under Difficulties": Education and the Fugitive Slave in Canada.' *Ontario History* 74 (1982), 95–111.

Smith, T. Watson. 'The Slave in Canada.' *Collections of the Nova Scotia Historical Society* 10 (1989).

Solomon, Barbara Miller. 'The Oberlin Model and Its Impact on Other Colleges.' In Laser, ed., *Educating Men and Women Together*, 81–90.

Tyack, David B., and Myra H. Strober. 'Jobs and Gender: A History of the Structuring of Educational Employment by Sex.' In P. Schmuck, ed., *Educational Policy and Management: Sex Differentials*, 131–52. Academic Press 1981.

Welter, Barbara. 'The Cult of True Womanhood: 1820–1860.' *American Quarterly*, 1966, 151–74.

Winks, Robin. 'Negro School Segregation in Ontario and Nova Scotia.' *Canadian Historical Review* 50 (1959), 164–91.

Unpublished Papers

Butchart, Ronald E. 'Courage, Calling, and Color: New York Teachers Among the South's Ex-Slaves, 1862–1875.' Paper presented to the History of Education Society, Chicago, 27 October 1989.

Walton, Jonathan. 'Haven or a Dream Deferred for American Blacks: Chatham, Ontario, 1830–1880.' Paper presented at the Canadian Historical Association Meeting, 31 May 1978.